The New York Times

FASCINATINGLY FIERCE CROSSWORDS

The New York Times

FASCINATINGLY FIERCE CROSSWORDS
150 Hard Puzzles

Edited by Will Shortz

ST. MARTIN'S GRIFFIN ⚏ NEW YORK

THE NEW YORK TIMES FASCINATINGLY FIERCE CROSSWORDS.
Copyright © 2009 by The New York Times Company. All rights reserved.
Printed in the United States of America. For information, address
St. Martin's Press, 175 Fifth Avenue, New York, N.Y. 10010.

www.stmartins.com

ISBN-13: 978-0-312-56540-4
ISBN-10: 0-312-56540-2

D 10 9 8

ACROSS

1 Writing that lacks objectivity
16 Purveyors of spicy cuisine
17 "Hurry, you'll be late"
18 Tpks.
19 Full house sign
20 Patriot, e.g.: Abbr.
21 Old map abbr.
22 "Look ___!"
24 One going back and forth to work
26 Replacement raiser
30 Loses
34 When Nora leaves Torvald in "A Doll's House"
35 Man wearing une couronne
37 Follow
38 It's often hit at night
40 Musicians whom orchestras tune up to
42 Work unit
43 Daughter of Hyperion
45 Beat in November, perhaps
46 It's on the Rhone delta
48 Some tracks
50 Kind of cart
52 Sticking point?
53 Elicitors of little dances, briefly
56 Wing
58 Alternative to Rep. or Dem.
59 67-Across citers: Abbr.
62 August comment
66 Like Scorsese, but not Fellini
67 It begins "A well regulated Militia . . ."

DOWN

1 Member of the Allies in W.W. II: Abbr.
2 Expressed surprise
3 Former R.F.K. Stadium team, briefly
4 Proactiv target, informally
5 Aeschylus trilogy
6 Legendary 49ers receiver
7 Charles of CBS News
8 Uintah and Ouray Reservation inhabitant
9 Madrid maze-runner
10 Ices, maybe
11 Bakery output
12 John
13 "Last one ___ . . ."
14 Boarding places: Abbr.
15 Religious title: Abbr.
22 Start of an Ella Fitzgerald standard
23 Old map abbr.
25 Reply to "The phone's for you"
26 Mullah's decree
27 Fall shade
28 Composition of some nerves?
29 Ski-___
31 "The Other Side of Oz" autobiographer
32 Coup follower
33 Ways: Abbr.
36 Osteoarthritis treatment
39 Silent lawman?
41 Public
44 It might be filled with ink
47 Like guests at home
49 Message on a dirty car
51 Tons
53 "I'm pointing at it"
54 Act feeblemindedly
55 Disconnected, in mus.
57 Large moth
59 Inits. on many A.T.M.'s
60 Sheepskin leather
61 Volunteer babysitter, maybe
63 Inits. in '70s–'80s rock
64 Leg that gets whistled at
65 Net holder

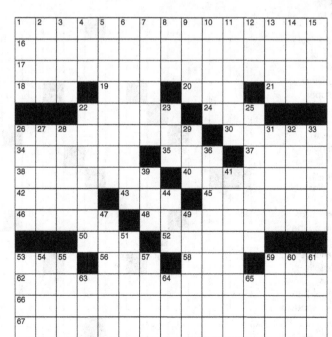

by David Levinson Wilk

2

ACROSS

1 Some pizza slices, e.g.
8 They employ speakers
15 Army E-7
17 One good at making faces
18 Moved like molasses
19 Plant holder?
20 Needles
21 1971 U.S. Open winner ___ Smith
22 Launch
24 It's sold in bars
25 A abroad
26 Modern company category
28 A abroad
29 Modified
31 Like British bishops
33 Time to attack
34 2004 P.G.A. Player of the Year
35 Dreamliner developer
37 Miss Gulch miffed her
40 Ovidian openings
41 Contact lens solutions
43 N.L. West team, on scoreboards
44 Home on the range: Var.
46 Moselle feeder, to Moselle natives
47 South-of-the-border spouses: Abbr.
48 End of ___
50 36-Down, por ejemplo
51 Island in the East China Sea
52 1995 Annie Lennox hit
55 "Maybe yes, maybe no"
56 Be made up
57 Worried about, slangily

DOWN

1 Anti
2 Satan, to Scots
3 Fictional swinger
4 When some people retire
5 Sud's opposite
6 ___ T
7 Whiny one
8 Infected
9 Chorus bit
10 Sponsorship
11 Lessor's list
12 Gloater's remark
13 Narrow, in a way
14 Lineate
16 Not impromptu
22 Caviar fish
23 Potential vote-getter
26 Pluto and others
27 Change places?
30 "___ get it!"
32 ___ Friday's
34 Auto options
35 Like some gardens
36 Ciudad Bolívar is on it
37 With lightness
38 Wipeout?
39 Bullyragged
42 Driving aid, of sorts
45 Hotel room amenities
47 ___ lot (is telling)
49 First drawing class, perhaps
51 Only
53 Mountain road section
54 Binding declaration

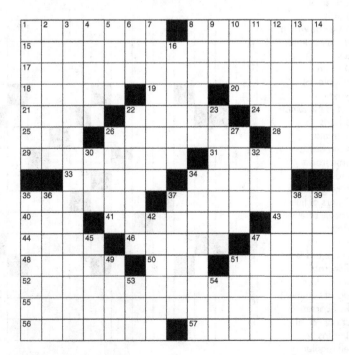

by Jim Hyres

ACROSS

1 See
5 Flexible prefix
9 Cries for attention
14 Summoning
16 With 13-Down, places for shooting stars
17 Bit
18 Take ___ (break)
19 They have African cousins
21 An eagle is on its flag
22 Pattern of scanning lines on a TV
23 They can be choppy
24 Bill for fine clothing?
27 Argonaut who slew Castor
29 "Bob & Carol & Ted & Alice" co-star
32 Hard-rock center
35 One in a shelter, maybe
36 ___ particle
37 Is in charge
40 Beautiful people of literature
41 "___ in the Park" (Rodgers and Hart song)
42 He wrote a hit Broadway musical with Weill
46 Parts of some joints
48 ___ ready
49 Rank last attained in 1950
53 Imminent, old-style
54 Harmless reptile with a dangerous-sounding name
55 "Somebody's Knockin'" singer ___ Gibbs
56 Wannabe's efforts
57 Easy ___
58 Auto performance factor, informally
59 Start of Massachusetts' motto

DOWN

1 Beards
2 Repay, in a way
3 "See?!"
4 Dwarf
5 Piles
6 Entangle
7 Not merely warm
8 Like some commerce
9 Far Eastern female servants
10 "Good night, sweet prince" speaker
11 Now level
12 Cold northerly winds of southern France
13 See 16-Across
15 ___ lot (very little)
20 Late
24 Sans subtlety
25 Jedi protector
26 Many a surfer
28 Cold war abbr.
30 Abbr. in a birth announcement
31 Med. specialty
32 Whiz
33 Premium product
34 Mediterranean succulent
38 Early form of Greek
39 Understanding, of sorts
43 Transportation in a 1941 hit song
44 Military toppers
45 Amazon warrior killed by Achilles
47 One of Hamlet's courtiers
48 Novelist Tina McElory ___
49 ___ morgana (mirage)
50 Behind
51 Down
52 Some bent pipes

by Eric Berlin

4

ACROSS

1 Soup line
9 Erased
14 One might request help getting started
16 Inclined . . . or flat
17 Makes something up
18 Roman land
19 Company once taken over by Carl Icahn
20 "So sorry"
22 Mr., abroad
24 Southwestern sign-off
25 Reminds a bit too much
26 Like Indians
28 Suffix with jardin
29 Irish Sea feeder
30 Jazz fan, most likely
32 Rubens painted her
35 Decor finish?
37 Figs. in identity theft
38 Goes off
42 Like a lottery winner, typically
46 Boomer's kid
47 He played J-Bone in "Johnny Mnemonic"
49 Quaint schoolroom item
50 "No ___!"
52 Belle's beau
54 Carmaker since 1949
55 Layabouts
58 Opposite of always, in Augsburg
59 Round window
60 Tender shoot?
62 First name in TV talk
63 Whip snapper
64 They're perfect
65 Cross the line?

DOWN

1 Best Supporting Actor for "The Fortune Cookie," 1966
2 She served eight days in jail for public obscenity
3 Sub-Saharan scourge
4 Year for Super Bowl LXXXIV
5 Exploit
6 Where the Enola Gay plane was built
7 Start of a Beatles title
8 Olympic team?
9 Vision: Prefix
10 DuPont trademark
11 Made impossible
12 Steams up
13 Hypersaline spot
15 In places
21 Sub-Saharan scourge
23 1986 Indy 500 winner
27 ___ forces
31 "Ixnay"
33 Italian province
34 Gets back to, quickly
36 Foosball locale
38 Look into
39 Like some copies
40 Mentor's companion
41 Manager's terse order
43 It's a short walk from Copacabana
44 Celebrity-spotting eatery
45 "A diamond is forever" sloganeer
48 "Key Largo" Oscar winner
51 Fee to enter a poker game
53 Daughter of Zeus
56 Period in sch.
57 Out-of-commission cruisers
61 Feather holder?

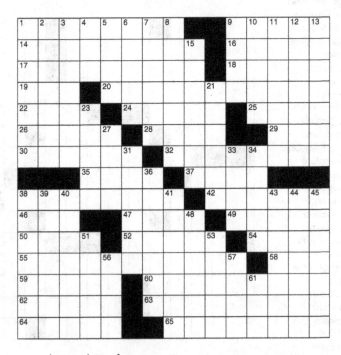

by David Quarfoot

ACROSS

1 Antique store?
7 Violin components
15 Make a ball
16 Ladle
17 Secrets
18 Holder of an afternoon service
19 French flag color, in France
20 "Shoot!"
21 Where workers may do the daily grind?
22 Excited pointer's comment
24 1999–2001 Broadway musical revue
25 Editorial cartoonist Rall
28 Listener
29 From, in some names
30 Former Washington duo
37 Stepped in like Superman
38 Somehow
39 Resort of a sort
40 Old TV control abbr.
41 Old protest grp.
42 2000 Olympic gymnast ___ Ray
45 Rhoda's sister on "Rhoda"
48 Passiontide time
49 Dogsbody, so to speak
50 Mark of distinction
54 Isabel Allende's birthplace
56 Meet, as expectations
57 Child's cry at a parade, perhaps
58 "Harrumph!"
59 Kids' game sites
60 Preceder of many a goal

DOWN

1 Unpopular worker
2 Cast
3 Sea predator
4 National headquarters of J. C. Penney, Dr Pepper and Frito-Lay
5 Paper strip for old computer data
6 Energy Star org.
7 Toledo twinkler
8 Command to a dog
9 Just so
10 Fail to keep
11 Surrounded by
12 "Dona ___ Pacem" (Latin hymn)
13 Plays for a sucker
14 Ancient burial stone
20 Popular snack chip
23 One of the Jacksons
24 Fates
25 Kind of salad
26 Zip
27 British title
29 Castle with many steps
31 Paper carrier
32 Part of a sentence: Abbr.
33 Showy bird's mate
34 Famous name in newspaper publishing
35 Like many a mistake
36 Kin of -ists
42 Fashion designer Perry
43 Olympus alternative
44 Hero of Charles Frazier's "Cold Mountain"
45 Topper with a tab
46 Voluptuaries
47 Places for many stained-glass windows
49 Tender in Tijuana
51 First name among clothiers
52 Huntsman Center players
53 Work with mail
55 Old TV's ___ Club
56 Narrow waterway

by Harvey Estes

6

ACROSS

1 Accusatory words
5 Certain red algae
12 Potting materials
14 Clicker
15 Native up north
16 Essayist whose motto was "Que sais-je?"
17 10 kilogauss
18 It has many soap slots
19 Plans to get back at
21 "Dog Barking at the Moon" painter, 1926
22 Comes back
23 Name on some briefs
24 Provide with new squares, perhaps
25 Insults wittily
26 It isn't repeated
28 Land at an Italian airport?
31 Captain of the Ghost, in Jack London's "The Sea Wolf"
34 William ___, secretary of commerce under Clinton
35 Casserole dishes
37 Day before a Jewish holiday
38 Passing legend
40 Go
42 They're treated by veterinarios
43 Turned over
44 Floor coverings, to a Brit
45 Pronunciation considerations

46 Cousin of Jane Eyre
47 One singled out before drinking
48 It's full of slots, briefly

DOWN

1 Martyred Carmelite nun ___ Stein
2 Music critic's bane
3 One tying up a turkey, say
4 Exercise, in Exeter
5 Brazilian port known for coffee
6 Artificial flavor base
7 Petal product: Var.

8 Number one
9 Not stopped
10 Many Madrileños
11 They're good at taking things down
13 Legally punishable
14 Starbucks slip-ons
16 Make a mess of
20 Woman in Chekhov's "The Sea-Gull"
23 Chart climber
25 Literary character who debuted in "The Curse of Capistrano"
27 Beat up

28 City on the Salentine Peninsula
29 Warner Music Group label
30 Looks up to
32 Involves
33 Order lover
34 Not be able to take
35 One way of fitting
36 Big bore
38 Pop singer McCartney
39 Leader of a 1970 military coup
41 Theme of Nabokov's "Lolita"

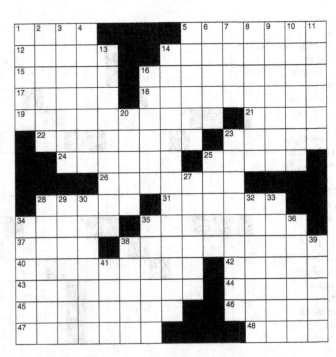

by Brendan Emmett Quigley

ACROSS

1 Didn't immediately go on
7 "Don't fall for that"
15 Title bandit in a Verdi opera
16 Postseason event
17 Some fertile regions
18 Bottle label
19 Disorderly type?
20 It doesn't require a full deck
21 Yvette's years
22 G.P.S. device, at times
24 Botanical beards
26 Shout to a cabbie
28 "Scarface" setting
29 Back together
32 Locks up
36 Comic introduction?
37 Figs. in bank records
38 Teller's area
41 Teaser
42 Not in harm's way
47 Best
50 "With Reagan" writer
51 Wall St. purchase
52 Better writing
54 Seven of 1,000,000
55 Arduous
57 Quickly
58 Checking one's territory
59 Beat one's gums

60 Antiphon
61 Like patent leather

DOWN

1 Piano trio
2 Playground retort
3 Loosen
4 Ruthless governor
5 One passing
6 Not straight
7 Native Nigerians
8 Big name in small trucks
9 Not just say
10 Record
11 ___ Friday's
12 Rappers' sounds
13 Emphatic concurrence

14 Annual celestial display
23 Kitchen aid
25 Sets a setter on, say
27 Spelling and others
30 Calling
31 "Is that a fact?!"
32 Wolf in sheep's clothing, e.g.
33 Something auto-dialed?
34 Star treks?
35 ___ Hills (edge of the San Fernando Valley)
39 Totals
40 Primary
43 Smooth, to Solti

44 Many of the Founding Fathers
45 Actress Chandler and others
46 Catch sight of
48 Gild
49 Long rides?
53 Cast leader?
56 Sometime PC supporter

by Sherry O. Blackard

ACROSS

1 Easily swindled sort
5 Baby with big eyes
10 They're not good
14 Like some hurricanes
15 ___ Island
16 Secluded spot
17 Fine-tuner
18 Midlevel math course
20 Some important decisions
22 Really let have it
23 Wreathes
24 Loud succession of sounds
25 It's debatable
26 Mouth burner
29 Goes over
32 Fictional mariner and others
34 Dam, e.g.
35 You might get into it before going under
37 Jet pump for fluid withdrawal
39 Carrier with Tokyo hdqrs.
40 George ___, German-American artist known for vitriolic caricature
42 Some wines
43 13-Down creator
45 Old empire member
47 Singer Cantrell
48 Leaves in the kitchen
52 Academy offering
54 Picture tube
55 Historic ship that sank on Christmas Day

57 Ned Beatty's role in "Superman"
58 Bureau: Abbr.
59 River through Newark, England
60 1955 Tony winner for "Quadrille"
61 Source of some pressure, maybe
62 Go (along)
63 Lummoxes

DOWN

1 It may hang on a pot
2 Like Filipinos
3 Not inadvertent
4 Some pianos
5 Appendixes, e.g.
6 For what purpose

7 Quick survey
8 Teachers' degs.
9 It's ball-bearing
10 Advance
11 Stalwarts
12 Two-time Newbery winner ___ Lowry
13 Funny number
19 Ones keeping a firm balance?
21 African beauty
24 Get going
27 Place for a tap
28 "___ to Hold" (1943 film musical)
29 Spoils
30 1990s transportation secretary
31 Just by scanning

33 Department store area
36 Soap opera creator ___ Phillips
38 Corporation whose stock symbol is KO
41 They send things up
44 Real bitter-ender
46 Compact
49 Mustered
50 Imagine
51 Animal shelters
52 Order ender
53 Carry on
54 Syrup brand
56 Big inits. in 1970s TV

by Dana Motley

ACROSS

1 "Regarding what was just said . . ."
16 Make it louder
17 "C'est la vie"
18 Hotfoots it
19 Milk sources
20 __ gratia (in all kindness): Lat.
21 Newspaper section
22 Some computer messages
24 Like la mer: Abbr.
25 Windy City rail inits.
26 Twist of the head?
27 It's read online
29 Large-minded
31 Family that founded America's first theme park
32 Some course requirements
33 "For __ be Queen o' the May": Tennyson
34 The right stuff
37 Stuffed sole stuffing
41 Like a good turkey
42 It comes with laurels
43 Member of a corp. board
44 Directional suffix
45 Bone brace
47 Like a mudhole
48 Dries, as hay
50 Loaded
51 Outcomes of some talks
52 "Possibly"
55 Set the record straight on something personal
56 Like a done deal

DOWN

1 Have some pull
2 1960s–'90s Indonesian president
3 Like some mathematical curves
4 They're usually placed in the middle of the table
5 Sen. Feingold
6 Quick
7 Noted erupter of May 18, 1980
8 Wagon train locale
9 Choppers
10 Nautical imperative
11 Play cat and mouse (with)
12 Very smooth
13 Unconscious
14 Distinguished
15 Chicken flavorers in a Chinese restaurant
22 Ishmael's people
23 On a mission for
26 Missionary writings
28 Whiz
30 Some Connecticut collegians
31 Store first opened in Detroit in 1962
33 Firm control, metaphorically
34 Ipecac and others
35 Italian violinist Giuseppe __
36 Kicker
37 Choose, as an icon
38 Like some rules
39 TV sponsor's concern
40 What Romeo and Juliet did
42 The Witch of the South
46 Used leverage
47 "Mountain," in Hawaii
49 "Land," in central Asia
51 Model behavior?
53 Hapsburg domain: Abbr.
54 Wanna-__

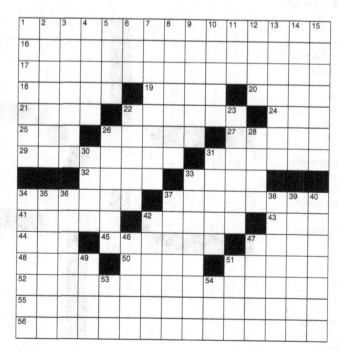

by Manny Nosowsky

ACROSS

1 Sheets
7 Rub
15 Flowering plant with prickly leaves
16 Funnelform flora
17 Like part of the heart
18 Periods of decline
19 Garage sale?
20 Neighbors of Indians
21 Breadwinner
22 Circus pioneer Ringling and others
23 Magazine contents
25 "___ Secretary," Madeleine Albright's 2003 autobiography
30 Lie very, very still
35 Wolfish
36 Be on the take
38 Throws off
39 Secret
40 Slaves
41 Bullied baby, maybe
42 Mouse manipulator?
43 It might hold the solution
49 Having the same concentration of salt as mammalian blood
54 Pounded
55 Cousin of a sego
56 "Fighting" collegiate team
57 Is older than
58 ___ Sea between Ireland and England

59 Concurring comment
60 O.K.

DOWN

1 Put on
2 Prefix with syllabic
3 Like rhinos vis-à-vis elephants
4 Like some elephants
5 Ride
6 They can cause eruptions
7 It's simple to solve
8 Inclines
9 Recipe parts
10 Kind of steak
11 Shrub of the genus Indigofera
12 Film

13 Trails
14 Latin infinitive
24 Its currency is the dirham: Abbr.
25 Number associated with a boom
26 Emblem of life
27 Prayer addressee, in Paris
28 Unwelcome dining discovery
29 Work well together
30 Surveyor's map
31 Italian island reef
32 Follower of myself
33 Cry
34 Travels at a speed of

35 Home of San José
37 It may involve a homophone
41 Yeast, e.g.
42 "Benjamin"
44 Drones, say
45 Dispensary stock
46 Pool
47 "The State and Revolution" writer
48 A famous one was issued at Nantes
49 Parenting challenges
50 1980s Geena Davis sitcom
51 City once named Provo Bench
52 Tendency, as of events
53 Moonfish

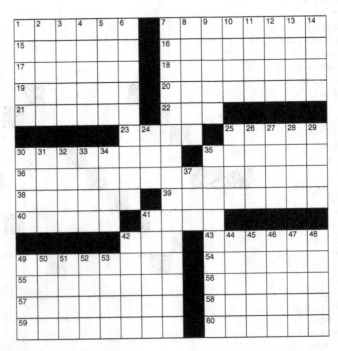

by Philip C. Ordway

ACROSS

1 Light show?
16 Small player
17 Big 12 team
18 Math ratio
19 It's made in Japan
20 Press
21 Bit of shrink rap?
24 Frequent portrait subject
26 Incoming clutter
29 Vet's memory, maybe
31 Rest of the afternoon
35 Coin with 12 stars on it
36 Often-dunked item
38 "I don't buy it"
39 Bug elimination
42 In danger of snapping
43 Belafonte catchword
44 Fool on the ice
45 Evergreen shrubs
47 Casual states?
48 European tongue
49 Jabba the ___ of "Star Wars"
51 Match maker?
53 Navy noncom
55 Farm butter
57 Quintillionth: Prefix
60 Kingdoms by the sea
65 Hogan's hero?
66 Pet expression?

DOWN

1 Pou ___ (vantage point), from the Greek
2 Tees off
3 Bones connected to fibulae
4 One whom everyone is for
5 Contents of some urns
6 Brother of un padre
7 Follower or Lenin or Stalin
8 "Our Gang" assent
9 They're often held under water
10 Cacklers
11 It might be struck south of the border
12 Annexation justification
13 Hebrew for "delight"
14 Highlander's weapon
15 Attention-getters
22 Form of ether
23 Like cornstalks
25 T'ang dynasty poet
26 Otto preceder
27 Relatively white
28 Rice-___
30 Road Runner cartoon backgrounds
32 More likely to retire
33 Does very poorly, in slang
34 Coy compliment response
37 "Now I remember!"
40 Steady
41 Move imperceptibly
46 Pace
50 Certain Sri Lankan
52 Kristy's "Little Darlings" co-star
53 Italian term of endearment
54 P.E.I., e.g.
56 Dramatic opening?
58 Mary in the White House
59 ___ cat
60 Year in the reign of England's King Stephen
61 Fictional uncle
62 Sparks setting: Abbr.
63 Drink additive?
64 Line part: Abbr.

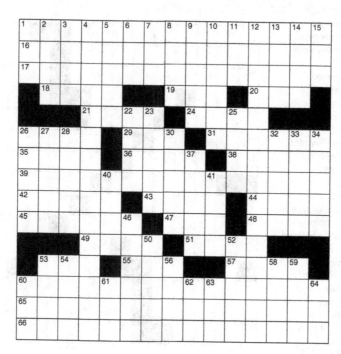

by Harvey Estes

ACROSS

1 You may pretend to pick one
10 Chewed stimulant
14 He had a 2004 #1 hit "Drop It Like It's Hot"
15 Capital 12,000 feet above sea level
16 Willful ones?
17 "Take ___" (office order)
18 NPR reporter Shapiro
19 Title boy genius of a 1991 film
20 It might be neutral
21 Gets hot
23 "Who'da thunk it?!"
24 One of Bolivia's official languages
26 Campus grps.
28 Surprises with a call
30 Adenauer's successor as German chancellor
32 Word of admonishment
33 Native New Yorkers
35 Taker of two tablets
36 No-parking area
39 Preferably
42 "Kiss Hollywood Good-by" memoirist
44 Introduction to chemistry?
45 Virtuoso
46 Idyllic spot
48 Keypad locales
49 Dickens
50 Middle-of-the-roaders: Abbr.
52 Multiple of VI
53 Baked, in Bologna
54 Erroneous claim about a superhero
56 Fatty liquid
57 Hoi polloi
58 Sable or Montego, for short
59 It's graded subjectively

DOWN

1 "Shall We Dance" co-star
2 Not right
3 W.W. II icon on a 1999 stamp
4 Landed
5 "___ Oxford" (Ved Mehta memoir)
6 Name holder
7 Blew the whistle
8 Yes-men
9 QB protectors
10 Twinings offering
11 It gets little consideration
12 Best Director of 1997
13 Kind of dye
15 Dinner spinner?
22 Bluff, maybe
24 "That's ___ excuse for . . ."
25 Word with white, red or black
27 Rupee earner
29 Volt per ampere
31 Gave out
34 ___-Off (windshield cover brand)
36 Fourth steps in some sequences
37 Stuck
38 Prehistoric stone chips
40 Some royal coats
41 Like the best outlook
43 They can be overloaded
47 "Battlestar Galactica" commander
51 Fix
53 Modern address part
54 Rock suffix
55 E.T.O. transport

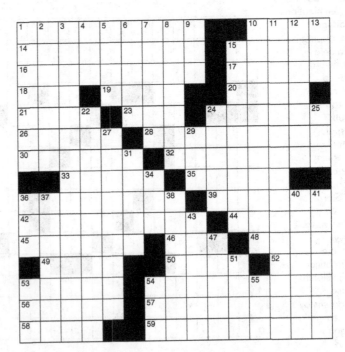

by David Quarfoot

ACROSS

1 Royal protection
12 Swift quality
15 Vitamin C, e.g.
16 "Another Green World" musician
17 1990s White House chief of staff
18 Largest U.S. youth org.
19 Certain connection makers
20 Gets the word out?
22 Whom auditors audit
23 Remiss
25 Hangouts
26 Spherical cereal
27 Little jingle
28 Custom
29 Representation of tuning fork sounds
31 List
33 Route markers
35 RR place
38 Infrangible
39 Directory data: Abbr.
40 Solara, for one
42 Friend of "Ralphie boy"
44 Words of resignation
45 Person who's authorized to shorten a sentence
46 Former New York senator
47 Tanning need
48 Alternative to eBay
52 Sight seer
53 1996 Emmy-winning role in a sitcom
54 Lottery-running org.
55 Game that involves opening a door

DOWN

1 Political columnist Thomas
2 Lacks of energy
3 One who sings but maybe shouldn't
4 Inflammatory stuff
5 Runners
6 What cribs are used for
7 Array on a bar shelf
8 It's fruit-flavored
9 Inked art, for short
10 Key word
11 Steadily took in
12 It always has a home
13 Raid targets
14 Warmed by the fire
21 Animate
22 Bird ___
23 Consumes with flair
24 Puts forth
26 It literally means "thing to wear"
29 Slangy greeting
30 Verb for a historian
31 Victorian-era novelist
32 Indiana-born composer/writer
33 Busy times at fast-food restaurants
34 Sets off
35 Composer of the opera "Brandenburgers in Bohemia"
36 Eight-line verse form
37 Newspaper inits. since 1851
38 Former Falcons coach Dan
40 Acquire
41 Put down
43 Word immediately preceding some signatures
44 More like a swami
46 The Great ___ (Victor Borge's nickname)
49 Some Eng. majors get them
50 Alma mater of NPR's Tom and Ray Magliozzi: Abbr.
51 Storm dir.

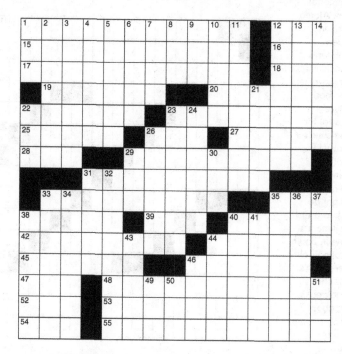

by Trip Payne

ACROSS

1 2005's "Bad News Bears" and the like
14 Firm up-and-comers
15 Saw about frugality
16 Wildcats' sch.
17 TV Guide listings: Abbr.
18 Johnny Cash's "___ Picture of Mother"
19 Pauperize
21 Resting places
24 They're game
25 Something rattled
27 Identi-Kit options
29 Church with elders: Abbr.
30 Commander at the Alamo
32 Brings in
34 Modern inhabitants of ancient Aram
36 Fast movement
40 Have bad posture
42 Material for some sheets
43 Legal V.I.P.'s
46 "That's ___!"
48 Woman with une nièce
49 It might be stuck to a dish
51 Longtime first name in South Carolina politics
53 Peter Gunn's girlfriend
54 Megalopolis with about 30 million people, for short
56 Pianist Maisenberg

58 It may finish second
59 Realize there will be no resolution
63 "Don't put words in my mouth"
64 Not here

DOWN

1 Place to get rolls
2 Letters of discharge
3 Turnabouts, slangily
4 Proscriptions
5 Like some transfers
6 Picks
7 Damp and chilly
8 Great time

9 People may take a pass on them: Abbr.
10 Chose to play
11 Lab locale
12 Like badlands
13 Cool red giants
14 When many resolutions are broken
15 Certain links
20 One of the Leeward Islands
22 Unable to get one's feet on the ground?
23 Makes an impression on?
26 It's twirled on a trail
28 Smash production?
31 Puts one over on

33 Caterpillar features
35 Breed
37 French copper
38 Many a senior
39 King of diamonds feature
41 Like Mad
43 Tests
44 Loving, as eyes
45 Backbone part
47 Gentlemanly
50 Bel ___
52 Intervening, legally
55 Proceed impulsively
57 Canterbury can
60 Up to
61 Ladies' room
62 Some racecars

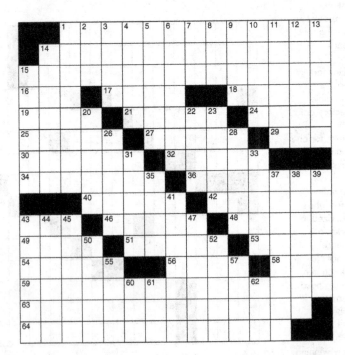

by Eric Berlin

ACROSS

1 Tanglewood's
___ Hall
11 Wet blanket?
15 Winslow
Homer's "The
Reaper," e.g.
16 After
17 Certain
secretary
18 When repeated,
a taunt
19 Standard
of living?
20 Place that may
suit you
22 After
24 ___ bourgeoisie
(gentry)
25 "It will come ___
surprise . . ."
28 Within: Prefix
29 Prefix with
business
30 End of many
a riddle
32 Isn't just a
licensee
34 The Seminoles,
in coll. sports
36 Hardly an
independent
thinker
38 Fail
40 But, to Brutus
41 Prefix with
drama
43 Political
convention
activity
44 Tow job
46 Mark of a ruler
48 It may have
a big head
49 ___ bar
50 Anago, in a
sushi restaurant
52 Hideous
54 One thrown at
a rodeo
58 Immoralist

59 Big blow to the
Japanese?
61 "This one's ___"
62 "Well, bless
my soul"
63 Forks
64 Place to wait
for a couple of
minutes, maybe

DOWN

1 ___ Pea
2 Marco Polo's
heading
3 Zinc oxide
may treat it
4 Giant bottle
5 Maya Angelou's
"And Still ___"
6 Mo. with
United Nations
Day
7 Get very close

8 Not recognizable
by
9 Wearied
10 Trojan ally, in
the "Iliad"
11 Wiesbaden
weekday
12 Confrontational
13 Cicatrix
14 Ticklee's
utterance
21 Mount in
Siskiyou County
23 Poet who wrote
"Don't send
a poet to
London"
25 Cobblers'
tools
26 Does it ever
hurt!
27 Voltaire, e.g.
31 Brunch beverage

33 Time to see
estrellas
35 Former empire
inits.
37 Ballet step
39 For all to see
42 Club with a nearly
vertical face
45 Check list?
47 Home of the
1988 and 2010
Winter Olympics
49 Best-selling author
of "Personal
Injuries"
51 Stiff-backed
53 Pass on
55 Starbuck's
orderer
56 Bilbao bull
57 Top
60 Application form
datum: Abbr.

by Manny Nosowsky

16

ACROSS

1 Boarders' spots
9 Excites, with "up"
13 Declaration from Mama Rose in "Gypsy"
15 Seethe
16 Resolution phrase
17 Nitwit
18 Italian TV channel
19 Sleuth's outburst
20 Richard's longtime partner on Broadway
22 Down-home entertainment
24 High, in a way
26 Served as
28 Drop off
29 Shade of bleu
30 Kind of infection
32 One and the same
34 Bygone epidemic cause
35 Asian peppers
38 Shared sleeping accommodations
39 Serengeti creature
40 Some are made with chocolate
43 Pie chart dividers
44 Pardner's mount
45 Proves otherwise, briefly
49 Sugar amt.
50 Tell off in no uncertain terms
52 Burrow
53 Letter opener
55 Series of articles, maybe
57 "Give ___ hug"
58 Bannister's length
59 Overhead
62 Big hearts?
63 Bums

64 "Over here"
65 "Not necessarily"

DOWN

1 Guide
2 Bar
3 Vitamin C provider
4 1999 best seller "___ Road"
5 208 people
6 Dress material
7 Supportive org. since 1965
8 Bluejackets
9 Lane with smooth curves
10 Michael Jackson autobiography
11 Can you top this? Why, yes!
12 Mo preceder
13 Following

14 L train
21 Like the "Wheel of Fortune" wheel, again and again
23 Mocha native
25 Turkey
27 Booted, maybe
31 Renal : kidney :: amygdaline : ___
33 Getting up there
35 Q*___ (vintage video game)
36 Office holders
37 Larval amphibians
38 Split
40 Flex, for example
41 Squirt
42 One-named singer with the 2002 #1 hit "Foolish"

46 One known for a bad hair day
47 Phil who was a five-time Gold Glove winner
48 Photocopier selections
51 Feat
54 Cold war faction
56 In and out, quickly
58 "The Amazing Race" prop
60 -esque
61 Hamburger's one

by Henry Hook

ACROSS

1 Rejected
10 Food whose name means, literally, "ring"
15 Personal
16 Title place in a Francesco Rosi film
17 Whistle blower?
18 Reach
19 Hit daytime show
20 Eustachian tube site
21 Mixer with O.J., popularly
22 In public
23 Ancient writers of hieroglyphics
25 Plunder, slangily
26 Chicken soup ingredient
28 Org. with a House of Delegates
29 Rankles
33 Sunken
35 Profits
36 Peppermint __
37 Means of introduction
39 Bad thing to be at
40 Calculator: Abbr.
41 Almost spills
43 Knights of __
45 Chasing
46 Buster?
50 "I Remember Mama" aunt
52 Swedish coins
53 It goes over the wall
54 Abominable
55 Not car-share
57 Space Invaders maker, once
58 "The devil's tools"
59 Joint part
60 Classic subject for rock 'n' roll lyrics

DOWN

1 "Gremlins" co-star, 1984
2 Fred's dancing sister
3 Shelf material
4 Game piece
5 Word said just before opening the eyes
6 "Make yourself comfortable"
7 Broken up
8 Travelers' headaches
9 __ City of book and film
10 Mendicates
11 Encourages when one shouldn't
12 Rot
13 1942 Allied victory site
14 Didn't settle
23 Sicilian dessert wine
24 More oozing
26 Attacks from a snow fort, say
27 "Sailing to Byzantium" poet
29 "Oho!"
30 Disappear
31 Good one
32 A winner may break it
34 Sports stat.
38 "I won't stand in your way"
39 Inveigle
42 Usually you try to hit yours
44 Julio's opposite
46 Family name in "A Tree Grows in Brooklyn"
47 __ friends
48 Divides
49 Trough's opposite
51 Score just before winning, maybe
53 Ditch with a retaining wall used to divide land
56 __ tho

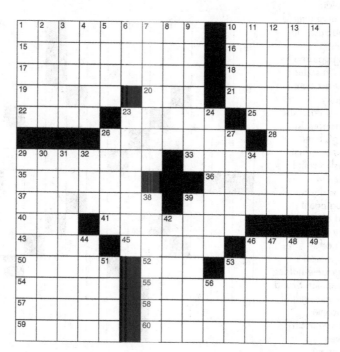

by Tyler Hinman

18

ACROSS

1 Working together
10 Level connectors
15 Ready to take off
16 Arita porcelain
17 Dig in one's heels
18 Risk
19 N.Y.C. subway line
20 "The X-Files" org.
21 The "R" in Edward R. Murrow
22 Cleaner
24 Item with a long spout
26 It follows directions
27 Plains natives
29 Schedule
30 Sheet of matted fabric used in quilting
31 Staging area for the Crusades
33 Post-accident inquiry
35 Dated database
37 Rare occasion
40 King's bane
44 Abu ___, first Muslim caliph, 632–34
45 Turns down
47 Drug agent
48 Part of the sch. year
49 Tick off
51 Stage lead
52 Vegetable holder
54 Depilation brand
56 Common gift of welcome
57 Newswoman Gwen
58 Frequent raid target
60 View
61 Green light
62 Beginnings
63 Really big job

DOWN

1 1994 literary autobiography whose first chapter is titled "Infant Prodigy?"
2 River pollutant
3 Meal replaced by M.R.E.'s
4 Grass part
5 Bricklayers' equipment
6 Monteverdi opera
7 Common childhood malady
8 Epic 1975 showdown, popularly
9 N, O or P, in chem.
10 Bad-mouth
11 Rachel of "General Hospital"
12 "Art of silence" performer
13 Ahead of
14 Start to knit
21 Very violent, say
23 Ethylene glycol product
25 Chip ingredient
28 Hustle
30 Railyard sight
32 Lost ground
34 Birth
36 "Act!"
37 Grill sites, briefly
38 Visa charge
39 Largest country wholly in Europe
41 Ignis fatuus, the fair maid of ___
42 Learning
43 Handle
46 Don who directed "Invasion of the Body Snatchers," 1956
49 Idiots
50 Copier setting
53 Responded in court
55 Trainee
58 Loan figure: Abbr.
59 Except for

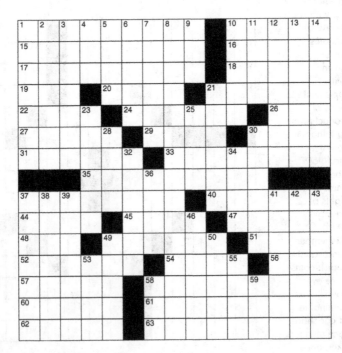

by Bob Peoples

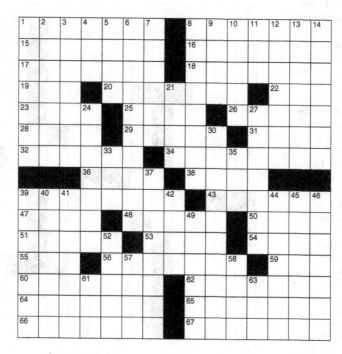

ACROSS

1 Idle
8 Crusade
15 One who might be in for a fall
16 Away
17 Err
18 Lacking the usual oomph
19 Shelley's fairy queen
20 Common alarm clock setting
22 Montemezzi's "L'Amore dei ___ Re"
23 Noted Americana lithographer
25 Storage site
26 Analyze
28 Strings run along one
29 Bob's partner
31 Good place to sit
32 Many a sled driver
34 Fibulae
36 Entrance part
38 MGM co-founder
39 Teetotalers
43 Environments
47 Official required to have a beard
48 Jefferson's portrayer in "Jefferson in Paris"
50 Old German duchy name
51 Actress Hedren
53 Gus who wrote "Dream a Little Dream of Me"
54 Broadcasting option
55 An agt.'s take
56 Awful, and then some

59 It may be raised by a rabblerouser
60 Belfast bloke
62 The Fonz, for one
64 Set against
65 Resonated
66 Worked
67 Speed-read

DOWN

1 Light yellow
2 Staff sizes?
3 Classic quartet leader
4 Sellers co-star in "A Shot in the Dark," 1964
5 Goes out
6 Avon peddlers, traditionally
7 1978 Glenda Jackson title role

8 "Isn't that unusual!"
9 Most fit to serve
10 Member of the Camelidae family
11 The Beatles' "___ Blues"
12 Serves
13 Ho-hum
14 Result of lack of sleep, maybe
21 Company famous for its safety record
24 Winter Olympics sight
27 A bit dense
30 Having I-strain?
33 They're often asked to look
35 ___ air
37 Negotiated

39 Not be satisfied, perhaps
40 A fraternity chapter
41 Afternoon, often, for a toddler
42 High-five, e.g.
44 Peak in New Hampshire's Presidential Range
45 Nth
46 Cut off
49 Exercise targets
52 "___ to Be You"
57 Hither
58 ___ place for
61 Masseur's workplace, maybe
63 "Kung Fu" actor Philip

by Kevin McCann

ACROSS

1 Fair trade
11 Words with "move on" or "life"
15 Baby shower
16 Draft choices?
17 Spaghetti sauce slogan
18 Actively trading
19 Through
20 Its highest possible score is 180: Abbr.
21 Inflict upon
22 Many are trained in childbirth: Abbr.
24 Slugger Williams and others
25 Looking frightened
26 It was uncommon at the Forum
27 Way to direct a helm
28 They might offer support in prayer
29 Unité politique
30 Ready for mounting
32 Characterize
34 "The nerve!"
38 Love, e.g.
42 First of a noted trio
43 First name in 19th-century outlawry
46 Grandson of Leah
47 Philadelphia's Franklin ___: Abbr.
48 Asian au pair
49 Plagues, with "at"
50 "Breezy" star, 1973
51 Ram home?
52 Pituitary hormone

53 Historic Thor Heyerdahl craft
54 Little Thief, for one
55 Snubbed person's comeback
59 Kids' TV character with a thick unibrow
60 Wipes out
61 Goddess who wed her brother
62 Physical component

DOWN

1 Shook
2 Last
3 Heads-up cry
4 Abbr. after Sen. Jack Reed's name
5 Label a bomb, perhaps
6 Letter run

7 "So-o-o sexy!"
8 Searched a trail, as a dog
9 Like some advertised films
10 "The Country Girl" playwright
11 Sides in an age-old battle
12 Smoke out
13 Go from 0 to 20 in three years?
14 Gets to
23 Luxury items for a king or queen
24 Pair from a deck, maybe
28 Knowledge
31 Property lawyers' concerns
33 Iowa college since 1851

35 More than look up to
36 Catches
37 Superlatively swank
39 Music critic's assignment
40 Raising Cain
41 Whip material
43 Star of the 1976 miniseries "I, Claudius"
44 Cries too easily, say
45 Zen enlightenment
49 Some cause laughter
56 Hi-___
57 Suffix with robot
58 Habitual scratcher

by David Quarfoot

ACROSS

1 Modern investor's option
7 Potluck supper offering
14 Where some bank deposits are made
15 Talkative one
16 Part of a frame
18 Deride
19 Ranger that cost about $2,500
20 ___-Saint-Laurent (Quebec region)
21 Fair
23 Gold medalist in Sarajevo and Calgary
24 Actress Polo of "Meet the Fockers"
25 Not sharp
26 A pair apart?
27 Co. founded by H. Ross Perot in 1962
28 Ask
29 Something ventured
30 Calvins, e.g.
32 Nosy Parker
34 Hall-of-famers Bill Klem and Nestor Chylak, e.g.
35 "___-Ami" (Guy de Maupassant novel)
38 Milan-based fashion house
39 She's a plus
40 French writer François ___ de Chateaubriand
41 Ring side
42 Capricious conceits
44 Gray shade
45 Privy fixture
46 "Cómo ___?"

47 Sparing no expense
50 Flawless diamond display?
51 "Hooray for the red, white and blue!"
52 They may give players a stiff arm
53 Thrifty customer?

DOWN

1 Museumgoer, e.g.
2 Shined
3 Network devices
4 Emporio ___
5 Bathysphere reading
6 San Jose-to-Fresno dir.
7 No longer practicing
8 Bowed
9 Montreal-born comic who wrote jokes for J.F.K.
10 Booking letters
11 Desert rats
12 Disestablishes
13 Big news in the '40s and '50s
15 Short-hop specialists
17 "Room 222" actress Nicholas
22 Cause for an assignation
23 Griper's litany
26 Groaners
28 Many a prayer
29 Couldn't hide one's astonishment
30 Wait

31 Daniel Decatur ___, composer of "Dixie"
32 It supplies drivers
33 Renaissance man
35 Edge
36 As one
37 Pitch from Carlton or Merit
38 Cioppino ingredients
39 You can get down from them
40 Do a price check on
42 Basketball maneuver
43 Baseball's Little Colonel
45 Capital founded in 1191
48 Prefix with state
49 Judah's house in a Lew Wallace novel

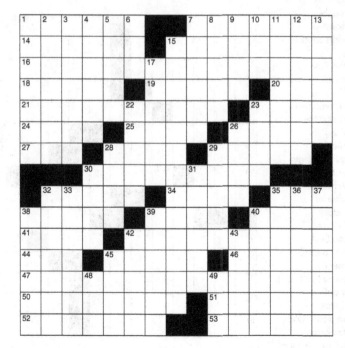

by John Farmer

ACROSS

1 Get close to
7 Shantytown shack material
15 Inuit garment
16 Singer of the 2002 #2 hit "Beautiful"
17 The silent treatment?
18 They take stock
19 Put on a lousy show, say
20 Common vending machine site
21 Snow in Nashville
22 Manual laborers in a convent
24 Mesopotamia dweller
26 Grp. concerned with defense
27 Luxury items
29 Strongly suggested
33 Middle square, say
34 1988 Bush campaign adviser
37 1951 play by Literature Nobelist Nelly Sachs
38 Three-time Masters winner
40 Theater lobby purchases
42 Author of the story collection "Little Birds"
44 Was naturally present
45 Manhunt assistants
50 Variable star in Cetus
51 Aria from "Otello"
52 "L'Évolution créatrice" author Bergson
53 Fairy tale parent
54 Signaled, on a quiz show
55 Screenplay skeleton
56 Axis nickname
57 How some medicines are administered
58 Reacted to a sudden pain, say

DOWN

1 Auto engine parts
2 Christian who does not believe in the Trinity
3 Unquestioned #1 status
4 Label obeyed by Alice
5 Lacking any curl
6 Spiky readout: Abbr.
7 Be reluctant to go
8 Fits
9 Efrem Zimbalist's birthplace
10 Home of the H. J. Heinz Co.
11 Overflowing with talent
12 Quarterback Rodney
13 Bug
14 Woodworking tools
22 Café addition
23 In a different way
25 Not permanent
28 Gull
30 Preparing (for)
31 "Dream Girl" playwright, 1945
32 Refused to recognize
35 Smart-looking, in British lingo
36 Great times
39 Inspirit
41 Puts another patch on
43 One of Poseidon's attendants
45 Argentine grassland
46 Toilet seats, e.g.
47 Dud
48 Title girl in a 1982 #1 John Cougar hit
49 Used a blade
52 ___ Bowl
54 Oil company facility

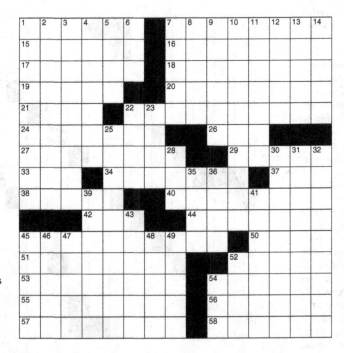

by Patrick Berry

ACROSS

1 World's longest wooden roller coaster, with "The"
6 Needle problem
10 W.W. I air ace, e.g.
14 "It's just between us"
16 Gymwear
17 Lackawanna's lake
18 It opens in Sept.
19 Dentist's request
20 One may be under development
21 Great Trek trekker
22 Secures
23 Like some craft show displays
24 Spirit that's willing?
25 #1 on Air Force One
26 Result of a quick revolution
27 Sunder
28 Place for I, O or U
31 Without aforethought
32 Cut-up
33 Popular New York City daily
35 "The sun," in 33-Across
36 Jours ___ (carnival days): Fr.
37 Fictional Jane
38 Cousin of a spoonbill
39 ___ Trammell, 1984 World Series M.V.P.
40 Heroine of Menotti's opera "The Consul"
41 "Just the opposite!"

42 Response to a brother?
43 Dog with a bone, maybe
44 Needles follow one
47 Fashionable wear
48 Lead-in to date or trap
49 Looie's saluter

DOWN

1 Just what is needed
2 Mercedes-Benz sedan
3 Take ___ (scram)
4 Parks in a pew
5 Shell contents
6 Girl, in song, "way down yonder in the paw-paw patch"
7 Support for a proposal
8 Business mag
9 Cleanliness, e.g.
10 Library supporter, maybe
11 Kitchen fixture
12 Leader of the Pacemakers in '60s pop
13 Get commands
14 "Hamlet" courtier
15 U.S. ___, known in New Hampshire as the Daniel Webster Highway
20 Infecund
21 "Neighbours" airer, with "the"
23 Shout before throwing a rope

24 Pleased
26 Heir lines?
27 Shopping sites: Abbr.
29 P's
30 Corleone portrayer
31 Freshen, as a stamp pad
34 Thirst
36 Mercury 6 occupant
37 Wildlife ID
39 Commodore computer
40 Less apt to speak
42 Slaving away
43 Tijuana locale
45 Literary monogram
46 7, on a phone

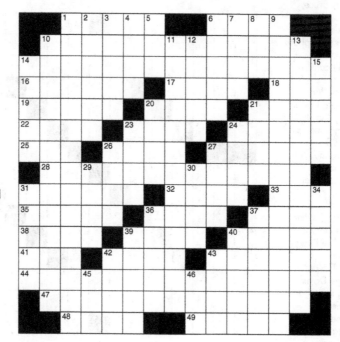

by Manny Nosowsky

ACROSS

1 Flirts with
8 Trying experiences
15 Eastbound waves?
17 "You and your conspiracy theories!"
18 Hera turned Antigone into one
19 Like the newspaper Al Shabiba
20 Main contents
21 Prefix with flop
22 Sea of ___, south of the Cyclades
23 Death to le roi
24 Space ball?
25 Six layers of a song?
26 Met number, maybe
27 Like arctic winds
28 Lenny Bruce, famously
29 Adjusts, as a magazine photo
32 Neckwear
33 Can't contain
34 Flock
35 Setting for Edward Hopper's "Nighthawks"
36 Paley's successor at CBS
37 Michelin guide no.?
40 E.P.A. output: Abbr.
41 Speed ___
42 Duster, for one
43 "The Story ___" (Pauline Réage novel)
44 "32 Flavors" singer Davis
45 Dog topper
46 Subjects of metaphysical research
49 "Picture Perfect" star
50 Permission slips, e.g.
51 Astrolabe alternative

DOWN

1 El Greco's "Bautismo de ___"
2 Milliner
3 Act on like a carbon filter
4 Barbie accessory
5 Buffet
6 Tabloid subj.
7 One of Chaucer's Canterbury pilgrims
8 Mexican beer named for its hometown
9 Marie, par exemple
10 Cabriolet maker
11 Portrait finish?
12 Ferretlike carnivore
13 Patriarch of the "First Family of Country Music"
14 Reel
16 Trammel
22 The biggest part of a large belt
23 Not pellucid
25 Person with a crystal ball
26 It was uttered in the past
27 Trapper's stock
28 Fashions
29 1985 Arnold Schwarzenegger film
30 Going rates?
31 Regular settings
32 Plants that are a natural source of cyanide
34 One who holds a note
36 "Sweet ___, run softly, till I end my song": Spenser
37 Where to begin
38 ___ Sea of California's Sonoran Desert
39 Terse demurral
41 Like the Rock of Ages
42 Focus of many an X-ray
44 Predisposed to fightin'
45 Multiple of CI
47 Georges Perec's 1969 novel "La Disparition" is written entirely without this
48 Compass dir.

by Byron Walden

ACROSS

1 See 17-Across
4 Beaux
10 Office figure: Abbr.
14 Old featherweight champion Attell
15 Actor Lyle of 1950s TV's "The Bob Cummings Show"
16 Half of a fish?
17 With 1-Across, mutual fund category
18 One way to shop
19 Quotation designation: Abbr.
20 Los Angeles Opera director beginning in 2000
23 Shrew
24 Hot topic of the 1992 presidential campaign
26 Service status
27 Shines
31 Deepens, in a way
34 Multi-generational diamond name
35 78 letters
36 Emulate 20- or 55-Across?
39 Fourth qtr. ender
42 Eavesdropping aid
43 Good guy
47 Banking officials
50 Daughter of Maggie and Jiggs
51 Keep under wraps
52 Latin masses?
55 One of two smashing siblings?
59 Barbara Kingsolver's "___ América"
60 Cross the novelist
61 Radar, say: Abbr.
62 Winners' flashes
63 Enter all at once
64 Opposite of AAA
65 Takes on
66 End table accompanier
67 Kind of deviation, in stats.

DOWN

1 Itch reliever
2 Eisenhower's boyhood home
3 Did footwork?
4 Far from demonstrative
5 Sykes of stand-up comedy
6 Sets apart
7 Footnote abbr.
8 Moral philosophy topic
9 Supporter of nature
10 Some ranges
11 Entertained, in a way
12 Grow by leaps and bounds
13 Some smiths work in it
21 Staked thing
22 Make happen
25 Green-keeping device?
28 Spire or obelisk, e.g.
29 Public offering
30 First name in linguistics
32 Saucy little girl
33 Body protector
37 Scratch (out)
38 Lack of excitement
39 ___ Peres (St. Louis suburb)
40 Was
41 Like many a reception
44 Cheers
45 Split and toasted treat
46 Bothered
48 Progress-impeding situation
49 Upright cousin
53 Chestnut
54 Smoother
56 Is off guard
57 Valéry's valentine
58 Wall Street Journal columnist Mossberg
59 Fertility clinic stock

by Gilbert H. Ludwig

26

ACROSS

1 Request made while pointing at a display case
5 Little bit
8 Kind of patch
14 Ups
15 #4, once, in Boston
16 Appear that way
17 Ltrs. may be written in them
18 One of 100 positions
20 What some of the letters in this puzzle seemingly have
22 Link
23 Sound at a spa
24 Sound
30 Zoom
32 Nickname for young Skywalker
34 Words of concurrence
35 An old Warner Bros. production?
37 Carried away
39 How you have to think to solve this puzzle
42 Volunteered
43 Sleeveless Arab garment
44 Go this way and that
45 Where Billy the Kid was born, believe it or not: Abbr.
47 River that rises in Monte Falterona
50 Argentine writer ___ Sábato
52 It's well-regulated
54 Drop
56 Spills out, in the Bible
59 Universal competitor
64 Language from which shawl and divan come
65 Astronaut Collins
66 Start of an apology
67 Not stick out
68 Feedback
69 Suffix with planet
70 Performed terribly, slangily

DOWN

1 Try to pick up
2 Striped animals
3 Do business with
4 She, in Venice
5 Words repeated at the start of the "Sailor's Song"
6 Hit 1986–87 R & B album
7 Movie with the opening line "I admire your courage, Miss . . . ?"
8 Reply in a juvenile spat
9 Elder, e.g.
10 Row makers
11 "Trust ___" (1937 hit)
12 Do, re or mi, in Italy
13 Tough problem
19 Sparkling
21 Nice brushes
25 Super Bowl souvenir
26 Map line
27 Robert who wrote "The Power Broker"
28 Kind of card
29 Coffee-to-go necessity
31 In eruption
33 Disadvantaged
36 Bombed
38 Opposite of "duh!"
39 Humdinger
40 ___-Ude, Russia
41 Afresh
42 Milk source
46 Really good one
48 "Hold on!"
49 Mario Puzo best seller
51 Dots on a map
53 "Suppose . . ."
55 "___ the bag!"
57 First name in humor
58 Whacks
59 Insect repellent ingredient
60 Delicious but fattening
61 Precollege
62 Ages and ages
63 Deferential

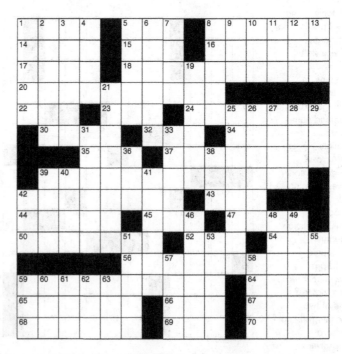

by Kevan Choset and David Kwong

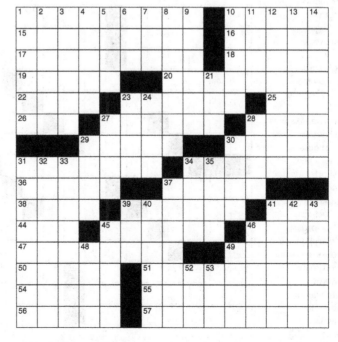

ACROSS

1 "The Art of Happiness" writer
10 Self-styled superiors
15 Joanie Cunningham portrayer, in 1970s–'80s TV
16 Universal product
17 It's just between us
18 Conform
19 Some shavers
20 Symbol of protection
22 Co-star of "The Witches of Eastwick"
23 Help in rounding up
25 Bug
26 Is down with
27 Bring down
28 Mexican plantation product
29 Actor Burton
30 Santa portrayer in "Elf"
31 United, for one
34 Like Playboy's Playmate of the Year
36 Standard partner
37 First name among diarists
38 Novel figure: Abbr.
39 Some old Acuras
41 Hrs. on the Mississippi
44 "Laggiù ___ Soledad" (Puccini aria)
45 Renounce
46 Daughter of Cap'n Andy in "Show Boat"
47 Daubs
49 "Gotcha"
50 Boy with a canine pal, in '50s TV
51 They're a big part of the life of Riley
54 Virtual transactions
55 He starred opposite Florence Henderson in "Fanny"
56 "Die Hard 2" director Harlin
57 Memorable

DOWN

1 Separate
2 "___ Arrives" (1967 soul album)
3 Petrol measures
4 Proximate, poetically
5 "___ corny . . ." ("A Wonderful Guy" lyric)
6 Drawing
7 Equal
8 Less green
9 Lackluster
10 Like some cards
11 Connecting point
12 Brand mentioned in "You're the Top"
13 Old fliers
14 Not with the others
21 Be up
23 Assess
24 Stuck, after "in"
27 Places to sleep
28 Penultimate letters
29 Bereft, old-style
30 x, y or z
31 One who's not the marrying type
32 Tuolumne Meadows locale
33 Lady's other half
34 Reason to bring out the chains
35 Net
37 Wrestle
39 Power: Lat.
40 Glucose, to fructose
41 Telling
42 Tawdriness
43 Unwanted buildup
45 Sans spice
46 Like some innings
48 1980s Lebanese president ___ Gemayel
49 Red, maybe
52 A hand
53 40-Down, e.g.: Abbr.

by Adam Cohen

28

ACROSS

1 Appear briefly, as a parade float
7 Spanish priest who famously opposed the conquistadors
15 Unbroken
16 She played a jilted wife in "Intermezzo," 1939
17 Note takers
18 Handyman's kit
19 TV, unflatteringly
21 Wrinkle-faced pooch
22 Went through the motions on stage, perhaps
23 Reaction to bad news
24 W shelfmate
25 Poor marks
26 Margin
27 Like Fagin
28 The ravages of time
29 King's card
30 She won the 1983 Oscar for Best Song
32 Went over the line?
35 Southeastern Conf. powerhouse
36 Memory unit, for short
39 Mantle's jersey number
40 ___ Lachaise (Paris's largest cemetery)
41 Builders at Uxmal
42 Underground treasures
43 Big moments
45 Land on the Arctic Cir.
46 Star of a "CSI" spinoff

47 Animal that's often exempt from "no pets" restrictions
49 Author of the Three Laws of Robotics
50 How chatterboxes talk
51 Togs
52 Diagnostic administered at home
53 Put in order

DOWN

1 Apothecaries' tools
2 Colonial home?
3 With a high grade
4 Star of a "CSI" spinoff
5 Watts's "King Kong" co-star, 2005
6 "I should say so!"

7 Famous first words
8 Desert dwellings
9 Hair confiner
10 Metal oxide
11 "The Lone Ranger" airer, 1949–57
12 City on the water
13 Soften
14 "Angle of Repose" author
20 Current location?
23 City founded by Mormon pioneers
26 Aloe additive?
28 Small-but-loud songbird
29 Actor originally slated to play Michael Corleone in "The Godfather"
30 Seals, in a way
31 Minded

32 Massachusetts senator succeeded by Kerry
33 Send another way
34 Earl in the Baseball Hall of Fame
36 Release from slavery
37 Blight
38 Flame-based cooker
40 Revolves
41 Akio ___, co-founder of Sony
43 Daughter in Inge's "Picnic"
44 Discrimination
46 Small bit of progress
48 Absolutely, in slang

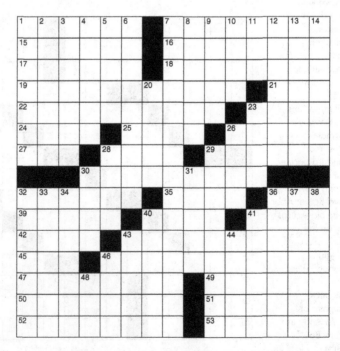

by Patrick Berry

ACROSS

1 Eclipse
5 Not reliable
15 Ophthalmologic study
16 "Really!"
17 Get back
18 Shrub with richly fragrant purple flowers
19 Lowlife
21 Festive time
22 Make use of
23 Guy's feminine side
24 100 kurus
25 Hoppers, e.g.
26 It's quite attractive
28 Dwarf galaxy orbiting the Milky Way
29 Member of a TV high-school clique
30 Fleeced
31 Pre-1939 atlas name
32 Some Congressional spending
33 Emotional upheaval
36 Ready to play
40 Harden
41 Stroke of luck?
42 Olympic gold-medal swimmer ___ Borg
43 Stew
44 Wag a finger at
45 Stern word to Spot
46 Movement part
47 Trial balloon
48 Fred MacMurray's "Singapore" co-star
51 Del ___ (Los Angeles suburb)

52 Figure in the Capitol's Statuary Hall
53 Rules, quickly
54 Having trouble staying up
55 Chinese menu possessive

DOWN

1 Time capsule ceremonies
2 As we speak
3 Where some vacations are spent
4 Rule that can be bent
5 "Our Man in New Orleans" jazzman
6 Behar of men's fashion
7 Putting in order
8 Beseech
9 White-striped antelope
10 Doctor's order
11 Buttoned up
12 Sign off on
13 Voice
14 Stamps
20 Isabella's realm
24 Hang over one's head
25 Result of a split, maybe
27 "What's ___?"
28 Small squirrellike animals
30 Modeled
32 Washed out
33 They often have strings attached
34 Decipher
35 Everyday
36 Feminine
37 Some are under plates
38 Live through
39 She ranks
41 Football conference
43 Sudden strike
46 Cousin of a shiner
47 Ward of Hollywood
49 "Really?!"
50 Wide spec.

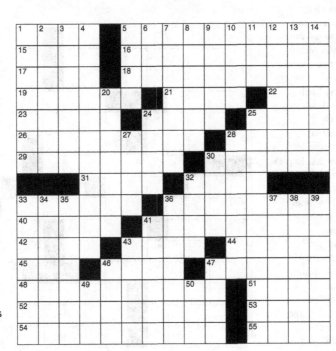

by James E. Buell

ACROSS

1 Electrical connectors
10 League parts
15 Sweet little thing
16 Lumberjack
17 Worked up
18 "The Name Above the Title" autobiographer, 1971
19 Volcano feature
20 Look that may include thick-rimmed glasses
22 Small goose
24 Seedy joint
25 Gossip
26 Lean on
27 ___ League
28 Try to get in
30 1980s sitcom starring Geena Davis
31 Large track
34 Jellied delicacy
35 Clutch
37 It may be sympathetic
38 Have ___ to pick
40 Herbal drink
43 Actress Louise
44 2001 winner of the Israel Prize
45 Bond girl in "Octopussy"
49 Some modern icons
51 Assaulted
52 Entrance area
53 "Ronzoni ___ buoni" (old ad slogan)
54 Earthen jar
55 Cause for exclaiming "That's it!"
59 Extraterrestrial
60 Usually
61 Played out
62 Person with a line?

DOWN

1 Passed without notice
2 Poe subject
3 1965 Yardbirds hit
4 Cornmeal concoction
5 H.S. biology topic
6 Old telecom inits.
7 "Uh-uh!"
8 One of 16 popes
9 Reinforces
10 Cheap
11 Big bets
12 Ancient Greek storage vessels
13 Pasta topper
14 Cineplex feature
21 Barely get
23 Bind
24 Stink
29 Currency replaced by the euro
31 Grinds
32 Worker's advocate, for short
33 Pharmacy solution
36 Stuff
39 Hornswoggles
41 Literary miscellany
42 Official magazine of the National Space Society
46 Yupik outerwear
47 Get by
48 Longshoreman, at times
50 Part of many a Halloween costume
56 Sorry
57 Sets
58 Two qtrs.

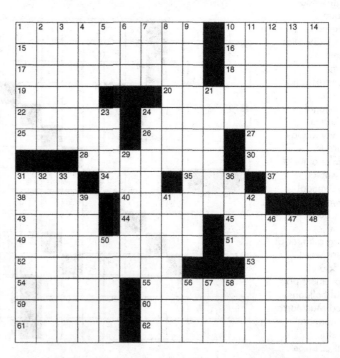

by Bob Peoples

ACROSS

1 Tiny margin
8 Tacit
14 Teens' hangout, once
16 Fret
17 Tribe around Lake Superior
18 College ___
19 Doesn't keep
20 Historical word forms
22 Hot rod?
23 "Lookee here!"
24 Joints
26 Francis ___, "Love Story" composer
27 "Which is ___ . . . ?"
29 "Holy Toledo!"
30 Over
32 Cost of something dear
35 Early lesson in foreign language instruction
37 Court session
38 Conference: Abbr.
39 Night spot
40 Recitals showing promise
44 Mint
45 Monodactylous
48 Old truck maker
49 Andean peak ___ Cruces
51 Query found in Matthew
52 The Philippines' ___ Archipelago
53 Endangered
55 Antique sources of light
57 Second shot
58 March Madness contest

59 They travel by air
60 Some soil contaminants

DOWN

1 Certain account
2 Refrain from piracy?
3 Post office worker?
4 Goes one up on
5 Poison source
6 Utter
7 "It's getting late"
8 Concentrated, in a way
9 ___-Kantian
10 Bath features
11 Place for cabins
12 Calligrapher's medium

13 Lot
15 Focuses
21 Landlord's entitlement, with "a"
24 Tropicana's parent
25 Whence maple syrup
28 Refuse
31 Oscar winner Davis
33 Children's author/illustrator Asquith
34 Cry made with a fist-pump
35 Court-martial candidate
36 Be supervised by
37 Brassy blast
41 "Plain Speaking" biographee

42 Signal for a good samaritan
43 Pickled specimens
46 Some sneaks
47 Gulf of Aqaba city
50 Musical kingdom
52 Siegfried and Sigmund's story, e.g.
54 Music for Mods and Skinheads
56 "Well, ___-di-dah!"

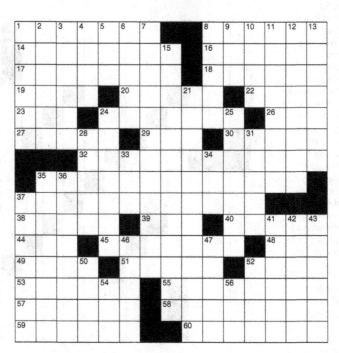

by Manny Nosowsky

32

ACROSS
1 Brilliant thinkers they're not
12 Some fallout
15 Hookup spot
16 Part of R.R.: Abbr.
17 Some tape-recorded interviews
18 Family V.I.P.'s
19 Deliver crosses, e.g.
20 It's next to nothing
21 They line some streets
23 Barron's reader, slangily
25 Creator of Genesis
27 Concerto component
28 Mideastern royal family name
30 NASA craft
32 Mil. list
33 Period in India's history
35 Hydrotherapy option
37 Vostok 1 passenger
41 Place for seeds
42 "Me? Harrumph!"
44 Org. in which decisions are awarded
45 You might tear it up
46 Some dairy stock
48 Abbr. in the real estate section
51 Choisy-___ (Paris suburb)
53 Employer of TV's Nash Bridges, briefly
55 1997 Bond girl Michelle
57 "ER" actress Freeman
59 100 sen
61 Miracle-___
62 Kind of student, for short

63 Versatile restaurant style
66 Neighbor of Telescopium
67 Song with the lyric "When you kiss me heaven sighs"
68 Turner of a page in history
69 Big top worker

DOWN
1 Unfriendly sorts
2 Like Swiss cheese
3 Muscular disorder
4 Picture within a picture?
5 Like some textbook publishers
6 Spot announcements?
7 Big Dutch export
8 Late stages, of sorts
9 W.W. II inits.

10 Course
11 More sharp
12 Georgian's neighbor
13 It's not measured in traditional years
14 1980 Pointer Sisters hit
22 Second youngest QB to win a Super Bowl
24 Ping and Pong are characters in it
26 Third of a Latin sextet
29 Show spunk
31 Not busy
34 Talk of swingers
36 Singer called the Texas Troubadour
37 No Mr. Macho
38 Cream additive

39 Mad-dogged
40 What's going on
43 It may follow a bridge
47 Grand alternative
49 Several departments, maybe
50 Far from bright
52 Dash follower?
54 Put on the back burner
56 One working on the cutting edge?
58 Tony's portrayer on "NYPD Blue"
60 ___ moth
64 Literature Nobelist Andric
65 What many an Indian is called

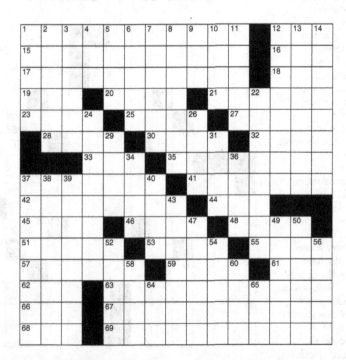

by Brendan Emmett Quigley

ACROSS

1 Goons
5 "Star Wars" villain, for short
10 Not solid
14 "Shoot!"
15 Others, abroad
16 Senate majority leader, 1985–87
17 Animated friend of the monkey Boots
20 It's not standard
21 Some are natural
22 1940s–'60s world leader
23 Mollify
24 Underhanded
25 Send over
27 A toast
30 Find one's place
31 Supergroup of the 1980s
32 Corrupted
35 Egyptian architect credited with building the Step Pyramid at Saqqara
36 Puts on a pedestal
37 Give money to
38 "Hits the spot" sloganeer, once
39 Up to
40 One of the Beverly Hillbillies
43 Some farmers
45 Caterpillar competitor
47 Battle of Britain fighter
49 Builder's need, often
50 Division of many a company
52 Vision: Prefix
53 Get ready to drive
54 Apple variety
55 Weak one
56 Blast from the past
57 Boss Tweed skewerer

DOWN

1 They're not standard
2 Move forward
3 Unrefined
4 Part of a flight
5 New Testament figure
6 Took in
7 Best-selling author of "The Gang That Couldn't Shoot Straight"
8 It's in for the long haul
9 Food garnish
10 "Beats me"
11 Evict
12 Skip
13 Informal possessive
18 Sign inside a state line
19 Renter
23 Stamp with a date
26 Are, in Arles
28 Drink with a straw, maybe
29 Cut
30 High parts
31 Mid-millennium year
32 Passbook abbr.
33 Windows file extension
34 5-Down and others
35 Dramatic football plays: Abbr.
37 Popped in
39 Take off a spindle
40 Aunt ___
41 Heathers
42 Sense
44 "We ___ please"
46 Senator of Watergate fame
47 It's got a flat bottom
48 Kind of platter
49 Nickname for José
51 ___ juris (in one's own right): Lat.

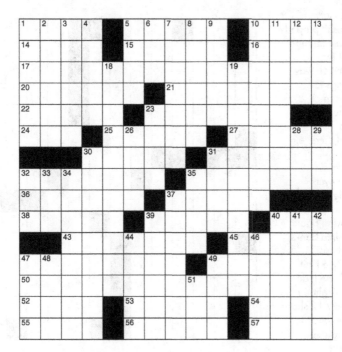

by Eric Berlin

ACROSS

1 Quick
4 Course yardstick
7 Standard pass
13 Hoity-toity
16 Unfrequented
17 Taking a grand tour, say
18 It's measured in radians
19 Buckthorn trees with medically useful bark
20 ___ Island, home for part of the Gateway National Recreation Area
21 Transistor electrodes
22 Stud
23 Postulate
24 Doesn't properly follow through
26 Not the common way
28 Things to pass in
33 Puffer's place
34 Flip
35 N.H.L'.ers, e.g.
38 Tops
39 Routs
44 Ran over
45 Volleys
47 Spam producer
48 Moving about
49 Go into banks, perhaps
50 1972 #1 hit with the lyric "I'm right up the road / I'll share your load"
51 Leaf sides
52 Person with a plan
53 Makes oneself appear smart
54 Actor Wass
55 Cape ___

DOWN

1 Caterpillar engager
2 Boater alternative
3 Need for a third degree?
4 Take illegally
5 Big fans
6 Beat poets?
7 Couple in a date
8 Signs
9 Privately
10 Does, as a Tennessee Williams play
11 Heirs, legally
12 Port on Massachusetts Bay
14 They bring tears to one's eyes
15 Big name in oil
24 Treaty violation, maybe
25 Place of debauchery
27 Media center?
28 William Gladstone, politically: Abbr.
29 Winning full house, for short
30 Shelled-out amount
31 Judge
32 Halloween costume
36 Natural
37 Potassium ___ (food mold inhibitor)
40 Cut back
41 Beauty spot
42 Pre-1962 British protectorate
43 Scribes
45 Mt. Agung locale
46 Demanding
47 Dwell

by Robert H. Wolfe

ACROSS

1 Unexpected birth
11 Somewhat
15 Four times what's left?
16 Guy de Maupassant's "Mademoiselle ___"
17 Pre-Gothic style
18 Like 101 courses: Abbr.
19 Staff members
20 Carriage trade-oriented
22 Wash tidally
24 Like the bar scene
25 Eco location
29 "The program's starting"
31 "The ___ Quartet" (Paul Scott work)
32 Lucknow dress
33 Guitar great Montgomery
34 "Let that occur," to Shakespeare
36 Defenseless
38 Deserted
39 Anti-insect application
40 Annie in "Klondike Annie"
41 Instrument made of turtle shell
42 "All that we see or seem / Is but a dream within a dream" writer
43 Relatives of the Missouria
45 Throws
46 Poker?
48 Shoulder ID
50 Army medics
52 Tie up
57 Kind of diagram
58 Near failure
60 Start of something big

61 No longer an issue?
62 Track numbers
63 Where to read about last night's game

DOWN

1 Game periods: Abbr.
2 "Did I just do what I think I did?!"
3 Owner/waitress in "Garfield"
4 Approximate
5 Like some heavy-duty tires
6 ___ hammer on (pounds)
7 Tech store purchases
8 Japanese plums
9 Goes off
10 Be loaded
11 Intensely interested
12 Early building gear
13 In some way
14 Some forwarded e-mails
21 Saul's general, in the Bible
23 Motley
25 "That would be my guess"
26 Like khakis
27 One unlike almost any other
28 Pre-euro cash
30 The duck in "Peter and the Wolf"

33 Took off
35 Destinación de vacaciones
37 Burmese cries
38 Secured
40 Had the intention of doing
44 Shout accompanied by pounding
45 Aviary racket
47 Some essays
49 Split
51 Lows
53 Climber's snack
54 Samoan capital
55 Like a Salmon P. Chase bill, slangily
56 90° from norte
59 TV control: Abbr.

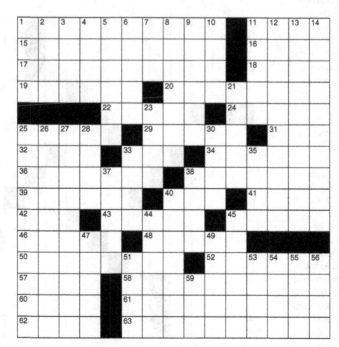

by Manny Nosowsky

ACROSS

1 Picnic side dish
11 Dosage abbr.
15 Defensive shell
16 Van ___ (Ohio county or its seat)
17 Difficult to eradicate
18 Ready to serve
19 Cutting-edge features
20 On pins and needles
22 "Momo" author Michael ___
23 It's often sweetened
24 A Pointer sister
27 On the way up
28 Springfield storekeeper on TV
29 ___ caramel
31 Sounding
32 Turn over
34 Blinds, essentially
36 Woodworking channel
37 ___ Kringle
39 MX-5, in the auto world
41 Pinup part
42 Country
44 Ponderosa choice
46 The Queen of Latin Pop
47 G.I. garb, for short
48 Make less threatening
49 Compound used to treat chiggers and scabies
53 ___ Sea (giant salt lake)
54 Jacqueline Onassis, professionally
56 It might be added with a twist
57 Surrendering sorts
58 Uses up
59 Requiring no preparation

DOWN

1 Fills out
2 State stat
3 Merganser relative
4 Hit list
5 It's detected by the Marsh test, in forensics
6 They can get caught in traps
7 Winged
8 Plaster base
9 Took a loss on
10 Gather
11 Ambiguous
12 Hill runner
13 Modern
14 Like some dads
21 Whom a bully may bully
23 "___ King this afternoon!": Emily Dickinson
24 Reverses course
25 Mozart's "La Clemenza di Tito," e.g.
26 Where visitors can barely relax?
27 Screened correspondence?
30 Jazz trumpeter Ziggy
33 Harris of "Seinfeld" and others
35 Approach
38 Remote hiding place?
40 Targeted
43 Shucked-to-order spot
45 Skipjack
47 High, in a way, with "up"
49 First name in gossip
50 Oklahoma native
51 Romance novelist Roberts
52 At first, once
55 Honour given to Joan Collins: Abbr.

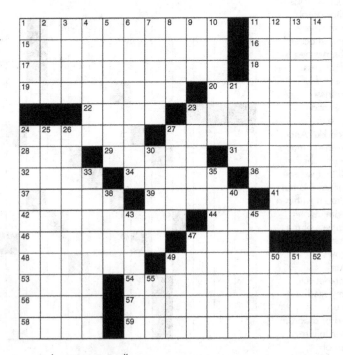

by James E. Buell

ACROSS

1 With 7-Down, an ordering principle
9 Program holders
15 Comic born John Sanford
16 Boeing rival
17 "For real!"
18 Least
19 Former sight from New York's Grand Central Parkway
20 The whim-whams
22 "Agreed"
23 Besteads
25 Going hand in hand
27 Area map
29 California's ___ Observatory
33 Oil, e.g.
37 ___ Van Duyn, 1991 Pulitzer-winning poet
38 Part of Hammurabi's code
41 First name in sportscasting
42 Yankee's home
43 Encase
46 Valid conclusion?
47 Picked up
49 Browning title character
53 Contribute (to)
56 Bivouac
58 Annoy no end
59 Military wear
61 Be sleepy
63 Saw
64 Gloss
65 II
66 Caribbean paradise

DOWN

1 Like the River Erne
2 "You ___ judge"
3 "The ___ is here to stay" (ill-considered corporate pronouncement of 1957)
4 Need for drugs?
5 With 9-Down, like some interviews
6 Reddish-brown
7 See 1-Across
8 Spare
9 See 5-Down
10 Service station sign
11 The basics, in a way
12 Follow
13 Cogitate
14 Former boomers
21 Special privileges
24 Cut
26 Japanese "thanks"
28 Comment of frustration
30 Not worth discussing
31 You might get a hand for it
32 Athletic support
33 Thrashes
34 Kings Peak locale
35 Drag
36 Drama often with masks
39 Prince Edward I. clock setting
40 Sporty car addition
44 Get set to bite
45 Fairy tale brother
48 Spoilers, at times
50 ___ Games
51 South American silver
52 Mont Blanc and others
53 The basics
54 Strike out
55 Popular 1940s radio quiz show
57 Shut (up)
60 French shield
62 "I am such a dummy!"

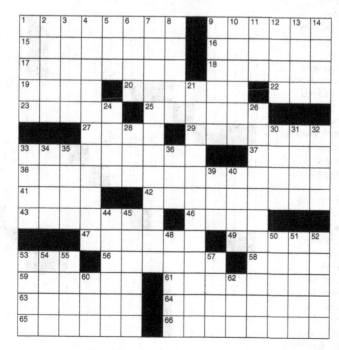

by David Quarfoot

ACROSS

1 He wrote "I have the true feeling of myself only when I am unbearably unhappy"
11 N.L. East nine
15 Lloyd's of London locale
16 It gets notions
17 Short-lived constructions
18 Natives call it Mongibello
19 It's no marathon
20 It's unlikely to be realized
22 Hall of fame
23 Takers of Tenochtitlán
25 Formed
26 Literally, "baked"
29 Inclines
32 Isn't delicate with
33 Editor
34 TV cop with a pet cockatoo named Fred
35 Word after "attached"
36 A week's worth of groceries, perhaps
37 German town
38 Lot
39 One may be striking
41 Bank security aid, briefly
44 Follow priestly orders?
46 Municipality, in some financial names
47 Maker of running shoes
48 "Way Out West" co-star, 1937

51 Move merchandise
52 Cramped locale
53 Units in Physics 101
54 Really bug

DOWN

1 Top-___ golf balls
2 Like some potatoes
3 Better
4 Make out
5 Half-sister of Eva?
6 Figures from 1 to 24: Abbr.
7 Stationer's supply
8 Stealthy ones
9 Not drop
10 Confounded
11 Bum

12 Substantiates
13 Casserole option
14 Old kingdom name
21 Noah Wyle's "ER" role
23 It has a slightly heavier British counterpart
24 Entrance march into a bullfighting arena
25 Gets through quickly, in a way
27 "I'm history"
28 Somewhat
29 Code bits
30 ABBA's "___ the Music Speak"
31 Robust
32 ___ que (because, in Brest)

34 Makes the rounds?
36 Buckthorn variety
38 Olympus competitor
40 It may hold the thé
41 Around
42 Really bugged
43 "It's Too Late Now" literary autobiographer
44 Comedian Chappelle
45 During
46 One calling the moves for a round dance
49 Bell part
50 Twa into twa

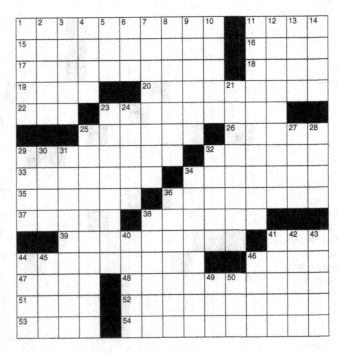

by Brendan Emmett Quigley

ACROSS
1 Top of the pops
10 In the loop
15 Flowering plant used in folk remedies
16 Toughness
17 Undeniable facts
18 Teacart goodie
19 "Hup, two, three, four" caller
21 "Ba-da-___, ba-da-boom"
22 ___ Williams, Huck Finn's female alias
23 Arranged anew, as paintings
26 One taken by an artist
29 Conception
30 Sand castle destroyers
31 Unpopular singer?
32 Baptism castoffs
33 Spaced (out)
34 War correspondent Ernie
35 Cows and bulls
36 Sound technician
37 Romantic hopeful
38 English portraitist who championed the Grand Style
40 It may add up
41 Tightwad
42 Hefty hammer
43 Telecommunications needs
49 Beam joiner
50 Backdrop of "What Price Glory"
51 Where a bungee cord might attach
52 Built for comfort
53 Emulated a coyote
54 Units of X-ray exposure

DOWN
1 Moving stock
2 One putting on finishing touches
3 Like kickboxing, originally
4 Isopods known as roly-polies
5 Oily compound used in dyes
6 Number of stars, perhaps
7 Getting 100 on
8 Radio Hall-of-Famer Rick
9 Certain Manhattanite
10 Warrants
11 Believer in the Rule of Three
12 Final Wilder/Pryor screen outing
13 Frequent target of old Ferrell "S.N.L." skits
14 Porcelain piece
20 Without leaves
23 Stage item
24 French sociologist Durkheim
25 Funny business
26 They comprise a part
27 "The Crucible" setting
28 Like disciplinarians
30 Excellent
33 Big name in jewelry
34 Gill-breathing amphibian
36 Symbolized
37 First word sung on the Beach Boys' "Pet Sounds" album
39 Wife in Fitzgerald's "Tender Is the Night"
40 Visit
42 Pool
43 Go
44 Former Royals manager Tony
45 Lawnmower handle
46 Break
47 Name meaning, literally, west island
48 Unleashes

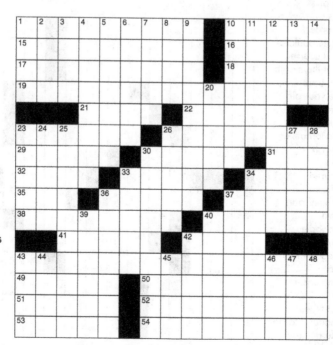

by Patrick Berry

ACROSS

1 Serious accident
10 Goal
15 Folk music scholar who helped popularize Woody Guthrie and Muddy Waters
16 Smashing
17 Dapple
18 "Jive at Five" composer/performer
19 Fall off
20 Very much for
22 Lukewarm reviews
23 American Airlines Ctr. team
24 Coasted at the Olympics?
25 Yanks
26 Dr.'s order?
27 Discombobulates
29 Took a course
30 City at the mouth of the Loire
32 "Take your pick"
34 Widely seen
36 Shade of black
37 Port alternatives
41 Waggish
45 Hacker
46 Treasured blankets
48 100 Bulgarian stotinki
49 Flapdoodle
50 Johnson who managed the 1986 championship Mets
51 Quiet types
52 Schooner's cargo
53 Hindu deities
54 Piano key, essentially
55 Complex unit
57 In one's spare time
59 Top-flight story
60 Intimate chats
61 Otterlike
62 Imbroglio

DOWN

1 Fossil remains of homo erectus discovered in 1891
2 Where Zelda Fitzgerald and Nat King Cole were born
3 Parade
4 Interlocks
5 Co-founder of the avant-garde Blue Four
6 Thick quaff
7 Words sung after "Hallelujah"
8 Flag
9 Critical analysis
10 0-198-61186-2, e.g.
11 1988 Meg Ryan thriller
12 "Popeye" cartoonist
13 Emperor beginning in 1989
14 "The Most Happy Fella" composer
21 Classic song that's the official anthem of the European Union
24 "A Study in Scarlet" inspector
27 Dahomey, since 1975
28 Drives off
31 Corn grower
33 Series finale
35 "Hubba hubba!"
37 Mexican rattlers
38 Southwestern salamander
39 Thaw
40 Grassland dotted with trees
42 Peridot, e.g.
43 Leaves the country
44 Major hurdle, metaphorically
47 Palace card
51 Quark-antiquark combo
53 Curtail
54 Shoot, slangily
56 Go out
58 It might turn up a lot

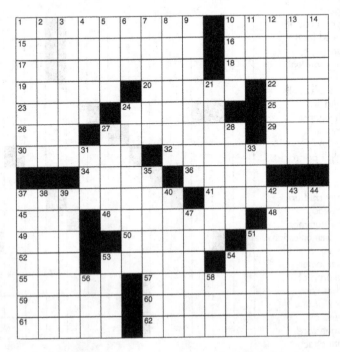

by Bob Klahn

41

ACROSS

1 First bishop of Paris
8 Can openers
15 "Good shot!"
16 It won't disappoint
17 Follow in the footsteps of
18 Top-notch
19 Bard's dark time
20 Ford product, briefly
22 Crazy Horse, for one
23 "___ the season . . ."
25 Pushing 90?
27 All-good filler
29 Brit. decorations
30 Revenuers, e.g.
31 Ancient
33 Start of many addresses
35 1980 Pulitzer-winning book filled with wordplay and paradoxes
41 Neon's lack
42 Having little talent for
43 Contents of some silos: Abbr.
47 Provider of immunity on "Survivor"
49 Zingers
50 Artists' stands?
53 Object in a courtroom
54 Latinum or Graecum
55 See 27-Down
57 Dot on a subway map: Abbr.
59 Total
61 Like some recordings
63 One out?
64 Celebrated

65 Most concise
66 Assigns a new ranking to, in a way

DOWN

1 Old-fashioned knife
2 "Pack it up"
3 R.F.K. Stadium team
4 Elusive one
5 Sitcom director Pitlik
6 Purveyor of chips
7 Be really sore
8 Endings to some e-mails
9 Marching sloppily
10 Newman's Own alternative

11 Relate
12 Flattened at the poles
13 Uttered loudly and sonorously
14 Cremona collectibles
21 Tobacco and others
24 Place for a horn
26 Archaic auxiliary
27 With 55-Across, auction alternative
28 London greeting
32 Sets apart
34 "No ___!"
36 Kind of ash
37 Luau entree
38 Many a suspect

39 Place for a pickup line?
40 City map abbr.
43 Cry after being held up
44 Restrain
45 Tailor, at times
46 Doesn't rest between pieces
48 Chief
51 Course in a German meal
52 Ooze
56 Sponsorship
58 Fliers' concerns: Abbr.
60 Leftover
62 Like Chopin's "Tristesse" étude

by Mike Torch

42

ACROSS

1 Bantered
7 Early Hebrew king
15 Rise
16 Sponsor of a historic expedition
17 Sticks in the supermarket
18 Potential to get around
19 Food filtered from seawater
20 Some sorority women
21 Sliding door site
22 Sloughs
23 Principle
24 Ceramic muralist for the Unesco building in Paris
25 1960s sitcom role for Felix Silla
26 U-Haul alternative
27 Common catalyst
28 Increase
30 Energetic
32 Beset by problems
34 Nostrum
38 Spam locale
40 ___ Farms, Maryland-based food giant
41 Stressful things?
44 Some execs
46 Kelly Clarkson's record label
47 Constellation appellation
48 Adams of Sinn Fein
49 Potential con
50 Touch of frost
51 Mayan commodity
52 Exchanged notes?
53 Sara Sidle's player on "CSI"
55 Labor class?
56 Drive off
57 Henry Fielding title heroine
58 Beat
59 Matthew who founded a college in 1861

DOWN

1 Northern pike
2 "Die Fledermaus," for one
3 It might get under your skin
4 Cooled things?
5 Count, now
6 Uninteresting
7 Nobel-winning poet Juan Ramón ___
8 Rarefied
9 Capital on the Atlantic
10 Bands of geishas
11 With 43-Down, très witty person
12 Niece of Sir Toby Belch, in "Twelfth Night"
13 Sites for some swearers
14 Is forbidden to
20 Series finale, in Stafford
23 Laid-back
24 Debbie ___, triple gold-medal Olympic swimmer, 1968
26 Archaeologists' interest
27 Battle site of 1914, 1915 and 1917
29 Franco's first
31 Lightweight boxer?
33 Birdhouse, of a kind
35 Pair above the kidneys
36 Daughter of Pope Alexander VI
37 1984, e.g.
39 Reproduced, in a way
41 Asian region whose name means "five rivers"
42 Blue Jay opponent
43 See 11-Down
45 Century 21 alternative
48 Succeed in spades
49 Apples, e.g.
51 Means of support
52 Nursery cry
54 Nose-in-the-air model?
55 Head, for short

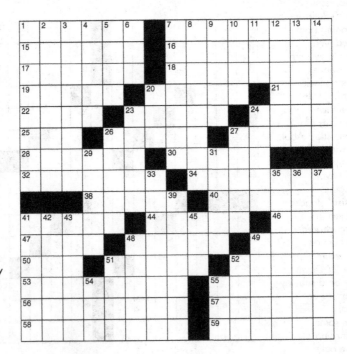

by Will Nediger

ACROSS
1 Having a bite
6 Crack heads
10 Well out of range
14 Shipwreck Beach locale
15 Playboy
16 Disneyland's Space Mountain, e.g.
17 Moves along
18 Three strikes and you're out, say
20 Dairy Queen orders
22 Price list word
23 Gallic title: Abbr.
24 Mork's language
26 Old swinger
28 Red-tags
32 Sight in the southern sky
33 Speck
34 Where tigers roam
35 Sweaters?
38 Sideshow attractions
41 ___-loading
42 Israir alternative
43 Parent
44 "Silent Night" adjective
45 Times of crisis
47 Pal around
50 Famous people
51 Resetting setting
52 Tear
54 Potsdam Conference attendee
58 "And . . ."
61 Drop off
62 A Balkanite
63 Has a hand out
64 Bottled spirit?
65 Track calculation
66 Tranquil scene
67 Elocute

DOWN
1 Range of some singers
2 Beef
3 ___ ether
4 Dating material
5 Small bar
6 Yearbook div.
7 What something has before it's dropped
8 What a seer may see
9 Clinton cabinet member
10 It might be framed
11 Work in pictures
12 Olmos's "Battlestar Galactica" role
13 Keep from desiccating
19 Inexpensive, slangily
21 Large seabirds
25 Come back
27 One who works for pin money?
28 45, e.g.
29 Straw poll setting
30 TV advertiser's prep work
31 Popular tea
36 "Sicut ___ in principio" (doxology phrase)
37 Old union members: Abbr.
39 Need for some drives
40 Pack carrier
46 "Get a move on!"
47 "In what way?"
48 Marveled aloud
49 Highest-grossing movie of 1942
53 Ole Miss miss, e.g.
55 Soviet space probe
56 Broadcast
57 A masked competitor waves it
59 "Dinner and a Movie" channel
60 Subj. for some future bilinguals

by Jim Page

44

ACROSS

1 Enclose
7 Plans out in detail
14 Unlikely beachgoers
16 Tyrant
17 Still, maybe
18 Goddess depicted holding a flute
19 Trisected
20 Real estate ad abbr.
21 "There ___ time . . ."
22 "A Heartbreaking Work of Staggering Genius" author
24 Heated competition?
25 Be sure of, with "on"
26 Bring in
27 Foaming at the mouth
31 Arrow poison
32 Heads
33 Blandished
34 Celsius who devised the Celsius scale
35 Most Marxian?
36 Bel ___
37 Plane-jumping G.I.
38 Auto loan nos.
39 Rant and rave
45 Needing a lift
46 Windjammer
47 Al-Anon member, maybe
48 Security personnel?
50 Heralds
51 If everything fails
52 Not moving

53 Picks again
54 Holders of conferences?

DOWN

1 Tasty
2 Actress Löwensohn of "Nadja," 1994
3 "Alias" airer
4 Ballerina-like
5 Naturalize
6 "I wouldn't have it any other way"
7 Gyroscope inventor
8 Associates closely
9 Refuse visitors
10 Burn up
11 Rules for allowing members of the opposite sex into dorms
12 Known to next to none
13 Like some swords
15 "Turn! Turn! Turn!" songwriter and others
23 Army of Hope member
24 Ancient capital on the Nile
26 Film maker
27 Historical Corsican family name
28 Soft support
29 Like English pronunciation in most of England
30 Sun-burned
31 Language of ancient Syria

32 Place to get paella
33 They can be carved out
35 Ringo's oldest son
37 Some cold ones
39 Kind of alphabet
40 Arabian capital
41 Legendary N.Y.C. club that launched punk rock
42 Woman from Chelsea, in the song "Cabaret"
43 Sam of "Wimbledon," 2004
44 Flying fish eaters
46 Spark
49 R.V. refuge org.

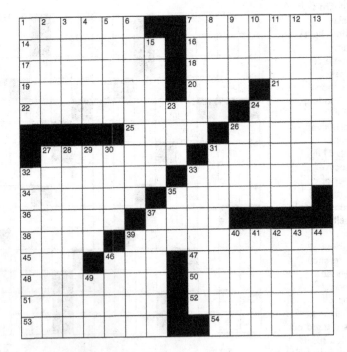

by Brendan Emmett Quigley

ACROSS

1 "Not to worry"
8 Plays pat-a-cake
13 Sinking of 1898
14 Become employed
16 Back and forth
17 Ships at sea
18 ___ Powers (negotiators between the U.S. and Mexico, 1914)
19 Sine ___ (timeless): Lat.
21 Opposite of brazen
22 Word said with a handshake
24 Order with a glass of milk
25 Women, slangily
26 Blues guitarist Sleepy John ___
28 Jockey Turcotte
29 Too much excitement
30 1966 musical about a taxi dancer
33 Makes things more interesting
36 Fuddy-duddy
37 Complain
38 Foot soldiers: Abbr.
39 Member of the Eastern establishment?
43 All in
44 Not just butterflies
46 Kind of candle
47 Allen wrench shape
48 Continuing annoyance
50 Familia relative
51 Undone
53 Attacker of colonies
55 "Most certainly, señor!"
56 Honor society rejectee
57 Playground retort
58 Objects of punches

DOWN

1 Where Jocasta was queen
2 Swinger, once
3 Org. founded by Dr. Nathan Smith Davis
4 Dress (up)
5 In place
6 "And while I'm on the subject . . ."
7 Reveal all
8 Mariner's aid
9 Bygone coins
10 Spot for a shot
11 Dove
12 Lot, e.g.
13 Buy and sell
15 Refuses
20 Any intelligence at all
23 Healthful food claim
25 Electromagnetism pioneer
27 Worry beads?
29 Agrippina, to Nero
31 Tee neighbor
32 Buying channel on TV
33 Ones clearing out?
34 Word of praise
35 High-mindedness
40 Poked (out)
41 Saucer contents
42 Pluck
44 Kind of feed
45 Cheap
48 Kiss: Sp.
49 Go for more duty
52 Insect egg
54 1969 Nabokov novel

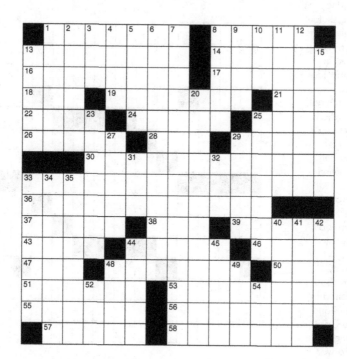

by Manny Nosowsky

ACROSS

1 Product line
16 One whose pieces are slanted
17 Post office department
18 It's full of x's: Abbr.
19 Puts down
20 Slip
21 Pernicious pets
23 First name among diarists
25 Operating
26 Put down
30 Cabeza, across the Pyrenees
31 Sparkle
32 Mini-shutout on the court
33 Repair shop stock
37 Parmenides of __
41 Some legal restrictions
42 Harsh calls
43 Sprays
44 They can be dulled
45 "__ lied!"
46 Burrow stash
50 There's a holy one every yr.
51 Variety show host inspired by the Grand Ole Opry
54 It might ward off a war
55 Flips

DOWN

1 Storage unit
2 Virginia Woolf's given birth name
3 Well-preserved one
4 Busy time in Saint-Tropez
5 1957 Jimmy Dorsey hit
6 Descendants of Ishmael
7 Coolidge Dam's river
8 Units of 100 ergs per gram
9 Part of a C.S.A. signature
10 Leather stickers
11 Annual opener
12 Relented
13 Stress, in a way
14 Takes to the other shore
15 Tax
22 Saskatoon-to-Winnipeg dir.
23 __ stands
24 Old march organizers: Abbr.
26 Parlor piece
27 Turn outward
28 Raid targets
29 Rousing cheers
31 Bound
32 The Eagle and others
33 Relig. institution
34 Buddy
35 Catalogs
36 Many a senior
37 East ender
38 Track climax
39 Caller ID aid?
40 One removing doubt
42 Not pertinent to
44 Browne-colored dog?
46 Communiqué segue
47 "The Man Who Wasn't There" director, 2001
48 Without repetition
49 Some old theaters
51 Deodorant variety
52 Ruling party
53 Max. or min.

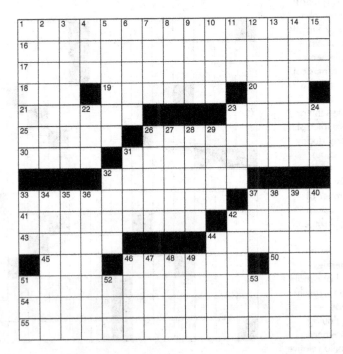

by Harvey Estes

ACROSS

1 Sec
6 What a germ may become
10 Heads, slangily
14 Former company with a torch in its logo
15 Georgia Tech's Sam ___ School of International Affairs
16 Uplift
17 Phileas Fogg, for one
20 London's place: Abbr.
21 Local supporter?
22 ___ whale
23 Telly giant, with "the"
25 Office stamp
27 Luyendyk of racing
28 Sounds of understanding
30 Topic at a family planning center
32 Hurdle for some srs.
34 A bit off, sadly
40 Company buyer of materials
41 In a precarious position
42 Place at which to board: Abbr.
43 Teutonic pronoun
44 ___ grass
45 Brick holders
48 Nucleotide chains
50 Here, in Honduras
54 Very pleasant places
56 Egyptian port
58 Abbr. on a pill bottle
59 Piano classic in C# minor
62 "Suicide Blonde" band, 1990
63 Hair removal option
64 Havens
65 "___ sow . . ."
66 Notice
67 Special delivery?

DOWN

1 One of the brothers Grimm
2 Ammonia derivative
3 Talent
4 TV watcher?
5 "___ turn"
6 Feature of many a stomach
7 Emigration aspiration
8 Posting need: Abbr.
9 Córdoba cordial flavoring
10 Hornet, e.g.
11 Equipped so as to prevent capsizing
12 Backfire
13 Desert land: Abbr.
18 Treats since 1936
19 Student's concern, for short
24 "The Temptation of St. Anthony" painter
26 "No clue"
29 Schemer's syllables
31 Pink-flowered plants often used as grafting stock
33 Designer for Lillian Gish
34 Some ship personnel, briefly
35 Society affairs
36 What most people believe
37 Former name in flight
38 Latin quarters?
39 Bon Jovi's "___ Rush"
46 Concentrated
47 Springboard for new comics, briefly
49 "Tumbling Tumbleweeds" singer
51 Virtual
52 Rte. that crosses Lake Michigan by ferry
53 "Not me"
55 ___ wave
57 Kind of suit
59 War stat.
60 Hoot and a half
61 Dogpatch demurral

by Alan Olschwang

48

ACROSS

1 "Sweet Liberty" director and star
5 Heroin, slangily
9 Air, in Augsburg
13 Free
15 Test versions
16 World War headgear
17 Prepare to take off?
18 Deserves a hand?
19 Less apt to trust
21 High in the Andes
22 Fiddles with
23 They may have private entries
26 September through April, to an oysterman
28 Superlatively severe
29 Snare
30 Tired-looking
31 Turner of records
32 Drew in
37 Operating expense?
41 Incentives
42 Least conventional
43 Possible result of infection
44 Very bright
45 Gushes, e.g.
46 Many cabins
50 Flat arrangement?
51 Viewers
53 Microwave feature
54 Told all
55 Honorees in l'Église catholique: Abbr.
56 Red-bearded god
57 Cold war grp.

DOWN

1 Colgate brand
2 Cut off the spine
3 Terse bit of advice
4 Inside
5 Sugar and salt, often
6 Gardener's supply
7 Suffix with polymer
8 Near the right answer
9 Soft
10 Applesauce
11 Opposite of raw deals
12 Where Can. shares are bought and sold
14 "The Saint" creator ___ Charteris
15 "Pee-wee's Big Adventure" director
20 Michigan college or its town
23 William who rode with Paul Revere
24 "That doesn't seem feasible to me"
25 She said "Life is a banquet, and most poor suckers are starving to death!"
27 Like L-O-N-D-O-N
33 Levies
34 South Dakota county or its seat
35 N.B.A.'er Mario ___
36 Analyze
37 Resort port where Alfred Nobel died
38 Ivy, e.g.
39 Unaccented
40 High beams?
47 Scores quickly?
48 King of drama
49 Info put on some schedules: Abbr.
50 Flap and Fuzz of "Beetle Bailey": Abbr.
52 Cry of impatience

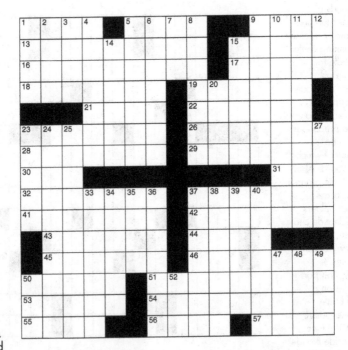

by Robert H. Wolfe

ACROSS

1 "You know . . . THAT woman"
16 "It's not an option"
17 Deviant, in a way
18 Sale word
19 It might help you make the cut
20 His kids' book "Falling Up" is dedicated to his son Matt
22 Fractions of watt-seconds
25 Increase, old-style
26 Respecting
31 Emergency advice
33 Lets have it
38 Was doomed from day one
39 Does some encroaching
40 Asian celebration occasion
41 Christian observances
42 Do-over
43 Range
46 It may get burned up
48 Low-___
51 Canadian coin image
53 Methodically, point by point
60 Meteorological phenomenon
61 Zones out, in a way

DOWN

1 Sounds of tsuris
2 "Aloha nui ___" ("Much love," in Hawaii)
3 It doesn't go off well
4 Like some milk
5 "Hill Street Blues" actress
6 Clark's "Mogambo" co-star and others

7 Hardy heroine
8 ___-Off (windshield cover brand)
9 High, in Heidelberg
10 Narcissus spurned her
11 Main outlet
12 Brown-___
13 Small island
14 Call letters?
15 Lux. was one of its charter members
20 BBQ annoyance
21 Stop, to a sailor
23 It's available in bars
24 Go places
25 German-born Dadaist
26 City northwest of Worcester, Mass.

27 1953 film whose title character says "A gun is as good or as bad as the man using it"
28 Was parasitic to
29 Praying figure, in art
30 Reduces to bits
32 Producer of a large mushroom
34 Passbook abbr.
35 High-grade group?: Abbr.
36 Sounds of sympathy
37 Sylvester, to Tweety
44 Part man?
45 Skiing gold medalist at Sarajevo

46 Nature calls?
47 Available
49 Narrow inlets
50 Start of some Jewish congregation names
51 Not fizzle out
52 Camp Swampy pooch
53 Mex. was one of its charter members
54 Hound
55 The '50s, e.g.
56 Something that may be packed
57 Pier grp.
58 Recording abbr.
59 Race conclusion?

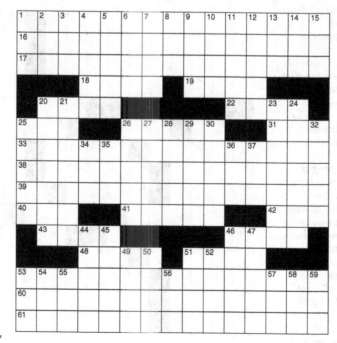

by Bruce Venzke and Stella Daily

ACROSS

1 Ivory Coast export
11 Literally, "king"
15 Neroli oil source
16 Blanchett of "The Aviator"
17 Acting, say
18 "Man of La Mancha" org.
19 Dynast
20 Primates, to humans
21 Bus driver's assignment: Abbr.
22 Featured performer in Berlioz's "Harold in Italy"
24 Instance, in Évreux
27 Good amts. to take in
30 Demonstration noise
31 Opposite of relaxed
33 Old Roman cry
35 Prayer pronoun
36 Instant
37 Doesn't do the job easily
38 Verbal flourish
39 Shadow
40 Dirt
41 They're put away in bars
42 Rub down
44 Bodily channel
46 This may bring in the big bucks
47 Divisions
49 Future shepherd's place: Abbr.
51 "Ariel" poet
52 1953 Eartha Kitt hit
58 Different
59 Road gripper
60 Goat's look
61 Celebrities
62 What dieters eat
63 Spots

DOWN

1 Fowl territory?
2 Little ___ . . .
3 Women's rights pioneer
4 "Rings ___ Fingers" (Henry Fonda film)
5 Go-between's business
6 Beat
7 Place in a Robert Redford movie
8 "Bond Smells ___" ("Diamonds Are Forever" soundtrack number)
9 Beersheba locale
10 Sheepish explanation lead-in
11 Composer of about 600 sonatas
12 Together
13 Gave evidence for
14 Serenity
20 "I could go for that!"
23 Does in
24 Was charming?
25 A wind chilled and killed her, in verse
26 Things that may wind down
28 Coon's age
29 Accounts of aliens, e.g.
32 Falls in drops
34 Stick together
37 Bank
41 Singer with the 1960 #1 album "G.I. Blues"
43 Cartoon cry
45 What's left behind
48 Practice run?
50 Corner cut, in Cambridge
53 Clean copy?
54 Models
55 Civil rights concern
56 "___ put it another way . . ."
57 Teutonic turndown
59 Some N.F.L. linemen

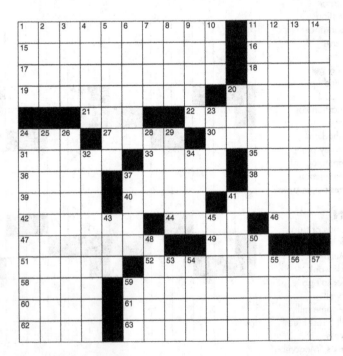

by Harvey Estes

ACROSS

1 Rotters
8 Fabled fliers
15 Royal aide in charge of horses
16 Pillar of a community
17 Drainageways
18 Polish national anthem, e.g.
19 Bully's retort
20 TV address for kids, briefly
21 Get tangled up
23 Baja's opposite
27 When repeated, a vitamin B deficiency
28 Sap
33 Requiring no care
36 It's not necessarily gold
37 Figure used by marketing planners
38 Military plane acronym
39 Virna ___ of "La Reine Margot"
40 Some sports drinks
41 Blemish
43 In addition to
48 Prepare pupils for examination
53 Buttress
54 Trial location
55 Turkish bath wear
56 Womb-related
57 "Probably . . ."
58 Goes in circles

DOWN

1 Seeks change, maybe
2 Pool shade
3 As required
4 Seals' meals
5 Sandblaster's target
6 Stew ingredient
7 Network: Abbr.
8 Brings up the rear
9 Embarrass
10 Iran's ___ Shah Pahlavi
11 Coveted
12 Revolutionary Michael Collins's country
13 Tut's kin?
14 Card game in which jacks are highest trumps
20 Harems
22 Senior moment, e.g.
23 Big name on the range?
24 NBC Thursday night staple, 1986–94
25 ___-Whirl (midway ride)
26 "To put an ___ disposition on": Hamlet
28 St. ___ Beach, Fla.
29 Broadcast workers' union
30 Opposite of baldness
31 Conductor Koussevitzky
32 Those in favor
34 Companion of Geo. or Wm.
35 Voting, it's said
41 More down
42 Whom a headhunter calls
43 About
44 Peel off
45 News
46 Screws up
47 Princess in a spaceship
49 Neighbor of Cygnus
50 Not much
51 Voice mail cue
52 Two in sixty-six?
54 Wine container

by Manny Nosowsky

ACROSS

1 Like the Marx Brothers in a 1935 film
11 Williams College athletes
15 It might include a built-in sharpener
16 Delivery after a delivery?
17 Drivers' surprises
18 Abbr. on old U.S. maps
19 Overcast sky, to some
20 See 52-Down
21 Pretentious one
23 Friend of Dr. Phil
25 Two-time Grammy winner Houston
27 He said "Champions aren't made in gyms"
28 French possessive
29 Pulitzer winner for "A Delicate Balance," 1967
31 He made a bust of Mahler
33 Grand
34 Component of some pools
35 It's supported by a cradle
38 Put
41 French possessive
42 Like many a campground
44 Some rules
46 "___ River"
47 One above a specialist: Abbr.
50 It may come out of a toy
51 Nickname in a 1970s crime drama series
53 Hall-of-Fame gridder Greasy
55 Immure
57 Sports fans' bonuses, briefly

59 Annual short-story awards since 1986
60 Major conclusion
61 Performers with dangerous acts
64 ___ end
65 Put under the table
66 Spoiled the surprise
67 When Mephistopheles appears in "Dr. Faustus"

DOWN

1 Sickroom chorus
2 ___ l'oeil
3 Old German coins
4 One carrying off carrion
5 Tithonus' abductor, in Greek myth
6 "Romeo Is Bleeding" co-star, 1993

7 Emergency response initiator
8 Some keys
9 Democrat Dellums
10 Turns over ice
11 Abbr. preceding a date
12 Daughters who became stars
13 Uncompromising
14 Like some wrists
22 Firth of Clyde river
24 Hamburger's home
26 Actuate
30 Shirt tag abbr.
32 Prayer start
33 Mine passage
35 Didn't straphang
36 Valentine figure
37 Like a Taser stun, usually

39 A train grp.
40 Brown alternative
43 1983 film about illegal immigrants
45 Cold war plan: Abbr.
47 One of the lives in Plutarch's "Lives"
48 Kearney's river
49 Security deposit payer
52 With 20-Across, writer who once lived with Gore Vidal
54 Gen. Ludendorff
56 Furnish
58 18th-century French marshal
62 Collier's work: Abbr.
63 Squiffed

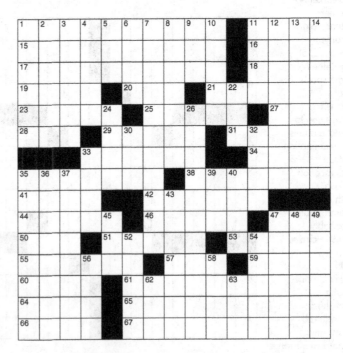

by Jim Page

ACROSS

1 ___ minimum . . .
4 Thunderbird grp.
8 First name in country music
14 1971 musical based on the Bible
16 Rifle effect
17 1984 David Lean film
19 Place to be picked up?
20 Inaugural oath starter
21 Match, in a way
22 Zidovudine, familiarly
23 W has one
25 Responder in a van: Abbr.
27 Letter abbr.
30 ___ Jorge, part of the Azores
31 Language that is mostly monosyllabic
32 Queens, e.g., informally
33 1982 Inspector Poirot movie
38 2003 trilogy completer, with "The"
39 W.W. II action film of 2001
40 Nitpick
41 Rtes.
42 Mens ___ (criminal intent)
43 Something overthrown shortly before the American Revolution
44 Kind of approval
45 Alien subject?: Abbr.
46 ___-bear
49 Davis Cup match-up
51 Place to relax
53 Wayfare

54 1980 film based on a Clive Cussler best seller
59 Subject of a temple at Delphi
60 Guaranteed
61 "No lie"
62 Welcoming
63 When doubled, a familiar cry

DOWN

1 Capital of Guam, old-style
2 Old Mercury
3 Not stand still
4 Brown letters
5 Mermaid setting
6 Painful ending?
7 Cut out
8 Box office sign
9 Bad job?
10 Bad spots?
11 Good news on an apartment rental
12 The last King Richard
13 ___ king
15 From Omaha to K.C.
18 How some meteors fall
23 Five-time baseball All-Star ___ Wills
24 French artist Pierre
26 Many Little League spectators
28 Cut back
29 Numbers
30 Dry spell
31 Some hooks
32 Lebanese valley
33 Like squirrels' ears
34 ___ cavae
35 Yadda, yadda, yadda, e.g.

36 A, to Samuel Morse
37 He purportedly said "Only one man ever understood me, and he didn't understand me"
44 Bleeds (for)
45 Start-of-meal urging
46 Poet Sanchez of the Black Arts Movement
47 Like a 100-mile-an-hour taxi ride?
48 Mike holder
50 ___ Royale
52 100 centavos
53 Heroic W.W. II grp.
54 Bowl sound
55 How to address a sgt.?
56 "Sesame Street" watcher
57 Burning sensation?
58 Hottie, perhaps

by Joe Krozel

ACROSS

1 Sonnet ender
7 Boardwalk locale
15 Yoga instruction
16 Noble and chivalrous
17 Transitional figures
18 Afternooners, maybe
19 Ball girl
20 Riviera, once
21 Thanksgiving follower: Abbr.
22 Pueblo vessel
23 Villain
24 Nicaragua's second-largest city
25 After
26 2005 Isabel Allende novel
27 Something to sing
28 Plug in overnight, maybe
30 Lincoln Lab locale
31 Bowdlerizes, in a way
32 Debriefed group?
36 __ pendens (pending lawsuit)
37 Like some guidance
38 Green spot
41 Event at which to ring necks?
42 Fitness advocacy grp.
43 PlayStation alternative
44 Sound studio job
45 Bulwer-Lytton's "Eugene __"
46 Cowardly fellow
47 Monarchy ruled by the al-Thani family
48 Prefix with lineal
49 Icarus, e.g.
51 Junk, so to speak
52 Cover again
53 Measure
54 Support structures
55 Is unacceptable

DOWN

1 Littoral line
2 Booted one
3 Whups
4 Marvin Gaye's record label
5 Robert __ Prewitt ("From Here to Eternity" soldier)
6 Real good-looker
7 Aid in drawing parallels?
8 Time Magazine's 1986 Woman of the Year
9 Like some gossip
10 Dundee of "Crocodile Dundee"
11 Sanctuary
12 What Zeus transformed Io into
13 Models sold from 1999 to 2004
14 Essential amino acid
20 They might scrape bows
23 Practices
24 Accept
26 3-D reference provider
27 Broadcast component
29 Screw
30 Dye-producing gastropod
32 Point of greatest despair
33 Open
34 Its fruit pulp is an ingredient in Worcestershire sauce
35 Rear-end, e.g.
37 Hair salon stock
38 Rural hauler
39 Exploitative type
40 Incursion
41 Take out of circulation
44 Swedish diplomat Wallenberg
45 First first name?
47 Alphabet run
48 Management issuance
50 Certain Coast Guard member: Abbr.
51 38-Down driver's cry

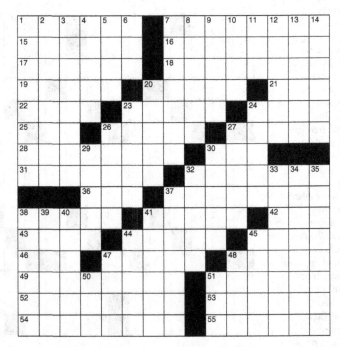

by Barry C. Silk

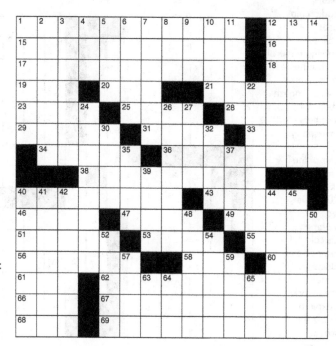

ACROSS

1 Party line?
12 Standard setting at 0° long.
15 Over
16 Over: Prefix
17 As is
18 Burmese opposition leader Aung __ Suu Kyi
19 Recognition response
20 Feminine side
21 Causing a rise?
23 Shred
25 "The League of Extraordinary Gentlemen" captain
28 Double crossed?
29 Pranks
31 Massenet opera
33 Prefix with pad
34 Patrick __, 1966 Tony winner for "Marat/Sade"
36 Finger-pointer
38 Producer of funny pages?
40 Man of steel
43 Could possibly be
46 __ Islands, west of Ireland
47 Is short
49 Rocks
51 Brings up, in a way
53 Chick follower
55 Fit to serve
56 Weigh
58 George Strait's "All My __ Live in Texas"
60 Lead investigator?: Abbr.
61 Son : Spanish :: __ : English
62 Admiral who went to an extreme?
66 HQ

67 Movie based on the book "Do Androids Dream of Electric Sheep?"
68 Floors
69 Concertgoers getting into the hits?

DOWN

1 Washington, D.C., university
2 2002 World Series locale
3 Place for a wicker chair
4 Possible defib performer
5 Too interested
6 Wedding trailer
7 Rock and Roll Hall of Fame co-founder and inductee
8 Station abbr.
9 Gone but not forgotten: Abbr.
10 "Little" girl in "David Copperfield"
11 Obsolete communication
12 Plaster preparations
13 Grilling aid
14 Novelty singer born Herbert Khaury
22 Follow
24 Blamed
26 Sat shiva, say
27 Hotel chain
30 Brand
32 Isn't idle
35 Brand kept near a toaster
37 Remains

39 Guitar effect
40 Really fill
41 Preceding
42 Good things to bring to the table
44 Household
45 Snob, maybe
48 Steam
50 Butterflies with eyespots on their wings
52 Rulers of the Nemanjic dynasty, e.g.
54 Bit of gravy
57 Take a turn, in some games
59 Took a turn, in some games
63 Something heard in a herd
64 Teacher's deg.
65 Ltr. accompanier

by Brendan Emmett Quigley

56

ACROSS

1 Became semirigid
7 Most likely to be hired
13 Liquor flavored with caraway seeds
15 Combat site of 1853–56
16 His tale follows the Friar's in "The Canterbury Tales"
18 Bow applications
19 Whence the word "futon"
20 Bothers
21 "A moment is a concentrated ___": Emerson
22 Carol starter
23 Playwright McNally
24 Canadian film awards
25 Litigation-prompting mineral
27 What businesses try to minimize
31 ___ Villa (English football club)
32 Two-seaters or four-seaters, e.g.?
34 Leader of the Connecticut Yankees in 1920s–'40s music
35 Bird named for its colorful breast and tail
42 Contacts go over them
43 Written work that explains one's actions
44 Prince ___ (frock coat)
45 Undoing
46 Life at a grocery store
47 Reading group
48 Keyed up
49 Holds high
50 Big jobs for a maid
51 Dry land

DOWN

1 Nozzle connected to a Bunsen burner
2 Consider comparable
3 One arranging things in large categories
4 "Blazing Saddles" villain Hedley ___
5 First name in 1970s women's tennis
6 Eat home cooking
7 Farmer's holdings
8 Least subtle
9 Heed
10 Release
11 Country houses?
12 Has a bit of
14 Precedent setter
17 California's Point ___
26 DNA sequence unit
27 Round numbers in England?
28 Peanuts and castor beans, e.g.
29 Cheapest traveling option
30 Roller coaster structures
32 1984 Maximilian Schell biopic
33 John Wayne had a little one
34 MTV owner
36 Like some notes on a music sheet
37 Record keeper
38 ___ Strait (water separating Australia and New Guinea)
39 Shining brightly
40 Water cannon target
41 Chuang-tzu, for one

by Patrick Berry

ACROSS

1 Gut feeling
12 Landmark Paris church La ___-Chapelle
15 Popular game on TV
16 #4 for Boston
17 Burned up
18 Was fast . . . or wasn't fast
19 Cipher org.
20 Bowmen's implements
21 Computer character set
23 It's sickening
25 Polynesian carving
27 Diorama
28 Misses in Spain: Abbr.
30 Long shot
32 Talk over?
34 Family tree word
35 Casting need
36 Opposite of down
40 Leaves alone
42 A Chaplin
43 Tease
45 Nipper
46 Movie producer?
49 ___ Secretary
53 Bob in the Rock and Roll Hall of Fame
54 Hardly Mr. Personality
56 Movie character whose first name is Julius
57 Welcome, in a phrase
58 G.M. and G.E.
60 Rubber-stamps
61 Computing-Tabulating-Recording Co., today
62 "Pink Cadillac" singer, 1988

66 "This is a Montague, our ___": "Romeo and Juliet"
67 Like what a person likes
68 Country singer England and others
69 Parts of medical checkups

DOWN

1 Smarts
2 Wound tighter
3 Rural vehicle
4 ___ tai
5 Come ___ surprise
6 Swindler
7 Dreadful
8 Like a lot of the U.S. oil reserves
9 Chicago setting: Abbr.
10 Laugh sound
11 Frequent feature of Emily Dickinson poetry
12 One who might win a spelling competition
13 Christmas tree circler, perhaps
14 Two-time U.S. Open champion
22 Boxed game equipment
24 Entered the pool?
26 Burned up
29 -ed, e.g.: Abbr.
31 Stay fresh
33 Vice president who graduated from Princeton at 16
36 Part of an egotist's self-description
37 Romantic
38 They may produce checks
39 Set down
41 Bottom line
44 Material
47 William Herschel discovery of 1781
48 Magazine holders
50 Shows excitement (over)
51 Band on foot?
52 Wanders
55 Bluenose
59 Broadway "score"
63 Quick
64 Rocky peak
65 A.L. Central team, on a scoreboard

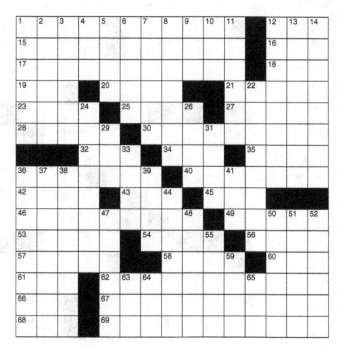

by Kyle Mahowald

ACROSS
1 Brings down
6 1969 film starring Dick Van Dyke and Mickey Rooney
14 Of the north
15 Literally, "sheltered bay"
16 Brit who gets an award for showing?
18 Not too long ago
19 Half of an old comedy duo
20 You might drop glass into these
22 "In no way, shape or form," e.g.
27 Important Indian
31 A lot of a handyman's work
32 Mercenary
33 Meteorologist's body?
34 Chemical dumping, e.g.
36 Unappetizing bowlfuls
37 It's charged at a fountain
39 Yemen Gate locale
40 Gets by rudely
41 Products of glaciation
42 1954–77 alliance: Abbr.
45 Like some ancient Greek victors
51 Cataclysm
53 30-Down nullifier
54 Mate's reply
55 They know the score
56 They're bound to land

DOWN
1 Public assemblies
2 First asteroid orbited by a NASA spacecraft
3 When Quadragesima occurs
4 Slow-moving
5 They're not up
6 Regarding that matter
7 Bricklayer's burden
8 White coat?
9 Duo that had a hit with "Unforgettable"
10 Cooking vessel
11 Sierra Club's first president
12 "Casablanca" name
13 Album unit
14 Crude container?: Abbr.
17 Center of a debate
21 1974 film that was Jonathan Demme's directorial debut
22 Shattering grenades, for short
23 Bizet opera priestess
24 Airstrip area
25 Modern city where de Soto landed in 1539
26 His 1488 voyage opened the road to India
27 Wrap up
28 "America" singer in "West Side Story"
29 Wears down
30 Red light
32 Binders
35 Poetic breaks
38 Grooms
40 Investigator
41 Tipped
42 Ward awarded two Emmys
43 "House of Frankenstein" director ___ C. Kenton
44 Bends
46 "Hellzapoppin'" funnywoman
47 Hungarian city or its river
48 Page
49 Blue Bell alternative
50 Violet, maybe
51 Cap
52 Mekong Delta dweller

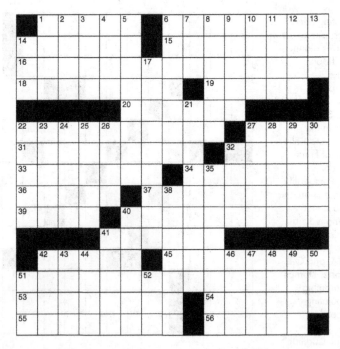

by Robert H. Wolfe

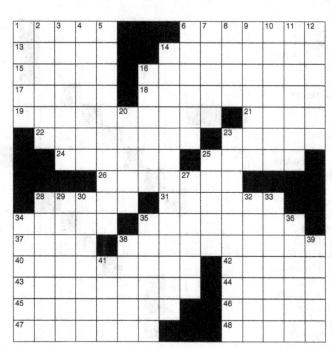

ACROSS

1 Handle holders
6 Bone near the shoulder
13 "Phenomenology of Spirit" author, 1807
14 Exposed
15 Make bank withdrawals?
16 State flower of Nebraska
17 Number of mari
18 Staple of a Rudolph Valentino film
19 Risqué business?
21 Do stuff
22 Pistols, e.g.
23 Beepers
24 Qajar dynasty's domain
25 Best Musical of 1999
26 Batters have them
28 Hesitant about committing oneself
31 Emulated Isocrates
34 Untagged
35 Like teeth after some dental visits
37 Flatten
38 Laundry challenge
40 Friendly snake?
42 It's a rush
43 Exercise routine
44 Not on the edge
45 Studs, e.g.
46 Event drawing intl. criticism
47 Falls off
48 Big name in oil . . . and oils

DOWN

1 "Through the Looking-Glass" game
2 Some soldiers' wear
3 What a big winner might be on
4 Shellfish contaminant
5 Certain shower gift
6 Relieves
7 Fruit drink
8 Fruit drinks
9 Rain gear
10 Raises
11 Strong and regal
12 Physicist Angström
14 Biker's cry
16 Joyful hymn word
20 Sick-looking
23 Greeting at the door, serving the hors d'oeuvres, etc.
25 Guinness Book listings
27 They're more than pinches
28 Haloes
29 They make things up
30 Teriyaki spices
32 Accord
33 Fixed
34 Football defense that employs five defensive backs
35 Gets with great difficulty
36 It makes a long story short
38 Orbiter of note
39 Meshed
41 Rosemary's love in a classic Anne Nichols play

by Sherry O. Blackard

60

ACROSS

1 Supporters of women's athletics
11 Gossip
15 Don't be cruel
16 Catch ___
17 Boardwalk buy
18 Leader in the Crimean War
19 Announcer who was the first to call DiMaggio "Joltin' Joe"
20 Hoaxes
22 It's a blast
23 Plot (with)
24 Ratify
27 Hits solidly
28 Greek island that was a source of fine white marble in ancient times
29 Meryl Streep's first film
30 Hotness
31 Mastermind
32 Steady worker
33 "Double Indemnity" writer, 1936
34 High no.?
35 Cone bearer
36 Babushkas
37 Landed
39 Disturb
40 Hittable
41 Whence the line "Whither thou goest, I will go"
42 Fast starter
43 1959 death row movie, with "The"
47 "What ___ for Love" ("A Chorus Line" song)
48 Number of people
50 Fall through the cracks?
51 Will Rogers's humorous self-description

52 Giant or D'back
53 Requests to compare and contrast, maybe

DOWN

1 Level
2 Crown
3 Amphitheater
4 Tie
5 They'll give you fits
6 Peace in the Middle East
7 "The Devil and Daniel Webster" writer
8 Eavesdropper?
9 Path across the sky
10 Put the pedal to the metal
11 Plug of half-smoked tobacco
12 Carefree
13 Face the people
14 Savvy
21 One out on a limb
23 Some commentary
24 Shade
25 1948 Ralph Richardson film, with "The"
26 Consort
27 Daiquirí resident
29 Sweetin who played Stephanie on "Full House"
32 Cabernet, say
33 Sweater choice
35 End of an epoch?

36 "It can't be!"
38 Hierarchy
39 Without bias
41 Jah worshiper
43 Remains
44 Goddess worshiped at the Temple of Philae
45 "South Pacific" girl
46 Fills the bill?
49 Directory listings: Abbr.

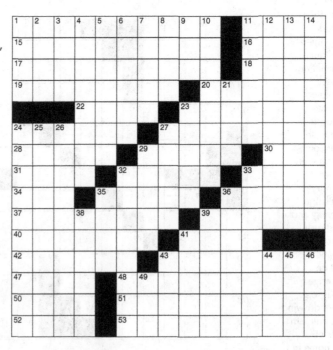

by Bob Klahn

ACROSS

1 Modern, efficient matchmaking process
12 Alimentary particle?
15 One who got held up, maybe
16 Old Testament book: Abbr.
17 Sensor
18 TV schedule letters
19 Director Craven
20 Pleads
21 Drawer freshener
23 Record collection?
24 Soothing art
25 "Nope"
28 Something you might part with overseas
29 Kmart acquisition
30 Popular wedding gift
31 N.F.L. Hall-of-Famer ___ Barney
32 Sans warranty
33 Slate evaluator
34 Biblical peak
35 Acre's setting: Abbr.
36 Stable parents
37 Like tigers vis-à-vis lions
38 Good as new
40 Washer setting
41 Arrives like a social butterfly?
42 Pinup's pride
43 Unspecified, but invariably unpleasant, alternative
44 Harry Belafonte cry
45 Regrettable
48 Fabled elephant abductor
49 "Impossible!"
52 The third to the fifth?

53 "Miss You Like Crazy" singer, 1989
54 Some tech. inst. grads
55 Worker around a furnace

DOWN

1 Raft
2 Like 24-Across
3 Are, in Alençon
4 Port. joined it in 1986
5 Old Japanese cars
6 "The Art of Arousal" writer
7 Northern constellation
8 Little jerks
9 "___ no idea"
10 Skeptical sort

11 Player of Joe the Bartender
12 Open-eyed
13 1974 David Bowie song
14 1953 hit that mentions "old Napoli"
22 Shipping unit: Abbr.
23 Mean types
24 You can see right through them
25 Falcon's home
26 Dessert with candied fruit, nuts and liqueur
27 Top secrets?
28 Placed
30 Oscar winner for "Two Women"

33 Like some wines
34 Bert Bobbsey's twin and others
36 Lost
37 Modernize
39 N.L. scoreboard abbr.
40 1960s–'70s antidiscrimination movement
42 Residents of ancient Alesia
44 ___ told
45 Throw below
46 Au fait
47 Rural road sign image
50 Windy City rail inits.
51 PX shopper

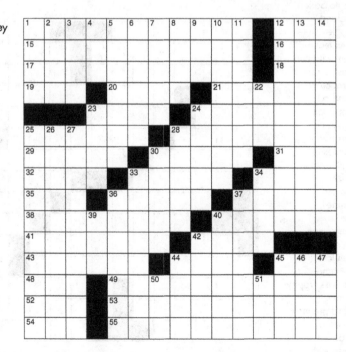

by Paula Gamache

62

ACROSS

1 Cranberry center
8 Runs through
13 Wears out
15 Inventories
16 Title for a duchess
17 Valuable fur
18 Settings for some TV dramas
19 Narcissists
21 Blame
22 Having very little kick
23 Protection
25 Not spontaneous
26 Make more sanitary, in a way
28 Sir Frank ___, historian of Anglo-Saxon England
30 People often leave them with cuts
32 Toast, after "a"
34 Vernacular
38 Handrail supporter
40 Halves of Córdoba couples
42 Legitimate
43 Relish
46 Two out of nine?
47 Like a string bean
48 Grunts
49 Postulate
50 Five-time Art Ross Trophy winner
52 Salad greens
53 Chiselers
54 To-do list
55 Asses with dorsal stripes

DOWN

1 Was logically consistent
2 Found the middle of?
3 Didn't stay dry
4 Tiny fraction of a British thermal unit
5 Tobacco farm employee
6 Some Siouans
7 Boils down
8 "The Rose Tattoo" Tony winner, 1951
9 Naval defense
10 Sevillian skills
11 Drafts, say
12 Some ID's
14 Leave
15 Apparently pleased
20 Fair selection
24 One being counter-productive?
27 They get punched
29 Result of a coup
31 Voiced bits of speech
33 Investigator who finds someone's birth mother, say
35 "I ___ you!"
36 Garden bouquet
37 Summons
39 Schoolwork
41 Get into easily
43 Tom Courtenay's "Doctor Zhivago" role
44 Characters in "Casablanca" and "Judge Dredd"
45 "___ roll!"
47 Poise
51 Line part: Abbr.

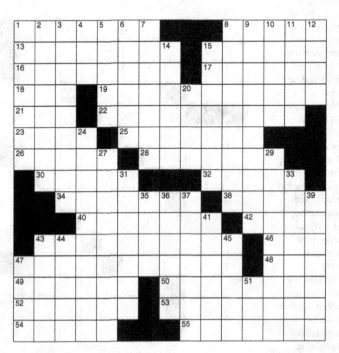

by Robert H. Wolfe

ACROSS

1 Declare one's intentions publicly
16 Job for one doing character studies?
17 Be in a very advantageous position
18 Old roadside name
19 Indication that one is being rubbed the right way
20 String along
21 Physics units
23 Deadlines on eBay are given in it: Abbr.
24 Verdi's "Un __ in Maschera"
28 River in "The Divine Comedy"
32 Quadrennial observation
38 Locales of frequent injuries
39 "F Troop" role
40 Fire, to Flavius
41 Point (to)
42 Old cable inits.
45 They're not in
48 Like some mail or traffic
52 Amorous bit
53 Image: Var.
57 Longtime La Scala conductor
60 It can take a lot of heat
61 Summer resort area famous for recreational boating

DOWN

1 "Am __ Man" (1960 Jackie Wilson hit)
2 Cramped urban accommodations, for short
3 "Do the Right Thing" pizzeria
4 Release
5 What that might be in Spain
6 Quiet
7 Where "Otello" premiered
8 Almost too late
9 Book between Ezra and Esther: Abbr.
10 Hot
11 Something that's often made up
12 Series ender
13 Some cough medicine: Var.
14 Lincoln in-laws
15 Kickoff
21 Sharp turn
22 Falling-out
24 Kind of crime
25 Ending to avoid?
26 Actor who roared to fame?
27 Brother of Nintendo's Mario
29 Rank
30 It's good to graduate with them
31 Transfuse
33 It means "red" in Mongolian
34 Kidney secretion
35 Village, in Würzburg
36 Tennis star __ Huber
37 It flows in Flanders
42 Thomas Paine's "Common Sense," e.g.
43 Grammy-winning Jones
44 Cracked
46 Big name in wine
47 Joins in space
49 Cabriole performer's wear
50 Dwarf planet just beyond the Kuiper Belt
51 "Cannery Row" woman
53 On Wilshire Blvd., say
54 Furnace
55 Like a line, briefly
56 Quibbles
58 World
59 Not fare well

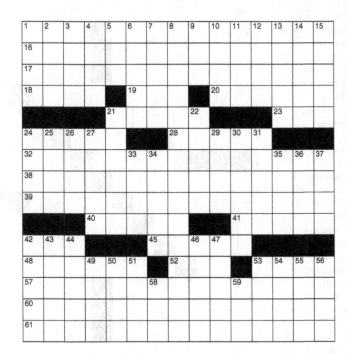

by Sherry O. Blackard

64

ACROSS
1 Blind, in a way
8 Spain's San Isidro and others
15 Children's author who was a regular contributor to Punch
16 Nation of 181 square miles
17 Introduce
18 "Just So Stories" author's first name
19 When there's no other option
21 Recommendations
22 Hospital dogsbody
23 Brickmaking company
24 Adirondack chair part
25 "Jabberwocky" opener
26 1956 cult film from overseas
27 Frost lines
28 Burdensome
29 It lays its eggs in others' nests
33 Ticks
34 Spanish rice ingredient
35 They make tracks
36 Device that contains an electromagnet
37 Seriously break the trust of, slangily
38 Chlorophyll-containing microorganism
42 Landscaping supplies
43 Some Tate Modern pieces
45 ___ 500, annual list of the fastest-growing private companies
46 One that picks up the kids?
47 Kerosene
49 Itch cause
50 French rococo artist Watteau
51 Court stat
52 Some chocolate
53 Free throw, e.g.

DOWN
1 Putts that might be conceded
2 Talking-to
3 God worshiped in ancient Thebes
4 Most widespread
5 Frosted
6 People in trees
7 Had a tough time deciding
8 Capacitance units
9 Condition
10 The Christian Science Monitor founder
11 Brown condiment
12 Got credit for
13 High-and-mighty
14 Elton John hit that begins "Guess there are times when we all need to share a little pain"
20 Country name retired in 1949
23 Folk wisdom
26 Brinks
27 Like some air fresheners
28 Aesop character with a country cousin
29 Napoleon, e.g.
30 Exclusive meeting
31 Kansas State athletes
32 Squeezers
33 National instruments of Guatemala
35 Insignificant
37 Cross references?
38 Detectives check them
39 Not quite on time
40 Blue ___
41 Still
43 Home of the Calendar Islands, once thought to total 365 in number
44 Teen affliction
46 Be angry
48 Gob

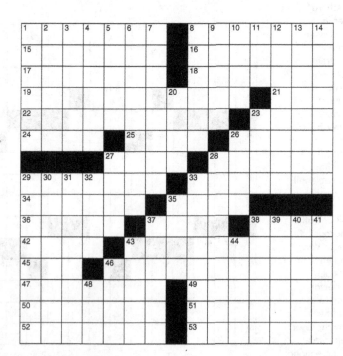

by Patrick Berry

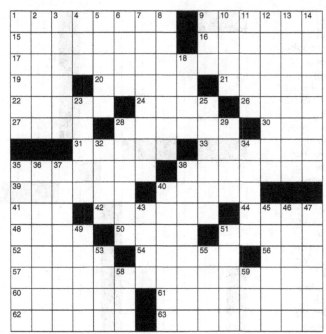

ACROSS

1 Plot device in some science fiction
9 Expedient
15 Saint born in Newark, N.J.
16 Modern site of an ancient Egyptian capital
17 Fictional character who says "I have measured out my life with coffee spoons"
19 ___ Nuevo
20 Cardio choice
21 ___ Lacs, Minn.
22 Discoveries in Al Hirschfeld drawings
24 Off the market
26 Whammy
27 Rack holder
28 Merry
30 Spawn
31 It's a free country
33 Descend, in mountaineering
35 Movie buff: Var.
38 1993 Peace co-Nobelist
39 Night sticks?
40 Western party
41 Computer key
42 Homer's home
44 One of the Bush brothers
48 Word with legal or lower
50 Home of the Hmong
51 Part of a French toast
52 Pan
54 Thomas of the N.B.A.
56 Flagstaff-to-Tucson dir.
57 Early Jesuit
60 Moving vehicles
61 Wagner opera setting
62 One side in the Battle of Thermopylae
63 Drill command

DOWN

1 Music style that often includes an accordion
2 "Terrible" czar
3 Longtime TV role for Danson
4 Generator output: Abbr.
5 Partner of all
6 Specialty
7 Weathers
8 National car care chain
9 ___ particle
10 Switch letters
11 Trinidadian, e.g.
12 The Barsetshire novels novelist
13 Doing very well moneywise
14 Sure thing
18 Popular caramel candy
23 Dealers' requests
25 Browbeating
28 George of old vaudeville
29 "Mame" director of stage and screen
32 Biblical verb
34 Joint assemblies
35 Busts a gut
36 First opera to premiere at London's Savoy Theatre, 1882
37 Rather close
38 Parent's stern order
40 Like some consonant stops
43 Flock member
45 Store, in a way
46 Word of emphasis
47 Eye libidinously
49 Some lampshade shades
51 Abbas I, II and III
53 Wife of Shiva, in Hinduism
55 Toll unit
58 "The Puzzle Palace" org.
59 One of the Ewings on "Dallas"

by Karen M. Tracey

66

ACROSS
1 Lock locale
6 Licks
11 Some rocket fuel
14 One lost through divorce
15 He said "Marriage is nature's way of keeping us from fighting with strangers"
16 Not disparate
17 Pooh-bah
18 Matching, with "the"
20 Chat room info
21 Mournful
22 Potluck panfuls
23 Words before a sarcastic "ha ha"
24 Now
26 Part of a pound
32 Put on again
33 Review unfairly
35 Political leader from Georgia
36 Driving range device?
43 Name in high fashion
44 Trigger, e.g.
45 Nickname in tabloids
46 Eyelet creator
47 Deux or trois lead-in
48 Chewed on
49 Of a pelvic bone
50 Some store officials
51 Knight's list
52 Peter and Paul, but not Mary

DOWN
1 In opposition to
2 Kind of price
3 American painter of sports scenes
4 Half of an old comedy duo
5 Deck chair part
6 Radial alternative
7 Supplements
8 Most vile
9 Breaks with service?
10 Producing bullets?
11 World capital on a river of the same name
12 Woman in a "Paint Your Wagon" song
13 Shows no sign of abating
19 Otto's preceder
25 Lions and tigers and bears
26 U.N. beachhead during the Korean War
27 Stout
28 Water
29 Part of an Ethiopian emperor's title
30 Columbus discovery of 1498
31 The Big Easy
34 Most coveted position
37 Brazilian beach resort
38 Crumble
39 Foreign dignitaries
40 British chemist's solution strength
41 Maze marking
42 Chancel symbols

by Harvey Estes

ACROSS
1 Multiple-choice choices
6 "Then again" follower
14 More within reason
15 Something to get sent off with
16 100 öre
17 "Possibly"
18 Ford's predecessor
19 Band's lineup
20 Collectible sheet
21 Begin to form
22 Drive away
23 Where to go for a cup
25 Bourbon flavorer
26 Response to an impatient person
27 Dating service datum
28 Broadcaster from 1995 to 2006
29 Hardly windy
30 Ships
33 Exclamation in a locker room talk
37 River of Troyes
38 "Phooey!"
39 Through
40 Single or double, say
41 Tenor Bostridge and others
42 Form 1040 fig.
43 With 10-Down, ocularist's offering
46 Old boom makers
47 Choice for the indecisive
48 What "-" may signify
49 A sigh
50 Olympics event
51 Having no match
54 Emerge
55 It may be password-protected

56 Derby wear
57 They've been on the road many times
58 Heretofore

DOWN
1 Display some interest in
2 Frequent USA Today features
3 Like people in the front row of a group photo, often
4 Get further Details?
5 Company
6 Suit request
7 Stop or touch follower
8 Rocher of cosmetics
9 Cannonball Adderley's specialty
10 See 43-Across
11 "Eraserhead" star Jack
12 Home to Hill Air Force Base
13 Transformer creator
15 Yellowstone feeder
22 Lit
23 Receivers of cuts
24 It helps one keep one's place
26 Trailer makeup
27 Indians, e.g.
31 Behind someone's back
32 His self-titled book has 24 chapters
34 Cookout fare
35 In heat?
36 Some problems to solve
43 Infomercial cutter
44 Winds
45 Period of douze mois
46 Cut
47 Bottom
49 Geometric figure
50 You can get a charge out of it
52 Landing site
53 Boxer's org.

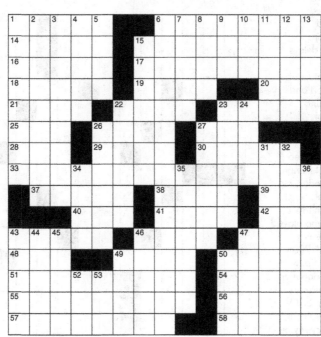

by Mike Nothnagel

ACROSS
1 Flooring?
10 Main character of TV's "The Pretender"
15 Occasion to reserve a table for two?
16 Singer/songwriter ___ Mandell
17 Greeting spot
18 Ready to be used again
19 Volcano part
20 Old cereal brand
21 "Wow!"
23 Boosler of stand-up
25 "___ for That" (1939 hit song)
26 Output of Tintoretto, e.g.
27 Small force
28 Dud of an idea
31 Slated
33 Reasons for some delays
34 Notice
35 Indicators of comfort and handling
38 Hall of introductions
41 British officer's wear
42 Patriot Putnam
46 Tournedos, e.g.
49 Part of a Latin trio
50 Eric who played Hector in "Troy," 2004
51 Temple player
52 Bank donation?
54 Mischievous
56 Saturn S.U.V.
57 Pig stealer, in a nursery rhyme
58 Literally, "first generation"
59 Key
62 Some gowns
63 Old World pigeons with markings around the neck
64 Contemporary of Arp and Miró
65 Prada alternative

DOWN
1 Marinara alternative
2 Andy Warhol subject
3 Superhero of 1960s TV
4 Kind of state
5 N.B.A. star Brand
6 American coot
7 Short-lived TV spinoff of 1980
8 Chevron sporter: Abbr.
9 Neighborhood in the Bronx
10 Actress Ryan of "Star Trek: Voyager"
11 Sour, fermented liquid
12 Getaways
13 Ragtime dance
14 Highly agitated
22 Eye irritants
24 Wine info
25 O.K., maybe
29 Locale in a classic Frank Sinatra song
30 Heavenly field?: Abbr.
32 Some ironware
36 Jam ingredients?
37 Capital of Fiji
38 Refluent phenomenon
39 Formal introduction
40 Eisenhower's Texas birthplace
43 Old Ford model
44 Dry-eyed
45 Like some connections
47 Stunning slaps
48 Poinsettia's family
53 Tips
55 Word with Star or Sun in product names
56 Means of escape
60 Writer ___ Pera
61 Tee, e.g.

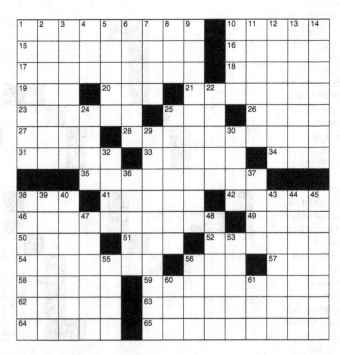

by Karen M. Tracey

ACROSS

1 Basic teaching
4 Sirens
9 Ruthlessly competitive
14 Start of a Tennessee Williams title
15 Red as ___
16 Spendthrift's joy
17 ___ de guerre
18 Whip on the high seas
20 Slows down
22 ___ Tech
23 Airline with the King David Lounge
24 Slander, say
26 Like "Brokeback Mountain"
30 Fix, as a pump
32 Org. with the annual Junior Olympic Games
34 Nosh
35 Hotter than hot
37 Stooge
38 Vandal
41 See 25-Down
43 Underhanded
44 Orchard Field, today
46 Buzz
48 Film pooch
49 Kind of party
50 Drug used to treat poisoning
54 Place of disgrace
56 E.T.S. offering
58 Unaccompanied
59 Spot for Spot?
60 Takes in
62 Unplanned
67 Word between two names
68 Get around
69 Military operation
70 Loaf on the job
71 Six Flags features
72 To the point
73 Some city map lines: Abbr.

DOWN

1 Lowly post
2 Something that may need boosting
3 Inner selves, to Jung
4 Annul, as a legal order
5 Apollo 13 astronauts, e.g.
6 Organization that no U.S. president has ever belonged to
7 Designer from China
8 Stop: Abbr.
9 Guiding light
10 Some fed. govt. testing sites
11 N.L. West team, on scoreboards
12 Business card abbr.
13 Venice's ___ Palace
19 Light shade
21 Cook up
25 With 41-Across, title for this puzzle
27 Reward for waiting?
28 List ender
29 ___-eyed
31 Track down
33 Arith. process
36 Still red inside
37 Burger topper
38 Show-off
39 "Here comes trouble"
40 Org. with troops
42 Ones going home after dinner?
45 Meat dish with a filling
47 100 centavos
49 Jazz buff
51 Carnival treats
52 Notwithstanding
53 Mathematical groups
55 MS. enclosures
57 Slot car, e.g.
61 Old dagger
62 Serve, as a banquet
63 Year in Trajan's reign
64 Kept
65 St. Paul hrs.
66 Rush

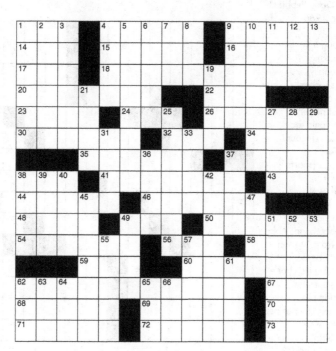

by David J. Kahn

ACROSS

1 Faucet with a rotating plug
9 Top with a quip, maybe
15 Convenient, in a way
16 Observer
17 Kids
18 Bibliographer's term
19 Tolerate
20 Product with the old jingle line "One little can will keep you running free"
21 Curved nails
22 The '80s, say
23 Time up
25 Chow fixer
26 Whips
28 Some Oscar-night gowns
29 Rig-___, Hindu sacred book
30 "The Sand Pebbles" actor, 1966
32 See
33 Lacking light
36 "Speaking personally . . ."
38 Ones with gifts who don't care about presents
39 Embryonic sac
41 Air___, discount carrier
42 Top-___ (sports brand)
43 Banff Natl. Park locale
47 It's in the neighborhood: Abbr.
48 He wrote "A man cannot be too careful in the choice of his enemies"
49 Seaside flier
50 Olympic competitors since 1900
52 ___ Strait, east of Canada's King William Island

54 Nabokov novel
55 Soon
56 "Really?!"
58 Form of boxing using both the hands and feet
59 Tiger's quality
60 Wailed
61 Genetic condition known medically as ephelides

DOWN

1 Guitar strings, e.g.
2 Ballerina Karsavina
3 One of 2.7 million Japanese
4 "Here Is Your War" author
5 Mil. rank
6 Punch lines?
7 Bow-making time

8 Gas in fluorescent lamps
9 Angle symbols, in geometry
10 Go after
11 Knit, maybe
12 Enthusiastic response
13 Checked
14 Conjoined area
24 Knot
27 Belittling act
28 ___ gratia
29 Actress Bloom of "High Plains Drifter"
31 Some football linemen: Abbr.
32 "Ick!" evoker
33 Indication to look down
34 Forum characters
35 Stretch in the 90's, say

37 Word of disgust
40 Area under a halter
42 Two-___ (strong)
44 Protein source
45 Sad
46 Bugs
48 Parting request
51 "Voice of Israel" author
53 Being abroad
54 Lies together?
57 Latin pronoun

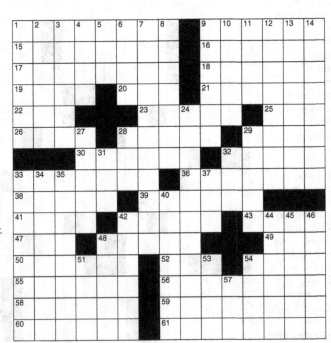

by Rich Norris

ACROSS

1 White-bearded, red-capped patriarch
10 G.I.'s sod
15 One with spin control?
16 Famous last word
17 Lexington Center centerpiece
18 Open
19 Concert equipment
20 Substantial bill
22 Toshiba competitor
23 Place for a swing
24 Recording standard
25 Club alternative
27 He came out of retirement in 1980
28 Doom
29 Decca rival
30 Flooded
32 Set right
33 Symbol of contrasting principles
34 Alongside, nautically
37 Floods
38 Eye site
40 Stretch
41 Slip acknowledgment
42 Form letters?
43 Org. whose logo is a torch
46 Lead seeker: Abbr.
47 Seminoles' sch.
48 See
49 Bill of Rights subj.
50 Churn
52 Doctor's orders
54 Crimson and white school, for short
55 Setting of van Gogh's "Bedroom"
57 Wally Schirra commanded it in 1968
59 All-natural abode
60 Car-jacking aids
61 Garish glowers
62 Plain

DOWN

1 Marine menace
2 Sagacity
3 Put spirit into, with "up"
4 Hooded menaces
5 Pop of Jamaica
6 The Elite Eight are associated with it
7 Piece of silver
8 Silver State city
9 One who's made a pledge
10 Subject of some sightings
11 Hindu trinity member
12 About three grains
13 Corridor to be kept clear
14 Quartet in a string quartet
21 Subject of some sightings
24 Change course
26 A little after, timewise
31 Hero of several Clancy novels
32 Good sign?
34 Environmental awareness topic
35 Cry when you think you've got it?
36 Cactuslike tree of the Southwest
39 Show a thing or two
40 Modena misters
43 They may keep the show going
44 Words on a heart
45 Philosopher Pascal
51 Oil magnate Hess
53 Capital where tala are spent
54 Staten Isl., e.g.
56 Emergency letters
58 Fried

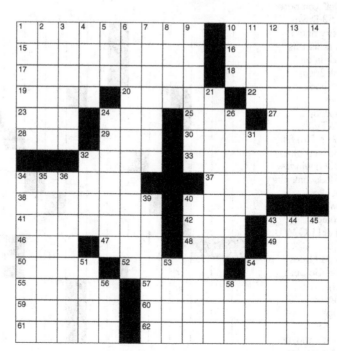

by David Quarfoot and Katy Swalwell

ACROSS

1 Fix . . . or damage
7 Deltiologist's purchase
15 Connected
16 U.S. city whose name is pronounced differently from its foreign namesake
17 Got around
18 "Two Years Before the Mast" star, 1946
19 Green marker?
20 Silver holder
22 Broke down
23 Year in the papacy of St. Pius I
24 Part of Bach's oeuvre
26 "Hänsel und Gretel" composer
28 See 53-Down
31 Literary name with a dieresis
32 Prince in an L. Frank Baum "Oz" book
33 Nerve
34 "Saturday ___," 1976 Earth, Wind & Fire hit
35 Something often laid at a window
36 1971 documentary about Ravi Shankar
37 Decamps
38 Part of I.L.G.W.U.: Abbr.
39 Like best buds
40 & 41 Go out nicely
43 Distinction
44 "Judge ___, . . ."
45 Western ___
48 A pinch, maybe
49 52-Across, for example

50 Sour orange, in French cuisine
52 White 49-Across
54 Intro to an unvarnished opinion
55 Cutthroat
56 Like centurions, typically
57 Benders

DOWN

1 Marked difference
2 Coupling device?
3 Jump-started
4 Interject
5 Runs through
6 Charm
7 Groundwork?
8 Standard offering of old
9 European two-seater
10 Pacific Coast evergreen
11 Super Bowl XLI winners
12 "___ Full of Sky" (2004 Terry Pratchett novel)
13 Coaster, e.g.
14 Georgia Tech football coaching great Bobby
21 Many an 11-Down fan
25 "Farewell, ___," 1965 top 10 Joan Baez album
27 Chiffon creations
28 It might singe a knight, in legend
29 Sizable, as a hamburger patty

30 Candlenut and buckeye
33 :D, in an e-mail
35 Sweep the competition
39 1967 Peter Fonda film written by Jack Nicholson
41 Gag rule, of a sort
42 Scoring leaders?
43 Savannah bounder
45 Waist products
46 Muscovite, for one
47 Richard of "The 300 Spartans"
51 Pip location
53 With 28-Across, ___ Caraïbes (Guadeloupe setting)

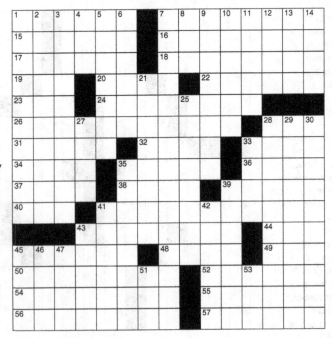

by Byron Walden

73

ACROSS

1 1971 hit with the lyric "He danced for those at minstrel shows"
12 Big shot? Hardly!
15 Film in which Ford was president
16 1998 Tony winner for Best Play
17 Clowns
18 Agatha Christie's "___ M?"
19 Flower with a bulb
20 Have insomnia
22 Tough guys
26 Group on Miles Davis's "Birth of the Cool," e.g.
27 Boxer's training equipment
30 Playwright Connelly who won a Pulitzer for "The Green Pastures"
31 Torah's beginning?
32 Grammy winner Blige
34 Like arctic winters
35 Least interesting
37 Issue
39 Curved nail
40 Seen enough
42 Launch of 1986
43 Title boy in a 1964 Disney film
44 McIntosh cousins
46 Improves
48 Most of Mauritania
49 Makes obsolete
51 "The X-Files" fodder
55 A, in Aix
56 Oscar winner between Tom Hanks and Geoffrey Rush
60 Victoria in London, e.g.: Abbr.
61 Subject of "The Double Helix"
62 Id follower
63 Protected areas

DOWN

1 Google heading
2 Bring to a boil
3 Crow
4 In the distant past
5 ___ A. Bank, menswear retailer
6 Constellation near Norma
7 Big A.T.M. maker
8 Topic in oil exploration
9 Tiffany who made Tiffany lamps
10 Relative of -trix
11 Body type
12 Girl group with the 1986 #1 hit "Venus"
13 "Buy now," e.g.
14 Emergency equipment
21 Creation of Genesis 2:22
23 Some pitchers
24 Stern School degs.
25 Author of "The Sot-Weed Factor"
27 Dome site
28 Supreme rulers
29 Malice aforethought
33 Film knights
34 Misanthrope
36 Given (out)
38 Gold digger's destination
41 Skater dude's exclamation
45 Wall treatment
47 Erstwhile Vegas hotel
48 After-dinner request
50 Brown with a blue pencil
52 Pan, for one
53 Give a body check?
54 Meets
57 Ultimate outcome
58 One of the Khans
59 "___ who?"

by Randolph Ross

ACROSS

1 Extracurricular activity traditionally for men
9 Measure of reflected light
15 Digitalis source
16 Manage adversity
17 Fresh
18 Kind of case
19 Fix at a farrier's
20 Confident affirmation
22 "Princess Caraboo" star, 1994
23 Set
24 Is peaked
25 Opera heroine with the aria "Einsam in trüben Tagen"
26 Singer Stubbs of the Four Tops
27 Murphy of "To Hell and Back"
28 Valium, generically
31 Place for buttercups
32 Overdo it at the gym
35 Withstands
37 Tognazzi of "La Cage aux Folles"
38 Opera that opens on Christmas Eve
40 Best Actor nominee for "Affliction," 1998
42 Life sci.
43 Captain of Stubb and Flask
47 Old World duck
48 Split
49 Ready
50 County holding part of Yosemite National Park
52 Old-fashioned letter opener: Abbr.

53 Less likely to fly?
54 Complex component
56 Having a hint
57 Paramount
58 Bigots
59 Not fleshed out

DOWN

1 Jet pilot's concern
2 Owner of Maybelline
3 Has substance
4 Einsteins
5 Awards for some campaigns
6 Set apart
7 A.C.C. member
8 Hold
9 Arabic name that means "servant of God"
10 He wrote "There was an old man of Thermopylae / Who never did anything properly . . ."
11 River craft
12 Author of "The Greedy Bastard Diary: A Comic Tour of America"
13 President who claimed to be a voodoo priest
14 Pirates' domain
21 Loose
23 Shameless hussies
26 Newswoman Logan
27 Band switch
29 Princess loved by Heracles

30 "Earth's Children" series author Jean
32 Colt handler
33 Extreme bovarism
34 Accepting
36 Ogrelike
39 Brother and husband of Tethys
41 Qualm
44 Greet cattily
45 Hindu drink of immortality
46 German astronomer who was the first to measure the distance to a star
48 Wades through
49 Precipice, say
51 ___ review
52 Remote option
55 Puma prey

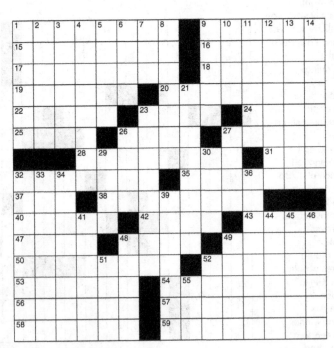

by Karen M. Tracey

ACROSS

1 Energy source
11 Troy Aikman, John Elway and others, in brief
15 Home of the National Automobile Museum
16 Self-styled world salsa capital
17 First lady who was once a prominent radio actress
18 Catch
19 1899 gold rush site
20 Tick off
22 Bull Halsey's org.
23 Rap sheet abbr.
24 Machu Picchu, for one
25 Swell
27 Certain campus Greeks
30 Ages
31 X maker, at times
32 Two Ralph Waldo Emerson collections
34 Political payoff, perhaps
36 Word with speed or fire
38 ___ P. Halliburton, founder of the Halliburton company
39 Pops
43 Sandinista's foe
47 TV chef Deen
48 JetBlue competitor
50 1994 Peace Nobelist
51 "The Beverly Hillbillies" star
52 Gambler's option
54 Spots
55 Trawler equipment
56 "Gulliver's Travels," e.g.
58 Remain
59 With 4-Down, longtime jazz record label
61 One who deals in futures
63 High places
64 Construction equipment
65 Break
66 Angels

DOWN

1 Pineapple, e.g.
2 Takes back
3 Brutes
4 See 59-Across
5 ___ roll
6 Object of a miracle of Jesus
7 Pennsylvania, e.g.
8 En estos lugares se habla español
9 "Oklahoma!" girl
10 "You ___?"
11 D.J.'s, at times
12 "Survivor" setting, 2004
13 Drub
14 Gentleman of Verona
21 Wrap
26 Dawn-of-mammals epoch
28 Tell
29 Modern dwellers of ancient Ebla
33 ___ Hill
35 Protective agcy. since 1974
37 Place with cages
39 Where drinks aren't on you
40 Singer with the 1975 #1 hit "Lady Marmalade"
41 Scraps
42 Turns in
44 Tramp
45 Highlands relative of an elk
46 Maintains
49 Some hogs
53 Villa ___
57 "Sorry to intrude . . ."
58 Winner of Wimbledon for five consecutive years
60 Store sign abbr.
62 Yardbird

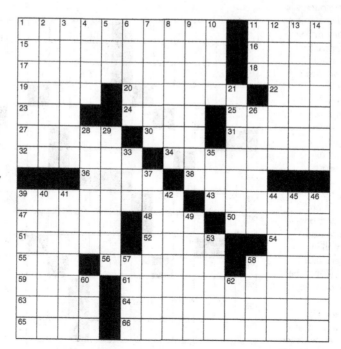

by Nancy Joline

ACROSS
1 Landscaper's aid
7 Woodcutter's aid
15 First in line
16 Woman who's just too cool?
17 Food brand with a sun in its logo
18 1978 Stephen King novel made into a miniseries
19 Fisherman's supply
20 They may come from the wings
21 Defibrillator users, for short
22 [Just like that!]
23 Follow
25 Falls at the hands of
27 Acted impulsively
31 Passed-down strands
33 Offer courses for
34 Kind of furniture
35 Money maker
37 Breakfast fare
38 Three-star officer: Abbr.
39 Perfect
42 Satisfied
43 Composer Frederick
44 Turgite or limonite
46 Delaware, the ___ State
48 Slight progress, after "from"
51 Bologna oils
54 Son of Leah
55 Grimalkin
56 Where many people may lie
58 Schubert works
59 Place to order rolls
60 Store, in a way
61 Further evidence
62 It might ask "What comes next?"

DOWN
1 Does a job on
2 Marsh denizen
3 Like some T-shirts and eggs
4 Returning to an old beat
5 Persians, e.g.
6 It might let off some steam
7 Place
8 Want in the worst way
9 Minute to the max
10 Administration ctrs.
11 It contains the auricle
12 Printer's amount
13 Thrilled
14 Breaks off
20 Run
23 The first one gets you going
24 It's near Fort Bliss
26 Shakespearean opener
28 Wicker work
29 Resin source
30 Exactly
31 Computer exec Michael
32 It has ports in Port.
36 Residence of some Indians
37 Provide money for
39 Went for
40 Words from the wise
41 Actress Anderson
45 Least known
47 Out
49 J.D.'s of the future
50 Uniform part, maybe
51 Architectural projection
52 Sauce thickener
53 Nonsense
55 Roulette play
57 Brief connection?
58 Floral offering

by Joe DiPietro

ACROSS

1 Tollbooth option for Northeasterners
7 Pennsylvania town that was the longtime home of Rolling Rock beer
14 Ogle
15 Plans named for a Delaware senator
16 One concerned with school activities?
18 Comment after "So"
19 Itself, in a legal phrase
20 Dating concern
21 Martini go-with?
22 Approve
24 BusinessWeek topic: Abbr.
26 N.F.L.'er or N.B.A.'er
27 Mathematician seen on a Swiss 10-franc note
29 Lounging terrace
31 "The Last of the Plainsmen" novelist
32 Judge's declaration
33 Yes-men
37 Worn rocks
38 Cold evidence
39 "Blade Runner" actress Young
40 Give an invitation for
41 A challenger might go after one
42 Cheer starter
45 Word with time or tone
46 Plays first
48 Steel guitar sound
50 With 9-Down, albeit, poetically
52 Length of a kids' fun run, briefly
53 Kind of wind
54 Disneyland attraction since 1955
57 Sweethearts
58 It may sit near a jack
59 "After you"
60 Deck reply

DOWN

1 College in south central New York
2 Extremist
3 Be wiped out
4 Easter baby, maybe
5 Birthplace of the first giant panda in North America to survive to adulthood
6 Abbr. on many Québec road signs
7 Slacker
8 Bearer of scales and plates
9 See 50-Across
10 Capital on the Daugava River
11 Fresh
12 Link between DNA strands
13 Round fig.
15 Collector of bizarre facts
17 Books with many cross references?
23 Cause for some fluff filling
25 Suave, and then some
28 Addict's bugbear
30 Japanese P.M. Shinzo ___
32 "Cryptonomicon" novelist Stephenson
33 Some coll. seniors take it
34 Have as a boss
35 The orange variety is black
36 One with the force: Abbr.
37 Maker of a wake on a lake
39 Source of strength
41 Showed anxiety
42 Flint, e.g.
43 Tomorrow
44 Cool
47 Locations for declamations
49 Certain chess piece, informally
51 Collector of couples
54 Rangers' venue: Abbr.
55 Cooler
56 N.Y.C. airport

by Mike Nothnagel

ACROSS

1 Classic nursery song opener
8 Wall hanging
15 Manly neckwear
16 Leading man in "The Marrying Kind," 1952
17 Rust producer
18 Zero
19 Mil. branch
20 "Steinbrenner!" author Dick
22 Canal
23 Circa
25 Lanford Wilson's "The __ Baltimore"
26 German pronoun
27 Old
29 Offshoot
31 Long times: Abbr.
32 Braces
34 Cry of exasperation
36 "Chill!"
38 Cry of discovery
41 Call for
45 Kind of column
46 Bit of choreography
48 Freewheeling
49 __ Phair with the 2003 tune "Why Can't I?"
50 Hoi polloi disdainer
52 Level
53 Mathematician Napier, for one
55 NASA component
57 __ seul (dance solo)
58 Hip
60 They may be moving
62 By and by
63 Together
64 Some Civil War guerrillas
65 Coldwell Banker employee

DOWN

1 Teems
2 Season ticket holder's prize
3 Zeitgeist
4 Cabinet div.
5 Flight data, briefly
6 Purple __
7 Warm up
8 "Holy smokes!"
9 Not true
10 The Chi. Cubs play games on this
11 Course
12 Fired up
13 Theme from "Peter Gunn" composer
14 Pilot's certification requirement
21 Clueless
24 Lurched
28 Year the Ostrogoths were defeated at the Battle of Taginae
30 It has a code
31 Ransom demander
33 Some N.C.O.'s
35 Like some juries
37 Countdown elements
38 Colt's place
39 Foodie
40 Designated a new use for
42 Pattern in prosody
43 "Oh, yeah?!"
44 "Where's Charley?" composer
47 Obviously unhappy person
51 Ralph who wrote "Have Yourself a Merry Little Christmas"
54 Rossini protagonist
55 Like some vases
56 First name in humor
59 __-eyed
61 Barn dance participant

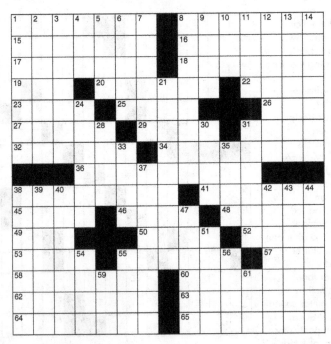

by Bob Peoples

ACROSS

1 Sitcom character with a leather jacket that's now in the Smithsonian
8 The New Yorker cartoonist William
13 Taxing preinitiation period
15 Childish retort
17 Have no dinner companions
18 Make
19 They're numbered in golf
20 Fasten firmly
22 Prefix with lateral
23 One prepared for church: Abbr.
24 Quintillionth: Prefix
25 Thai currency
26 2004 Brad Pitt film
28 Agitate
30 Scream
31 Felicitous
33 1974 Chicago hit
35 2002 sci-fi role for Hayden Christensen
39 Teacher's request of a publisher
40 Capitol Records owner
41 Dancer Limón
42 Moves laboriously
44 New York Cosmos' sports org.
48 Linear, briefly
49 Send a high-tech message
50 Kind of season
51 They, to Thérèse
52 Classic arcade game character who hopped around a pyramid
54 "David ___" (1934 Will Rogers film)
56 Seat of Hillsborough County, N.H.
58 Nintendo game with exercises for mental acuity
60 Treats similar to Mallomars
61 Local election campaign staple
62 Basketball defense
63 Some shorts

DOWN

1 Believer
2 One catching some waves?
3 California air station where Nixon landed after resigning in 1974
4 Glazed dessert
5 Mouse catchers
6 Latin leader?
7 Crown
8 Garment worn over a choli
9 Bygone carnivore
10 "I should ___ die with pity": King Lear
11 Drawing medium
12 Ends one's travels
14 Omaha and Spokane were once in it
16 Competitor in a harness
21 Initial venture
24 Ad directive
25 Player of Dr. Kiley on "Marcus Welby, M.D."
27 Ran on and on
29 Giants are in it: Abbr.
32 Snap
34 Flight
35 Makes contact with
36 Glower?
37 One with a taxing job
38 Avalanche
43 Hollywood crowd?
45 Not stout
46 Ernie Bushmiller comics character
47 Light measures
52 Survey part: Abbr.
53 Follower of the bottom line?
54 Screen
55 "As I Lay Dying" character
57 It ended when Francis II abdicated: Abbr.
59 Ernst contemporary

by Mike Nothnagel

80

ACROSS

1 Where to find the Mercury line and the Girdle of Venus
5 Small wonders
15 Novel that ends "By noon, the island had gone down in the horizon; and all before us was the wide Pacific"
16 Dirt
17 Frill
18 Alley oops
19 Historical succession
20 Millet, for one
21 Antarctica's Prince ___ Mountains
22 Many G's
23 Ray, Jay or A
24 Word with building or burial
25 Uncouth
27 Title for Camilla
30 Shade of red
31 Writer who was a source for Verdi's "Rigoletto"
32 Be profligate, in a way
38 Like Pompeii, once
39 Kind of service
40 1961 film also known as "The Job"
44 Numbered 31-Down
45 Bourbon order
46 Proofs of purchase, often: Abbr.
47 Part of the Dept. of Justice
48 Predecessor of the boliviano
49 "Tout le monde en ___" ("Everyone's talking about it": Fr.)

51 With 54-Across, black magic
52 It can keep ballfields dry
54 See 51-Across
55 Lots to offer
56 Invite letters
57 Bank holdings?
58 Like porridge

DOWN

1 Controversial study
2 Title city in a 1983 George Strait hit
3 Ordinance
4 TV tavern
5 Check for credibility, in modern lingo
6 Hardened
7 Polaris or Procyon
8 Furry tree-dweller of the Amazon
9 The river Pison flowed from it
10 Austrian article
11 Squelch
12 Unpleasant way to catch one's spouse
13 They're found by the C's
14 Does the math
23 Bowls
26 Good bud
27 Result of too many rusty nails on the road?
28 Melees
29 Some Microsoft employees
31 See 44-Across: Abbr.
33 "Weeds" channel, briefly
34 Line struck through by a winner

35 Aral Sea feeder
36 Starchy bite
37 Beats narrowly and unexpectedly
40 Somewhat
41 Sobieski of "Joan of Arc"
42 He wrote "The heart has its reasons which reason knows nothing of"
43 Most-nominated Best Actor (eight times) never to win an Oscar
44 Burning the midnight oil
46 Built up
49 Uptown
50 Lola in "Damn Yankees," e.g.
51 Actress Maryam
53 Plugged in

by Byron Walden

ACROSS

1 Actor whom People magazine erroneously declared dead in 1982
10 Aid in retriever retrieval?
15 Persian's gift
16 Gull-like
17 Basis of "America"
19 "Get ___" (1967 hit for the Esquires)
20 Filmmaker Morris
21 Barrel statistic
22 Turkey dough?
24 "The Christmas Song" co-writer
26 Univ. research grantor
27 Crack
28 Military V.I.P.
30 Slippery as ___
32 Deserve consideration
33 The last novel featuring him was "Stopover: Tokyo"
34 Fugitive's fear
37 "Let's be reasonable . . ."
38 Annular seals
39 Water softener
40 Sensation
41 Cheekbone
42 Syst. of unspoken words
45 Muffin holder
46 He served between Hubert and Gerald
48 First name in college football coaching
50 Pizzeria chain since 1943, informally
52 Val d'___ (French ski resort)
54 "La ___," 1946 Dolores del Rio film
55 Punish publicly, perhaps
58 Way to stand
59 Place for a vacuum
60 Rocker Patty who married John McEnroe
61 Felt suppressed rage

DOWN

1 Land bordered by the Congo
2 Having some replacement parts?
3 Last
4 Line of motor scooters
5 Pier grp.
6 Springiness
7 Implication
8 Home to Rosa Parks Blvd.
9 Bad way for a ship to be driven
10 Govt. probe
11 Plaster
12 Get plastered
13 Not at all fond of
14 Result of cross-fertilization within a population
18 Dartboard material
23 Discards, with "off"
25 Designate
29 Couple's word
31 Home of Silver City: Abbr.
32 Stack on a pallet: Abbr.
33 Melvin of the Orioles
34 Film studio department
35 How some people walk
36 Hammer activator
37 Avalanche setting
39 Something taken before practicing
41 Dough must be squeezed out of them
42 Distinctive director
43 Light up at a dance?
44 Paged
47 Sticker
49 "Affliction" star, 1998
51 It's splintered
53 Graphic artist Nolde
56 Letter wearer: Abbr.
57 Milkweed part

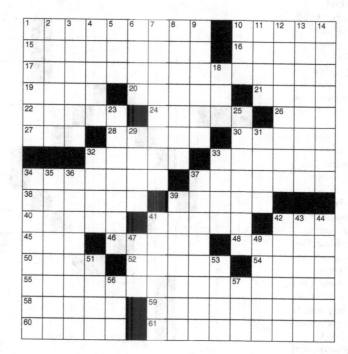

by Pete Mitchell

ACROSS

1 Magellan, e.g.
11 Three-time Gold Glove winner ___ Otis
15 Enthusiastic welcome
16 Undergo ecdysis
17 Imparts artfully
18 "Put your wallet away"
19 Word with age or weight
20 Surveillance setup
22 Bricklike
25 Idolized artist in Ouida's "A Dog of Flanders"
26 Bad combustion
29 Sorority letters
31 Shatt al Arab port
32 Put away
33 Many a Degas portrait
35 Skipper, to Barbie
36 La Grande Jatte, e.g.
37 Zolaesque imputation
38 Duct opening
39 Outboard motor inventor Evinrude
40 Release a bulletin?
41 TV role for Bamboo Harvester
42 Attack
44 Basketball court's three-point line, e.g.
45 Rumble in the Jungle setting
46 Whizzes
48 One who's more than attentive
50 Its flag depicts a plow, shovel and pick
52 Contend (with), in the country

56 St. ___ (Cornwall resort town)
57 Doctor, at times
60 Fröbe who played Goldfinger
61 Cosmopolitan alternative
62 ". . . maybe more, maybe less"
63 Supporters of roads

DOWN

1 Some Muslims
2 Shut (up)
3 Dictionary word before a variant spelling
4 Mount
5 Eternal
6 Toss
7 "V for Vendetta" actor, 2006
8 ___-Tab (PC window-switching shortcut)
9 Gained popular acceptance
10 Quaint note opener
11 Simple life?
12 Casa dei Bambini school founder
13 Show tune sung by a stevedore named Joe
14 Relinquishes control
21 Tula moolah
23 Track wager
24 Toss
26 Words to leave by
27 Did a dog trick
28 Aids in closing deals
30 Lath cover
33 It may lack stars
34 Northwest Terr. native
37 Pre-election group
41 Zabaglione ingredient
43 Decides one will
45 Hound
47 Sassers
49 Result of a handshake, maybe
51 Pick ___ (pettifog)
53 Record label for Sam & Dave and Booker T. & the MG's
54 Sourdough's dream
55 Period pieces?
58 ___ crusade
59 Dude

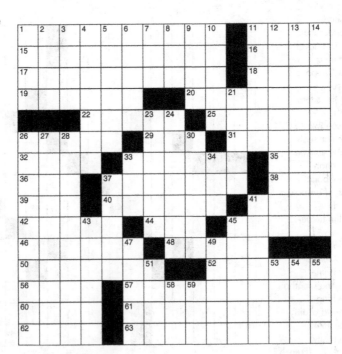

by Todd McClary

ACROSS

1 "On the other hand . . ."
8 Quaint cry from a caught crook, with "The"
15 Between here and there
16 Hot
17 Go for, as a ball
18 Film director's discovery
19 Powwow place
20 Wrong
22 Town outside Harrisburg
23 Topless?
24 "Le Bon Bock" artist
26 Times on the History Channel?
27 Cusp
28 Sony debut of 1979
30 Swallowed the bait?
31 Spandex and Lurex
33 Hurt
35 Works with
36 "What's the ___?"
37 Seashell hues
40 1940s fashion
44 Smart figures?
45 1938 Daphne du Maurier novel
47 Layer
48 Neighbor of Mex.
50 Ohio city whose name means "hospitality" in Greek
51 Dog
52 High country
54 Popular ISP
55 Slog
56 Wrong
58 Natural gas components
60 "___ Place"
61 Be at rest
62 One who tries
63 Bawls out

DOWN

1 Favorite
2 Backtrack on, as a rug
3 Certain multiscreen cinema
4 Quieted (down)
5 Overwhelming
6 Viscosity symbol, in physics
7 Figure on which royalties are based
8 What to do if you can't beat the suckers
9 Night spot
10 Thomas ___, last royal governor of Massachusetts
11 1919 Broadway musical that set a record for most performances up to that time
12 Southwest Arizona's ___ Desert
13 Howl
14 Content
21 Puts one's John Hancock on
24 What X+Y signifies
25 Cassava product
28 Having learned a lesson
29 Mex. is in it
32 Port pusher
34 Hypotheticals
36 How most farm animals behave
37 Very much
38 Zebras, e.g.
39 "___ Daughter," 2003 Judi Hendricks novel
40 Greek philosopher who founded Stoicism
41 High-elevation areas
42 1983 Randy Newman song
43 Ready to be proofed
46 Carrier
49 Earth, in sci-fi
51 Grain threshing tool
53 Legendary siege site
55 Author Silverstein
57 Saccharide suffix
59 7-up, e.g.

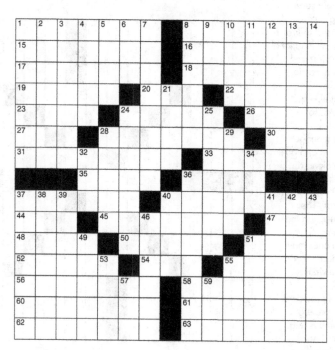

by Manny Nosowsky

ACROSS

1 Player in three 1970s Pro Bowls
9 Dispersion devices
15 Infernal
16 Any of six popes
17 It's heard at many a wedding
18 San Francisco neighborhood, with "the"
19 Basketball analyst Elmore
20 Former Shea players
22 Neighbor of Isr., once
23 Threaded holder
25 "Christ's Entry Into Brussels in 1889" painter
26 Snow on an album cover
27 Sigmoid curves
29 Trough site
30 "Please," to Franz
31 Swiss multinational
33 Didn't just nosh
35 Kind of carriage
37 Molotov cocktail, e.g.
40 Shucks, so to speak
44 Mets manager Minaya and others
45 One along an autobahn?
47 Aunt who sings part of "The Farmer and the Cowman"
48 High ones may produce a roar
49 Cape wearer's field
51 Focus provider?
52 Canyon, e.g.
53 Columbus, e.g.
55 Educ. Testing Service offering
56 "Not right now"

58 Picasso mistress and subject
60 Where Antonio and Shylock litigate
61 Ingress
62 Tequila brand with a red sombrero bottle top
63 Levied

DOWN

1 Waldenbooks alternative
2 It's sweet, it's said
3 Ways of access
4 Lower, in a way
5 Tombstone, e.g.
6 Fresh face at a firm
7 Easterners
8 "Hey!?"
9 Edsel model
10 Intake optima: Abbr.
11 Return address abbr.?
12 Orient
13 Plant of the arrowroot family
14 View coral reefs, maybe
21 Not false
24 Mountaineering aids
26 Word in a cameo-filled movie's credits
28 Folks guilty of disorderly conduct
30 "Goin' to Chicago Blues" composer
32 Ranch extension?
34 "Of the," in Oviedo

36 Campaign staple
37 Not hold something against
38 Select for a case
39 Runaway
41 Advertisers' output
42 Cookout setting
43 In sequence
46 Curtain fabrics
49 One of the Gospels, in a Spanish Bible
50 Cadbury-Adams brand
53 Minute: Prefix
54 Thin
57 RNA is a topic in it
59 Family V.I.P.'s

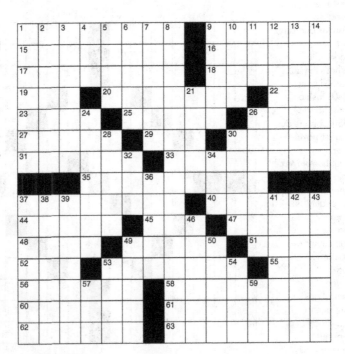

by Victor Fleming

ACROSS

1 Positive
10 Vacuum maintainers
15 Like some fruit bats and petrels
16 Cornrow component
17 Whine
18 Royal jelly consumer
19 Jungian principle
20 Samoan, e.g.
22 Kind of party
23 Top of a stadium
25 Comic character
26 From Niger to Zambia: Abbr.
27 Hacker of the Middle Ages
28 "The Dram Shop" author
29 Squeals
30 Start of a Spanish Christmas greeting
31 Certify
34 Unwelcome discovery on a credit card statement
36 Period to find out more
37 Tough companions?
38 Minor leader?
39 Carving in an Egyptian tomb
41 Relief may follow it
44 Botanist's beard
45 Unproductive
46 Rubberneck
47 Where cell phones don't work
49 Weed-B-Gon maker
50 200 milligrams
51 Popular reference work
54 Match point?
55 "Shoot!"
56 Name on a truck
57 Loser in a casino

DOWN

1 Opportunities to run away from home
2 Gustavo's good
3 Require
4 Female role in "Chicago"
5 "Paint the Sky With Stars" singer
6 Suffix with proto-
7 Abbr. on a key
8 They're back on board
9 City on the Permian Basin
10 Extend awkwardly
11 Sparkle
12 Cousin of a hyena
13 Be what you're not
14 Be a night watchman?
21 Manhattan ave.
23 Sudden impact
24 First home of the University of Nevada
27 Firm assistant, briefly
28 Couple of pizzas?
29 Revelation exclamation
30 Work unit: Abbr.
31 Black-and-white
32 Spent from all the conflict
33 Webbed
34 Generation-to-generation information
35 Poet Seeger
37 Otherworldly one
39 It's appetizing to aphids
40 What ochlophobists fear
41 Big-league promotional event
42 For some time
43 Drinks a toast
45 It's massive and relatively hot
46 ___ Waitz, nine-time New York City Marathon winner
48 King Claudius, e.g.
49 Artist John, known as the Cornish Wonder
52 Malay Peninsula's Isthmus of ___
53 Publicity

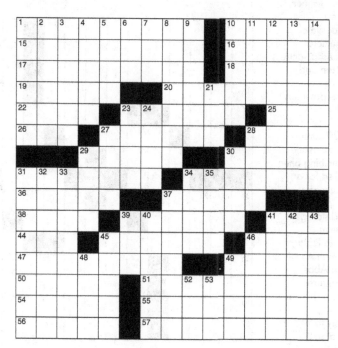

by Barry C. Silk

ACROSS

1 Faux pa?
11 Fortifies
15 Helpful figures?
16 Not yours, in Tours
17 Retinue
18 One given a staff position?
19 Enough for everyone to have seconds
20 Options for salting away, briefly
21 They're taken out in an alley
22 Purveyor of hot stuff
24 Med. specialty
25 Target of some antibiotics
27 2002 French Open winner Albert
28 Opposite of ephemeral
30 "Moesha" actress Wilson and others
32 Jump provider: Abbr.
33 G.P.S. fig.
34 1920 Summer Olympics site
38 Something often looked for on a rainy day
42 ___-Meal (vacuum food storage system)
43 ___ la Plata
45 One photocopier tray: Abbr.
46 DC figure
48 De ___ (Dallas suburb)
49 Reply to "That so?"
50 Libretto accompaniment

53 French painter of Napoleonic scenes
54 Little shooter
55 Shaker formula
56 Became adjusted
57 Whack
58 Something to crack

DOWN

1 Stir-fry vegetable
2 Calling
3 Dove's desire
4 Tool parts for bending and shaping
5 Rite aid?
6 He's a doll
7 Special-___ (football players used only in specific situations)
8 French novelist d'Urfé
9 Chaos
10 Ready to be used again
11 Italian for "sleeves"
12 Love lover
13 Blandness
14 Breaks in the heat?
23 Scaling aid
25 Abalone
26 The first one ruled 1547–84
29 How a mob acts
31 15th-century prince of Wallachia
34 Gives out
35 Uncommitted
36 Dessert Calvin doesn't like in "Calvin and Hobbes"

37 Train, say
38 Specially
39 Almost at
40 Not au naturel
41 Weave a raised design into
44 Peaceful
47 Snack cake brand since 1967
48 Cashew family member
51 It can leave you red-faced
52 "Futurama" creator Groening

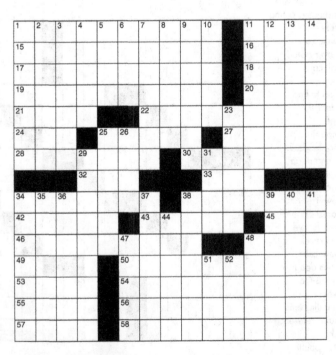

by Raymond C. Young

ACROSS

1 Breakers communicate with them
4 Medevacs, in military slang
9 Shop coat?
13 Gets a move on
15 Officer slain in the Old Testament
16 Ear-relevant
17 Sharply outline
18 Prefix with -hedron
19 Carpenter's groove
20 Avignon infinitive
21 City of canals
23 Roseanne's mom on "Roseanne"
24 Things wheeled in supermarkets?
27 Kind of therapy
29 Cow
30 Judge, e.g.
31 Rock and Roll Hall of Fame inductee known as the White Lady of Soul
36 Tactful
37 Nebulous stuff
43 Words to live by
44 People people
46 Billboard listing
49 Puts together in a hurry
50 Wood smoother
51 Food whose name is Italian for "feathers"
53 Rip off
54 Cry of vehement denial
56 Reservation dwelling
58 Aged Frankfurter?
59 Maestro Masur
60 Make more interesting
61 Future shoot
62 Janitorial tool
63 Big band era standard
64 Kind of ice

DOWN

1 Half of a 1970s–'80s comedy duo
2 Went kaput
3 Opposite of openness
4 Quarrel
5 Treats often taken apart
6 Scuba gear
7 Palestinian group
8 Cadet's topper
9 Plot thickener?
10 Very, very hot
11 Like some highways after construction work
12 Furniture protector
14 What rain might fall in
22 It contains the elastic clause
25 Absorbed
26 Debugging discovery
28 C ration replacer
32 They, in Marseille
33 Thing to be picked
34 Former telecom giant
35 Cop
37 Metal in the points of gold pens
38 EarthLink alternative
39 It's celebrated in late January or early February
40 Socially dominant ones
41 Put a new bottom on, in a way
42 Black & Decker offering
43 Classroom sneeze elicitor
45 Express
47 Country singer McCoy and others
48 Get divorced
49 Grill brand
52 Astronomer's study
55 Motor Up alternative
57 Cleaning product with the slogan "It's that fast"

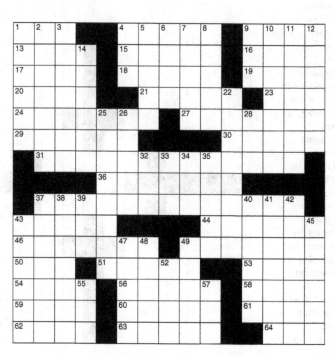

by John R. Conrad

ACROSS

1 Claimed as one's own
8 Paper binder
15 Sandlot game
16 Draft pick
17 Looking ragged
18 Lined with trees
19 Rock guitarist born David Evans
20 Mike Brady of "The Brady Bunch," e.g.
21 Half a nursery-rhyme spider's description: Var.
22 Longtime "What's My Line?" panelist
23 "Go jump in the lake!"
25 Begin, as an enterprise
26 1947 semi-documentary-style crime drama
27 Aces
29 Communist federation: Abbr.
30 Common site of archaeological remains
31 They mean nothing
35 Red stain in a lab
37 Dance in a pit
41 Running wild
43 "It's true!"
45 Carrying on
46 First name in electrical engineering
47 Run-in
49 Made happy
50 Bigger and stronger
51 Class struggles?
52 Sanctions
53 Pro performer

54 Others
55 Expose and destroy

DOWN

1 Guinness Book weather record category
2 Former home of the N.F.L.'s Rams
3 Cooling-off period
4 Spoils
5 Immobile in winter
6 Not wait for an invitation
7 Eye sore
8 Bath and others
9 Carnegie Mellon athletes
10 King of Belgium
11 Races

12 Pantries
13 "___ and Franklin," 1976 biopic
14 Makes flush
24 Drum accompanying a pipe
25 The ___ Marbles
28 Island said to be the home of Homer's tomb
31 "Again?!"
32 With no time to lose
33 Celebrity chef
34 Scoundrel
35 Young members of a convocation
36 Melville's Ishmael, e.g.
37 Comes through successfully

38 Bristol Cream ingredient
39 Guide feature?
40 Control tower equipment
42 Purrer
44 Links with
48 Once, long ago
49 Woodwind instrument: Abbr.

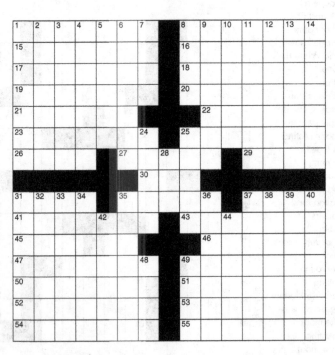

by Manny Nosowsky

89

ACROSS
1 Celebratory cry
9 It can leave you breathless
15 Two-time Nicaraguan president Chamorro
16 Draw successfully
17 County whose seat is Redwood City
18 "Ya got me!"
19 Union in D.C., e.g.
20 Sets up
22 Cleanse
23 Beaucoup de Louises
25 Dismiss as unworthy
26 "Well, I declare!"
27 Three Stooges' actions
29 ___ man
30 San Francisco mayor Newsom
31 Skeleton part
33 Handicap, say
35 "The Da Vinci Code" sequence
39 Sly slur
40 Motor additive?
41 They have five sects. of multiple-choice questions
42 Temp takers
44 ___ Bay (South China Sea inlet)
48 Court interferences
49 Out there
51 Gabrielle's sidekick, in a TV series
52 Place for 42-Across
53 Undercover wear?
55 Prescription notation
56 Bottle

58 Horror cry
60 Religious leader who wrote "Peace With God"
61 Baseball coverings
62 Jennifer Lopez title role
63 Bakes

DOWN
1 Salutation abbreviation
2 Stuff in a bomb
3 Flower named for a German botanist
4 Hackberry relative
5 Pseudologue
6 "Soap" family
7 Breakless, in a way
8 Derogatory term popularized by George H. W. Bush

9 Superman, for one
10 Head makeup
11 Play whose star won the 1990 Best Actor Tony
12 The Wars of the Roses ended in his reign
13 Dwarf
14 Soothing things
21 Prime Minister Nouri al-Maliki, e.g.
24 Salad bar binful
26 France's first minister of culture, 1959–69
28 They can make waves
30 Iona College athletes
32 Stop O.K.'ing

34 Hope offerer: Abbr.
35 They might follow the drill
36 Wobbly
37 Note offering good advice for life?
38 Information holder
43 Help in getting up
45 Come to pass
46 "How dare you!"
47 Treat affectionately
49 Belief in Hinduism
50 "___ have no . . ."
53 Sturdy, twilled cotton fabric
54 "Look Forward in Anger" comedian
57 Word before some animal names
59 Books, for short

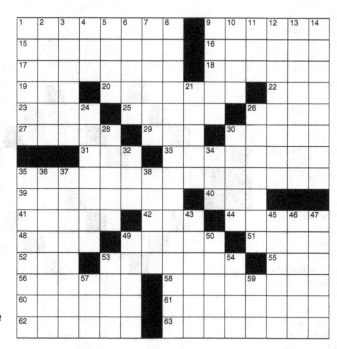

by Charles Barasch

ACROSS

1 First
16 Dante characters?
17 The "she" in the lyric "And when she passes, I smile"
18 Relinquish
19 Central square, maybe
20 50 Cent cover
21 First word of "Shrek"
22 Its capital is Porto-Novo
24 "Lo, here ___, / Never to rise again": "Hamlet"
25 ___ Digital Shorts (late-night comic bits)
26 One way to work
27 Drawing of the heart?
29 See 58-Down
30 Discoverer of the law of quadratic reciprocity
32 Disparage
34 Sideshow staple
37 Strong aversion
38 With 55-Across, $MgSO_4 \cdot 7H_2O$
40 Afternoon ora
43 Stop: Abbr.
44 Amber, for example
45 Capital of New Zealand: Abbr.
47 Food eaten with gravy
49 Mallow family members
51 "Vogliatemi ___" (aria from "Madama Butterfly")
52 The Green Hornet's real first name
54 Some stipend recipients, for short
55 See 38-Across
56 Interdisciplinary college major
59 Patch alternative
60 Last

DOWN

1 Galas
2 Saint-___-du-Mont, church containing the remains of the patron saint of Paris
3 Place for some prospects
4 Hardy one?
5 Break
6 Place for a stirrup
7 They may take a few yrs. to mature
8 Villain in the book of Esther
9 Brought out
10 NE for SW, e.g.
11 Jazz trumpeter/composer Jones
12 "Trip to ___" (1968 Susan Sontag book)
13 "Over the Rainbow" vocalist Ray
14 Be extant
15 Like some disappearances
22 Chihuahua fare
23 Chromosome home
26 Wampum
28 Gatorade choice
31 Olympics theme composer Arnaud
32 Person on the left?: Abbr.
33 Bolt measures: Abbr.
35 Charity carnival feature
36 Higher calling?
39 Former Mercury model
40 L.A.'s ___ Tower, tallest building in the West
41 Nickname on "Cheers"
42 Not together
44 Headache
46 Bring down
48 Leather band
50 Eastern royal
51 ___-Württemberg (Stuttgart's state)
53 Co-founder of the Non-Aligned Movement, 1961
55 1970s rocker Quatro
57 N.L. Central team, on scoreboards
58 With 29-Across, highest-quality

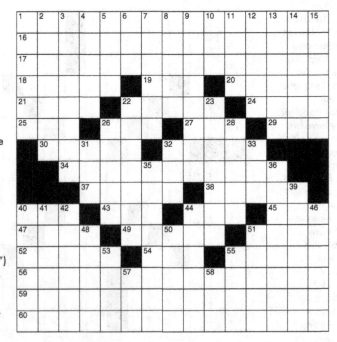

by Byron Walden

ACROSS

1. Oblong dessert
12. Compositions
14. Wizards and Magic, e.g.
16. "Heat traps" in houses
17. Suitable for hypertension sufferers
18. Liquid used in canning
19. "The ___ the limit!"
20. Traditional know-how
21. Skull Island denizen, for short
22. Mushy ___ (British dish)
23. Drab and colorless
24. Geom. measure
25. Kind of dish
26. "___ Now" (1968 R & B album)
27. Old masters reside in them
29. Court staff
32. Bully's target, maybe
33. Biblical figure who says to God "Make me understand how I have erred"
36. Takes on
37. Overlook
38. Baker v. ___ (landmark Supreme Court voting rights case)
39. Memo heading
40. Square dance partner
41. Long known for playing football
42. Doesn't stay on topic
44. Gelato sans milk
45. Hiding one's true feelings

47. French-born architect who designed Washington, D.C.
48. 1930 novel that takes its title from Shakespeare's "Twelfth Night"

DOWN

1. Bankrupting
2. For the ___
3. Potential heiress
4. Congressional output
5. Grab ahold of
6. It separates the Bering Sea from the Pacific
7. Spreads out
8. Compartmentalized box's contents
9. Two-time football Pro Bowler Leon
10. White sheets
11. Take from a book, say
12. Female prison official
13. "From Russia With Love" org.
14. Sweet, glazed cake
15. "G'bye!"
19. It leaves an impression
22. D.C. players
23. Wilbur Post's "pal"
25. "The Odd Couple" director
26. Is shown
27. Ice cream flavor
28. Lie
29. Early "astronaut"
30. It reveals who's on first
31. Undependable
33. Paleontologist's discovery, maybe
34. Show the ropes to
35. Jeremy ___, 1980s–'90s portrayer of Sherlock Holmes
37. Gets into a single lane, say
38. Stock holder
40. Romance or horror
41. 1992 Nicholson title role
43. Highlands weapon
44. Soft rock?
46. Many a retirement gift

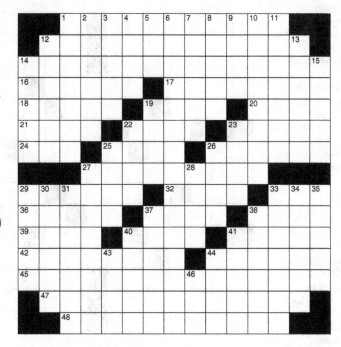

by Patrick Berry

ACROSS

1 Whole ___
8 Place on a Monopoly board
15 What goes around
16 Gain or loss
17 Line from a scam artist
18 Tablets site
19 Where the African Union is headquartered
21 Headache intensifiers
22 Patient status
23 Slicer locale
24 Little sucker?
25 Dept. store stock
27 Fictional salesman of '80s ads
31 Shrink
34 It's hard to fail
35 Grammy category
36 Biographical subject of the Best Picture of 1936
39 A driver might dip into it
40 Farm housing
41 Place for a clown
42 Tap type
44 He beat Botvinnik in 1960
45 Unlikely to break the ice
46 Firm wheel: Abbr.
48 Per ___
52 1988 chart-topping country album
54 Resident of Chinese highlands
56 Hero's welcome
58 Jambalaya
59 Relief pitcher Armando
60 Went over

61 Substitute for some snack foods
62 McDonald's mascot before Ronald

DOWN

1 Misses at fiestas: Abbr.
2 Group of 6-Down
3 Exercise of a sort
4 Best Supporting Actress of 1997
5 Some defenders: Abbr.
6 See 2-Down
7 Relative of a loon
8 Mutualism
9 Cry before disappearing
10 Univ. class
11 Sportswear company whose logo is three parallel stripes
12 Like a well-kept lawn
13 Science fiction author Greg
14 Number of wives of Enrique VIII
20 Mideastern news source
24 Sex therapist's suggestion
26 Smart
28 One held in an orbit
29 ___ Corporation (jewelry retail giant)
30 Hair salon option
31 Corp. bigwigs
32 Jambalaya

33 Monkshood
34 Co-star of Broadway's "Fanny"
37 Indefinitely large
38 Like many a road map
43 Clarifying words
44 Pump alternative
47 Boeing personnel: Abbr.
49 On the outs (with)
50 Virtual meeting of a sort
51 Patrick with a Tony
52 Cyborg's beginning?
53 First name in motorcycling
54 It may follow convention
55 Oft-framed piece
57 Cousin of TV

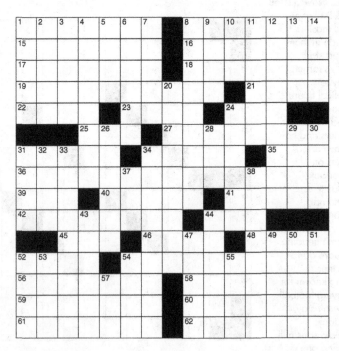

by Karen M. Tracey

ACROSS

1 You can sink your feet into them
12 Bus line?
14 Caribbean cruise port of call
16 Diwali revelers
17 Sprinted, perhaps
18 Home of the Cotopaxi volcano
19 Early film actress Pitts
20 Rolling Stone cover subject
21 Abbr. after an author's name, maybe
22 Marty's mentor in "Back to the Future"
23 Where Japanese shares are bought and sold: Abbr.
25 Mountain
26 Utah's ___ Mountains
28 Comparable to a wet hen
32 Pointed warning?
34 This-and-that recording for a friend or a party
36 Time immemorial
37 Van ___ of "Double Team" and "Double Impact"
39 Some "wax"
40 ___-Bo
42 Beer may be on this
43 Cement layer's work
44 Word before and after "against"
47 Marvel Comics series
49 Profile on a 19¢ stamp
50 Major component of kidney stones

52 Hula-hoop, say
53 Start of a series
55 ___ diet, food plan emphasizing olive oil, fish, fruit, vegetables and red wine
56 Gulf war offensive

DOWN

1 Star performer's reward
2 Got together
3 100, say
4 Classic cars with 389 engines
5 Hotel room option
6 Draw
7 Birds with a name from Greek myth
8 Squirt
9 Title aunt in a 1979 best seller
10 Most affected by pathos
11 Leaves alone, sometimes
12 It's guarded in a soccer game
13 "Copacabana" antagonist
14 Coffee alternative
15 Third-longest river of California
19 Daydreamed, with "out"
22 Pulled off
24 Partner of Coburg, historically
26 Major in astronomy?
27 Site of the King Hussein Mosque
29 Language of India with a palindromic name

30 Home of Lawrence University
31 Accessories for a secretary
33 Go ahead of
35 Dennis the Menace, for one
38 Accepted bad treatment
41 Heat up
43 Like someone who's been fooled before
44 Wickiup, for one
45 Self-styled "Family City U.S.A."
46 Like 1-Across
48 Scrooge McDuck, notably
49 Sleep: Prefix
51 National competitor
52 Swatter's target
54 Places for gurneys, for short

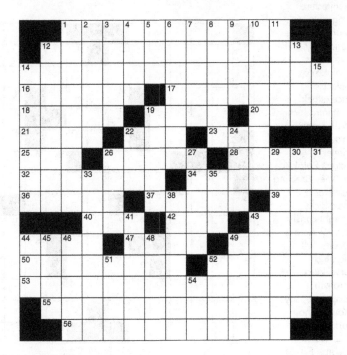

by Roger Barkan

ACROSS

1 Adoption option: Abbr.
6 Settled down securely
12 They're often unpaid
14 Do further work on a bird?
15 Construction material
17 Applies polish to?
18 Some sit on pads
19 Parcel part
20 Face with stone
21 It may be usurious: Abbr.
22 Waite ___, Hall-of-Fame Yankees pitcher
23 Hospital supplies
24 Feature of some classical architecture
26 Fragrant heartwood
27 James Bay native
29 Five atoms in a ulexite molecule
31 Face attack
35 Writ introduction?
36 1988 tennis Grand Slam winner
37 Actress Pataky
38 Cockney greeting
40 Relatives of pollocks
44 It might consist of a 19-Across
45 Become full
46 High-tech surveillance acronym
48 Soapstone, say
49 "You betcha, Bartolomé!"
50 "___ Work" (George F. Will best seller)
51 Early
54 Some bygone roadsters
55 Blue Angels member, e.g.
56 Fluish, perhaps
57 Less like a yo-yo

DOWN

1 Some poles
2 Fight
3 Relatively fresh
4 Water fleas, barnacles, etc.
5 Lee of Hollywood
6 Grant
7 Filter holders, briefly
8 1932 Garbo title role
9 Give shades to in advance
10 Who's a critic?
11 Strikes
12 Certain rose creator
13 Banjolike Japanese instrument
14 Leaf part
16 Auto option
25 Julie Harris's "East of Eden" role
28 Machination
30 So as to avoid getting shot
31 Eastwood played him in five films
32 Out
33 Thighs may be displayed in it
34 Thighs may be displayed in it
35 Water polo teams, e.g.
39 Conductor Segerstam and novelist Enger
41 As yet uncollected for
42 It rises in the Black Forest
43 Graduated
47 Galley countermand
49 Sharp rival
52 Old washday choice
53 The Platters' "___ Mine"

by Jim Page

ACROSS

1 "It's all here" sloganeer, once
4 Frisky one
8 Marie Osmond or Loretta Young
14 "Elijah" or "The Creation"
16 Key on a cash register
17 Drop a few positions, maybe
18 Overprotect
19 Maker of Kiwi Teawi
20 Mystery author Dexter
21 The Pacific Ocean's only island kingdom
22 It was good for Sartre
23 One and only
26 They're staffed with doctors
30 Bad time for a tropical vacation
33 Lawyers with many assts.
34 I.T. firm founded by Ross Perot
35 Wine used to make zabaglione
36 Soviet ___
37 Member of an extended familia
38 Country that won the most medals at the 1980 Winter Olympics
40 Reluctantly accepting
42 First name in cosmonautics
43 Major U.S. Spanish-language daily
44 Rarely written-out Latin phrase
48 "Wozzeck" composer ___ Berg
50 What stare decisis upholds the validity of
52 Red line?
54 Set of guidelines
55 Mrs. Tony Blair
56 Put forward
57 Has trouble sleeping, maybe
58 ___ Ramsay ("The Black Stallion" hero)
59 Sorry

DOWN

1 Continue effortlessly
2 Dog in Disney's "Cinderella"
3 "Paradise Lost" character
4 Ultraloyal employees
5 Passed on by taletellers
6 Not full-bodied
7 Wingtip tip
8 Feeling no better
9 "Man is a ___-using animal": Thomas Carlyle
10 Pass under the basket, maybe
11 Is clueless
12 Stout alternative
13 Drift boat attachment
15 Highest-grossing film of 1986
20 Bridesmaid's accessory
22 Very disagreeable
24 Hear
25 Analytic work
27 Soul singer who was also a coronated king of Ghana
28 New rendering
29 Near the bottom of the drawers?
30 Take one more shot at
31 It may be bid
32 One of the "10 Attic orators"
39 Tate ___ (London art gallery)
41 Team that won the first A.F.L. championship
45 1981 Literature Nobelist Canetti
46 Stocking stuffer
47 Fabric with the same name as a Scottish river
49 French district that lent its name to a foodstuff
50 "Fantastic!"
51 Ne plus ultra
52 Work within a company, say
53 Density symbol, in physics
54 Material at the basis of "Jurassic Park"

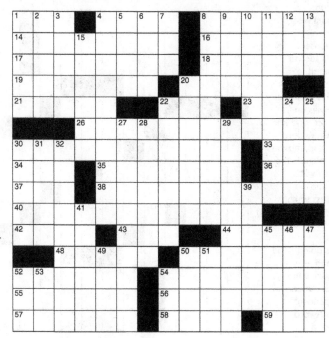

by Patrick Berry

ACROSS

1 "That may be true, but . . ."
11 ". . . there are evils ___ to darken all his goodness": Shak.
15 Visit
16 ___ Lemaris, early love of Superman
17 When a procrastinator tends to something
18 Exultant cry
19 Advance further?
20 Comic Boosler
22 Place of refuse
26 Tons of fun
27 It's built for a trial
31 Shot putters' supplies?
33 Player of June in "Henry & June"
34 Title locale of five 1980s films: Abbr.
36 Russian peasant wear
38 Chic
40 No-nonsense cry
41 King's second
43 Diamond, e.g.
44 Like petty offs.
45 She had brief roles as Phyllis on "Rhoda" and Rhoda on "Dr. Kildare"
47 Prize cup, maybe
48 Jazz pianist who played with Satchmo
50 Address south of the border
52 They're thick
54 Feast
59 Ones going head to head
60 Magazine that hands out annual Independent Press Awards
64 Part of a rebel name
65 Little redhead
66 "Buona ___!"
67 Puppet glue-ons

DOWN

1 Alexis, e.g.
2 Improve
3 Green's concern: Abbr.
4 Italian tenor ___ Schipa
5 Routine responses?
6 Soap actress Kristen and others
7 Money machine mfr.
8 Knock around
9 Pier grp.
10 Roy Rogers's surname at birth
11 Son of Elam whose name means "God the Lord"
12 Response to "I had no idea!"
13 Northeastern city named for a Penobscot chief
14 One concerned with the nose
21 Some of those who "hail the new" in "Deck the Halls"
23 Arrow of Light earner's program
24 Nostalgia elicitor
25 Cry "nyah, nyah!"
27 Engagement breakers?
28 Outlaw band member
29 Insignificant sort
30 Saki story whose title character is a hyena
32 Clammed up
35 Felix, e.g.
37 Bête noire
39 Modern provider of fast service, briefly
42 Nugget holder
46 Light reddish-brown
49 God commanded him to marry a harlot
51 Like some instruments
53 Like some instruments: Abbr.
55 "What's Going On" singer, 1971
56 What you may call it when you're wiped out
57 New Wave singer Lovich
58 Shore scavengers
61 Governing creative principle
62 Vietnam's ___ Dinh Diem
63 It's most useful when cracked

by Myles Callum

ACROSS

1 Be an agent of
7 Shock source, sometimes
15 Hawaiian "thank you"
16 Exchange for something you really want?
17 Handle, e.g.
18 Catholic
19 Wrestler Flair
20 They might just squeak by in a basketball game
22 Grooming brand introduced in 1977
24 Runners with hoods
25 Sound from a silencer
28 1965 Sonny Bono hit
31 "Berenice" author, briefly
33 Constellation seen on the flags of Australia, Samoa and Papua New Guinea
35 Club's cover
37 "___ Peak" (1997 Pierce Brosnan film)
38 Parliamentary address?
42 This, in Thüringen
43 Striking figures
46 Regulation targets for Theodore Roosevelt: Abbr.
47 "Deal with it!"
49 Catchers of some ring leaders
50 Hard up
53 Seraglio section
54 Void
57 Second chance
59 Opposite of diminish
60 "Let's have it"
61 Cardinals' gathering place
62 Violent

DOWN

1 Unscrupulous
2 Pantheon heads?
3 Fights with knights
4 Cool, in a way
5 Hockey player Tverdovsky
6 Youngest of the Culkin brothers
7 Gather
8 Scale developer
9 One-room house, typically
10 Skin pics?
11 Truncation indications: Abbr.
12 Skin pic?
13 Agent Gold on HBO's "Entourage"
14 It has pickup lines
21 It has many functions
23 Ancient meeting places
25 Cleaning product that may be useful after a party
26 Spray source
27 Amoco alternative
29 Short, close-fitting jacket
30 To ___
32 Desert Storm reporter
34 Home of Theo. Roosevelt Natl. Park
35 U.S.N. position
36 Eyebrow makeup
39 Speak explosively in anger
40 Dumps
41 Come back
44 Tree with double-toothed leaves and durable wood
45 Bad-tempered
48 Give a stemwinder
50 Bygone magistrate
51 Even ___
52 Lexicographic concern
54 "I get it" responses
55 See, say
56 Turbulent water stretch
58 Tribe visited by Lewis and Clark

by Paula Gamache

ACROSS

1 Backup
6 Squirts
10 Size in a lingerie shop
14 Music maker "played" by the wind
16 Basse-Normandie department
17 Stereotypical nerd
18 2004–06 poet laureate Kooser and others
19 Boards
20 Fluffy, perhaps
22 Tears
24 Trainee
25 Zodiac symbol
28 ___ Britannica
29 Navajo handicrafts
31 Car rental company founder Warren
33 Country with coups d'état in 2000 and 2006
35 Airline purchased by T.W.A. in 1986
36 Cellist who debuted at London's Wigmore Hall at age 16
39 Invite to one's penthouse suite
40 Robed dignitary
41 Fen bender
42 Availed
44 It lands at Landvetter
46 Holders of shoulders: Abbr.
47 Ancient Greek sculptor famous for his athletes in bronze
48 Inclusive pronoun
50 Cautious people stay on it
52 Shakespearean scholar Edmond
56 Problem ending
57 Expensive choice for a commuter
59 Big name in contact lens cleaners
60 "Madame Butterfly," updated
61 Peer on a stage
62 Being tossed, maybe
63 Statistical calculations

DOWN

1 Tio ___ (sherry brand)
2 Crazy
3 Set down
4 Bronc rival
5 Wrongful slammer sentence, say
6 Appreciation abbreviation
7 Curses
8 Palm smartphone
9 Smart
10 Fashionable resort area
11 Piñata decoration
12 Not put off
13 Raid victim
15 Instant success?
21 Indian lute
23 Like Shakespeare's Prospero, e.g.
25 Javanese chiefs
26 Salt halter
27 It'll knock you out after you knock it back
29 1996 Golden Globe winner for "Truman"
30 Variety listings
32 Like some diamonds
34 Lord of fiction
37 Beehives, e.g.
38 He wrote "In the country of the blind the one-eyed man is king"
43 Knot
45 Gomer Pyle expletive
48 Where the Fulda flows
49 Cartoonist Segar
50 Pioneering puppeteer
51 Place of honor
53 Grammy-winning merengue singer Tañón
54 Rialto sign
55 Coastal avifauna
58 Fed. property overseer

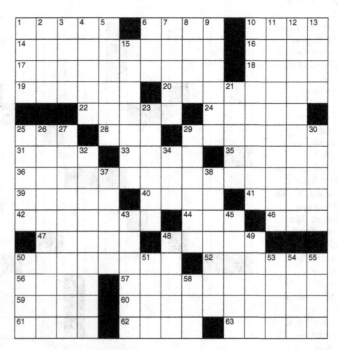

by Karen M. Tracey

ACROSS

1 Visits
8 French sentry's cry
15 Enter quickly
16 Ethically indifferent
17 "Again . . ."
18 With intensity
19 Four quarters, in France
20 Atlas sect.
22 Yugoslavian-born court star
23 Chuck
24 Purely physical
26 Show some spunk
27 Court
28 Curl tightly
30 When Hölle freezes over?
31 Pro sports team that moved from New Orleans in 1979
33 Shakes
35 Fat cat
37 Make tracks
40 Concavo-convex lens
44 UV index monitor
45 If it's regular, each of its angles is 144°
47 "Notorious" film studio
48 Memphis's locale
50 Grandparent, frequently
51 One raised on a farm
52 Some jackets
54 Philip of "Kung Fu"
55 Schwarzenegger title role
56 Outerwear fabric
58 Ding Dong alternative
60 Umm al-Quwain, for one
61 Pro Football Hall-of-Famer-turned-congressman Steve

62 Lured
63 Hides from the enemy, say

DOWN

1 Type of massage
2 Not removed delicately
3 Porthole view
4 The singing voice, informally
5 Old sticker
6 Overseas "-ess"
7 Authenticate, in a way
8 Tiger's-eye, essentially
9 Short family member?
10 "___ in the Morning"
11 Helped someone get a seat
12 Mayo's place

13 1974 Best Actress nominee Perrine
14 Champs ___
21 Approach to arithmetic that emphasizes underlying ideas rather than exact calculations
24 Not generic
25 Daughter of Ferdinand III
28 Greenland's Scoresby Sound is the world's longest
29 Classic American watchmaker
32 Insurance letters
34 Abbr. before many state names
36 "Go easy, please"
37 Had a problem with one's suits?
38 Model

39 Kind of intake
41 Got started, with "up"
42 Locale of the Carpathian Mountains, in part
43 "The New Colossus" and the like
46 Blarneyed
49 When most Capricornios are born
51 One beaten by a beatnik
53 Not split
55 No. of People?
57 A season abroad
59 Showing fatigue

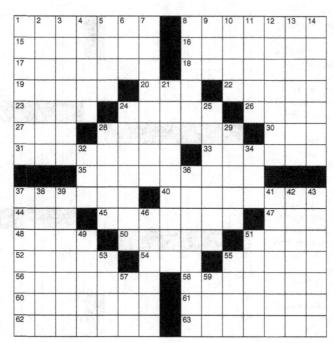

by Barry C. Silk

ACROSS

1 African city with famed botanical gardens
8 Riddle ender
15 Yosemite setting
16 Still oblivious
17 It has a fast, easy gait
19 Things you enjoy doing
20 Having new tournament rankings
21 Marxist quality?
29 Dish with tomato sauce
36 Area of W.W. II fighting
37 Like Dacron
38 Pros
39 Football helmet features
47 One working for a flat fee?
54 Has an accommodating spirit
55 Island just north of the Equator
56 Advances
57 Activity of an organism in response to light, e.g.
58 Puts away

DOWN

1 Spanish 101 verb
2 Wedding invitee
3 Wedding rentals
4 ___ Davis, first African-American to win the Heisman Trophy
5 Music symbol
6 Set (in)
7 "Ah, Wilderness!" mother
8 PBS station behind Charlie Rose
9 British general in the American Revolution
10 "I'll raise the preparation of ___": Mark Antony
11 Square in a steam room
12 Bids
13 A runner might enter it
14 Some flawed mdse.
18 Spot from which you might see a bomb headed your way
22 Recipe details: Abbr.
23 Dr Pepper Snapple Group brand
24 Composition of some French chains
25 Drink preference
26 Editorial cartoonist Hulme
27 Antique gun
28 Harvard Science Center architect José Luis ___
29 Dry, in Durango
30 Reverse movement, of a sort
31 Cézanne's "Boy in ___ Vest"
32 Longtime "All Things Considered" host Adams
33 Itself, in a Latin legal phrase
34 Not secret
35 Compact
40 Things hypothesized by Democritus
41 Move shoots, say
42 Flaky Turkish confection
43 Some moldings
44 Canine line
45 Follow
46 Way down
47 Popular U.S. board game since 1959
48 He played Bob in "La Bamba," 1987
49 It goes on and on and on
50 Former
51 They're big in Hollywood
52 Rest stop sight
53 "___ Hombres" (ZZ Top record)

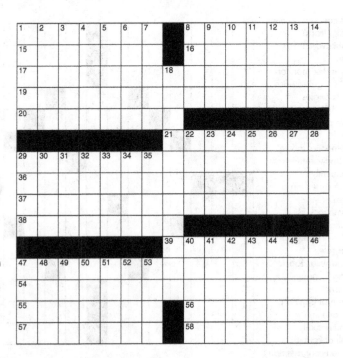

by Brendan Emmett Quigley

ACROSS

1 What you might do at the beach
10 Lethargy
15 Early inhabitant
16 Light smoke
17 Choked up
18 This is a test
19 Shaw who led the Gramercy Five
20 Muscleman with a 1980s cartoon series
21 Old-time actress Crabtree
22 Subject of interest in the question "Who are you wearing?"
23 Modern-day monarch, for short
24 Register
25 Brian known for 33-Across music
26 John who succeeded Pierre Trudeau as Canadian P.M.
28 Uris hero
29 Comment after getting something
30 Waves with long wavelengths?
33 See 25-Across
37 "Ash Wednesday" writer
38 Starry-eyed
40 Movie villain voiced by Douglas Rain
41 Miss ___
42 Spell checker?
44 Indian viceroy's authority
47 Damascus V.I.P.
50 Eventful times
51 "Take ___ the River" (Talking Heads hit)
52 Geometric prefix
53 Kip spender
54 Spanish kitties
55 Jerk

56 Doesn't support a conspiracy theory?
58 Deleted part
59 Oslo Accords concern
60 Gear
61 Frank Zappa or Dizzy Gillespie feature

DOWN

1 Forced feeding, as with a tube
2 Moon of Uranus named for a Shakespearean character
3 Like a romantic dinner
4 Big name in pest control
5 Get to
6 Jazz ___
7 Certain switch
8 Available
9 Small in the biggest way?
10 100 to 1, e.g.
11 Actress Nancy of "Sunset Boulevard"
12 Sandwich filler
13 Church piece
14 Old Tory
23 Fundamental energy units
26 "Vincent & ___" (1990 Robert Altman film)
27 Dailies, in the movie biz
29 ___-en-Provence, France
31 Groomed
32 Word before and after "in"
33 Swimming, surfboarding, etc.

34 Uncombed
35 Whitewall, maybe
36 Delays
39 Largest of the ABC islands
43 "The Tao that can be told is not the eternal Tao" philosopher
44 "Touché!" elicitor
45 Not accented
46 Important figure in the Gospels
48 Faulkner's "___ for Emily"
49 Out
51 1945 conference site for Roosevelt and Churchill
54 One might fight to the last one
57 Sonny's partner in "Dog Day Afternoon"

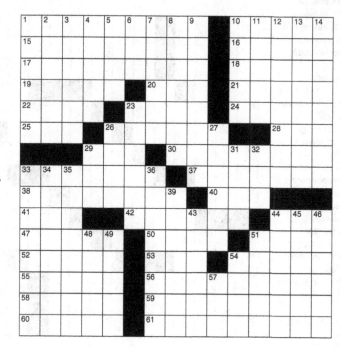

by John Farmer

102

ACROSS

1 Interest of Miss Marple
5 Blow-drying problem
15 Liner's locale
16 Slipping frequencies
17 Spot
18 Steering system components
19 "___ the glad waters of the dark blue sea": Byron
20 James Bond was kicked out of it
21 Eric of "Lucky You"
22 Contortionist's inspiration?
24 Aquavit flavorer
27 Risible
28 Paris fashion house since 1956
29 Seed's exterior
30 Off by a mile
34 1990s Indian P.M.
35 Where some addresses come from
36 Massenet's "Le ___ de Lahore"
37 Setting of Camus's "The Fall"
40 One yawning
42 Sign at some booths
43 Marina accommodations
44 Notoriety
47 Hansom cab accessory
48 Massive star
49 Half of doce
50 Something often smelled
51 Factor in a home's market value
55 Do groundbreaking work?
56 Carried by currents, in a way
57 Winetaster's concern
58 Serenity
59 Forum infinitive

DOWN

1 Shakespearean character who introduced the phrase "salad days"
2 Tattoo remover
3 Coffeehouse menu subheading
4 1959 #1 Frankie Avalon hit
5 Tested, as a load
6 Documentarian Morris
7 Elvis follower
8 Lot
9 Richard Gere title role of 2000
10 Basso Berberian
11 Sports champ depicted in "Cinderella Man," 2005
12 Counselor-___
13 Davis of "Cutthroat Island"
14 Theme
20 Fitch who co-founded Abercrombie & Fitch
23 Indication of disapproval
24 Novelist Potok
25 Tony winner for "Guys and Dolls," 1951
26 Detail on some tickets
28 Material used in making saunas
30 "Pink Shoe Laces" singer Stevens
31 "Elijah" and others
32 Bridle parts
33 Piercing glance
35 Coventry park sight
38 It's raised after a payment is collected
39 Disney doe
40 Pinches
41 Part of a laugh
43 Temporary property holder
44 Konica Minolta competitor
45 Elicit
46 Chick playing a piano
47 Isn't quite neutral
49 Toxin fighters
52 Symbol of industry
53 "Be more . . ." sloganeer
54 "Some Words With a Mummy" penner
55 Honourary title: Abbr.

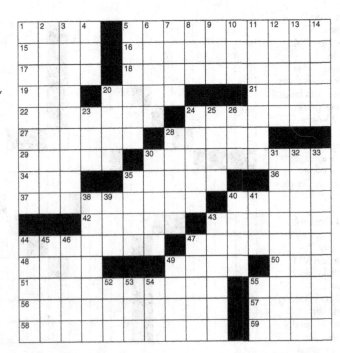

by Brad Wilber

ACROSS

1 Just the pits
16 Classic line of debate?
17 Just a bit, if that
18 Flag holder
19 In shape
20 Means: Abbr.
21 Songwriter Coleman and others
22 Illumination indication
23 Food whose name means "little sash"
28 Many an e-mail attachment
30 Sewn up
37 "The Ron Reagan Show" network
38 Determine
39 It'll change your mind
40 Drone
41 Dance move
44 Scratch
46 Winner of three consecutive Emmys for "Mission: Impossible"
47 Batman creator Bob
49 Woody Guthrie's "Tom ___"
53 Left-of-center party member
57 "I'll take whatever help I can get"
58 Pro team whose mascot is a blue bird named Blitz

DOWN

1 Thrashers' home in the N.H.L.: Abbr.
2 One just filling up space
3 Second of 24
4 See 52-Down
5 Arm raiser, informally
6 Vote for
7 In need of a sweep

8 Ragged edges, in metalworking
9 Lambs: Lat.
10 Destiny
11 String player?
12 Ottoman officers
13 Simple
14 Toot
15 Some specialize in elec.
21 They may give you a seat
22 Spring river phenomenon
23 Soundproofing material
24 Converse alternative
25 Yo-yo
26 Requiem title word
27 Alternative to a 23-Across
28 Somewhat, in music

29 Embarrassing way to be caught
31 1856 antislavery novel
32 Insult, on the street
33 Volt-ampere
34 Peculiar: Prefix
35 Relative of -ance
36 Perfect
41 He wrote that government "is but a necessary evil"
42 Gulf of Sidra setting
43 Like the Keystone Kops
44 "The ___ near!"
45 New Hampshire's ___ State College
46 Longfellow's "The Bells of San ___"
47 Rove in politics

48 Old man, in Mannheim
49 Rib
50 Prefix with -hedron
51 In ranks
52 With 4-Down, black magic
54 Raise a stink?
55 Billy's call
56 Logos and the like: Abbr.

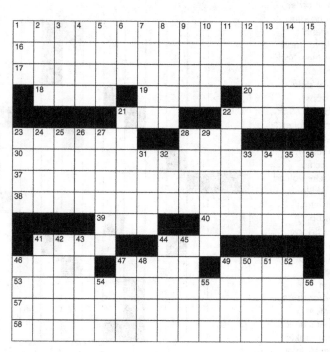

by Paula Gamache

ACROSS

1 Mad magazine feature
9 Spherical bacteria
14 Weekly since 1865
16 Financial V.I.P.
17 Martin of Hollywood
18 Quaint contraction
19 Puts in
20 Admits
22 Falls apart
23 Not quite up yet
24 Pick apart
25 1990s N.F.L. running back Curtis ___
26 ___ Paradise of Kerouac's "On the Road"
27 Keep in order
29 Ones needing fulfillment?
30 Locale for most of the New York Marathon
32 Kind of state
33 Rest stops?
36 Dobby or Winky, in Harry Potter
39 Solo
40 Hum follower?
41 "Pinocchio" character voiced by Mel Blanc
42 "That hurts!"
43 Played out
45 Rialto Bridge sight
46 One use for anise
48 Risqué
49 Not broadside
50 Mountain climber's need
52 Jaguar maker
53 When Hamlet first sees a ghost

54 Band active from 1995 to 2002
55 Providers of peer review?

DOWN

1 Figure in many jokes
2 Troop group
3 Arabs who are not in OPEC
4 Some sweaters
5 Smelling things
6 London's Covent Garden and others: Abbr.
7 Dicks
8 Daredevil's creed
9 Home of "The NFL Today"
10 Bishop Museum setting
11 Small sunfish

12 Help for a secret agent
13 Cantillates
15 1995 political book subtitled "Leader of the Second American Revolution"
21 When the kids are out
23 Old drive-in fare
26 "Happy Days" catchphrase
28 The General ___, "The Dukes of Hazzard" auto
30 Beyond oblivious
31 Turned
32 Half of a 1960s R & B duo
33 Source of lecithin
34 Chooses

35 Part of the Cablevision family
36 Current events around Christmas
37 Round steak, e.g.
38 Kind of crystals
41 Wine order
44 Rounds: Abbr.
45 Addition sign
47 It's hard to walk on
48 Rise by the shore
51 "The Partridge Family" actress

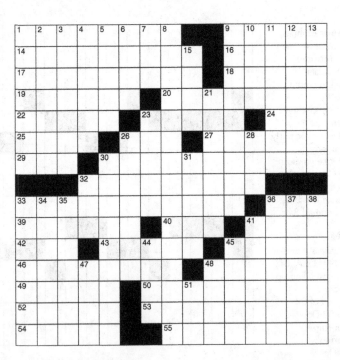

by Mark Diehl

ACROSS

1 Doesn't sit well
16 Class in which various schools are discussed
17 One way to solve problems
18 Pacer maker: Abbr.
19 Red sky, perhaps
20 "___ dispraise my lord . . .": Juliet
21 Expert in ancient law
24 City on the Natchez Trace
26 Not backing, in the backwoods
27 Lengthens, old-style
31 Retiree's coverage?
32 Basis for a suit
33 "30 Rock" creator
35 What a future American might take: Abbr.
36 Didn't paw
37 ___ grecque
40 Balloon attachment
41 Object in a Monet painting
42 Member of la famille immédiate
45 Floors
46 Frauen, across the border: Abbr.
47 Least spotted
49 Front wheel divergence
51 Hacker's cry of success
52 Something needed for your sake?
56 Gouge, say
57 Daydreaming, e.g.
62 Completely gone
63 Records of interest to real estate agents

DOWN

1 Distillation location
2 Suffix with cream
3 Encouraging remark
4 Predatory critter
5 Large accounts?
6 Place for jets
7 1968 folk album
8 Bit of moonshine
9 Adolescent outburst
10 Louis Armstrong's "Oh ___ He Ramble"
11 Initials of a noted "Wizard"
12 Go downhill
13 No follower
14 Drive along leisurely
15 Firmly establish
21 Like some shifts
22 Occasional clashers
23 Dakota tongue
25 ___ to be
28 Rather informal?
29 Help set up chairs for?
30 French study, e.g.
34 Take many courses
36 They're against each other
37 Relating to heraldry
38 Place
39 Kind of producer: Abbr.
40 It may contain tear gas
41 Emphatic turndown
42 Curly-haired "Peanuts" character
43 20th-dynasty ruler
44 Lois Lane player Durance and others
48 It may be wrapped in a bun
50 Astrologer with the autobiography "Answer in the Sky"
53 Iraq's ___ Ali Shrine
54 Grant
55 Business class, briefly
58 Hearing aids, for short
59 Now in
60 R.S.V.P. component
61 D.C. United org.

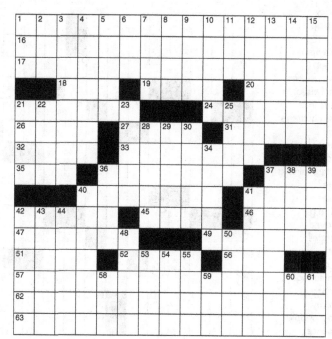

by Harvey Estes

ACROSS

1 When
9 Slip covers?
15 She was executed in 1917
16 100 centésimos
17 "Nonsense!"
19 Pentax Spotmatic, e.g., in brief
20 Boy in the comic strip "Rose Is Rose"
21 Parents
22 Parts of many jam sessions
25 Minute
27 African evergreen shrub
29 Vlasic varieties
30 Get ready to grill
33 Like VCRs in the 1970s
36 Delicacy
39 One-striper: Abbr.
40 Stuck with no way out
41 Kitchen pieces
43 Animal visitor to Paris in a classic children's book
44 Cornmeal concoction
47 One that takes a picture?
49 Crosses
50 Lead, e.g.
52 Engraved message?: Abbr.
55 "I'm not volunteering!"
59 Ring of anatomy
60 Boring people
61 On notice
62 "Tonka" star, 1958

DOWN

1 Withdrawal figs.
2 Joke writer for many Kennedy campaign speeches
3 Astrological set
4 Some husk contents
5 Understanding responses
6 Pusher
7 Botanical appendages
8 Fries, say
9 A telly may get it
10 Old Olympics award
11 Scarlett O'Hara's mother and others
12 W.W. II vessel
13 Cascades
14 Flip
18 Comment before turning in

23 Director of the Associated Press, 1900–35
24 Scale succession
26 Nicholas Gage title character
27 More
28 Tout's opposite
29 45-Down performers
31 How some hats are worn
32 Drawing, e.g.
33 Start of some countdowns
34 "Piece of My Heart" singer Franklin
35 Result of regular use
37 "Sin City" actress, 2005
38 Stagecoach puller

41 Body band
42 Flat part
44 17-Across, quaintly
45 See 29-Down
46 Parfait part
47 It's a big part of life
48 Do some tune-up work on
51 Aurora producer
53 2002 Literature Nobelist Kertész
54 Capital of Colombia
56 Land of "20,000 Leagues Under the Sea"
57 Dutch traveler's choice
58 Figure in the Sunni/Shia split

by Robert H. Wolfe

ACROSS

1 Navigation hazard
9 Coolness
15 Way off
16 Special delivery?
17 Married man who had long been a bachelor
18 Many a monthly check writer
19 Missing the point?
21 Car bar
22 W.W. II agcy.
23 Drawer units?
25 ___ Genevieve County, Mo.
26 Take off
29 When repeated, a "Funny Girl" song
30 Utterance when pointing to a woman
31 Chief
32 Famously fussy pair of diners
33 Any of les Trois Mousquetaires
34 Acts on a gut feeling?
35 Gold rush storyteller
36 Hardware store offering
37 In the style of: Suffix
38 Fishing boats
39 Island republic
40 ___ phenomenon (optical illusion)
41 Like most mammals
42 He wrote "A first sign of the beginning of understanding is the wish to die"
43 Top of some scales
44 Chump
45 Univ. offerings
46 Not having as favorable a prognosis
48 Main, maybe

53 Quiet craft
55 Dangerous places for correspondents
56 Bunny backer?
57 Where workers gather
58 Risers meet them
59 QB who was the 1963 N.F.L. M.V.P.

DOWN

1 Five-time U.S. presidential candidate in the early 1900s
2 One making firm decisions
3 Hombre, once
4 Some athletes shoot them
5 Like many an heir apparent
6 Goes under
7 If ever
8 Overdoes it
9 Not out of place
10 Importunes
11 Carnival follower
12 "Che!" title role player, 1969
13 Watch notch
14 Alternative that should be followed
20 Put under?
24 The Chi-___ (1970s R & B group)
26 "Pleasant dreams"
27 Seed-separating gizmo
28 Past prime time?
29 U.S. air-to-air missile
32 Navigation hazard
36 "C'mon, do me this favor"
38 Ordained

42 Post-Taliban Afghan president
45 Kind of scholarship
47 Mrs. Turnblad in "Hairspray"
49 Spanish hors d'oeuvre
50 Competing
51 Strip
52 Forum infinitive
54 Commuters' choices: Abbr.

by Lynn Lempel

108

ACROSS

1 Blockbuster alternative
8 Material for drainage lines
15 Just as anyone can be
16 What some bombs release
17 Early filmmaking brothers Auguste and Louis ___
18 What a cause might turn into
19 Noted 1915 West Point grad.
20 Bond type whose first purchaser was F.D.R.
22 Atkins diet no-no
23 "No god but God" author ___ Aslan
25 ___ Malfoy, bully in Harry Potter books
26 German city where Napoleon defeated the Prussians
27 States
29 Org. with a Council on Ethical and Judicial Affairs
30 Pitch problems?
31 May day events, perhaps
33 Big name in coffee makers
35 Ruffles
37 "Oh, I give up!"
41 Rot
43 Minus sign equivalent
44 Fractional currency
47 A sucker, for short
49 Layered dessert
50 Reunion gatherers
51 Apollo's birthplace
53 Be reminiscent of
54 Part of "the many," in Greek
55 Scull part
57 Printed
58 Noted Art Deco building in the Big Apple, with "the"
60 Dinar spender
62 Some
63 1962 hit with the lyric "Like the samba sound, my heart begins to pound"
64 Shop tool with pulleys
65 Has at a spread

DOWN

1 Annual sports event with seven rounds
2 Brandy
3 Mountain, e.g.
4 What many workers look forward to: Abbr.
5 Refuse
6 "The East ___" (1960s Chinese anthem)
7 Nissan model
8 Track warm-up leaders
9 Back of a leaf
10 "Red, White & ___" (2005 rock album)
11 On the plus side?: Abbr.
12 Deadly 2003 hurricane that hit North Carolina
13 It's far from a metropolis
14 Figure skater Sokolova and others
21 Foot type
24 Totally covered by
26 Miss No-Name
28 Relative of a cutter
30 Black, say
32 Hub NW of LAX
34 Buddy, in slang
36 Plant used as an herbal remedy for headaches
38 Rallying slogans
39 "Who'd a thunk it?!"
40 Paper that calls itself "America's Finest News Source"
42 Dialectal contraction
44 Brokerage giant
45 Zoological cavity
46 Criticize harshly and repeatedly
48 Like some books
51 Friend of Porky
52 "Pardon me," in Parma
55 Dropping sound
56 Tae ___ do
59 Bomb not bursting in air?
61 Bart Simpson's grandpa

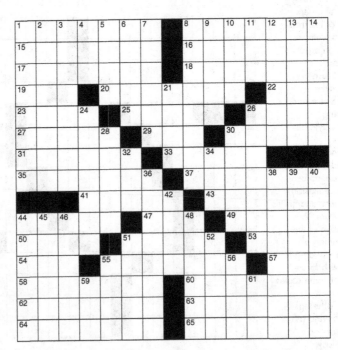

by Brendan Emmett Quigley and David Quarfoot

ACROSS

1 Stuck
8 "Not possible"
14 It might go off during a 30-Across
16 "Great taste since 1905" sloganeer
17 Rule broken in leisure?
18 He died soon after escaping from Crete
19 ___ dog
20 Dutch export
22 Van Halen's "Live Without ___"
23 Angle iron
24 TV series whose finale was titled "The Truth," with "The"
26 Unpleasant thing to incur
27 Squadron leader?
28 Swear words?
30 One can be tracked
31 2000 Olympics host
32 Recurring character who dies in the novel "Curtain"
34 Reveals
35 Dusting aid
36 Unesco World Heritage Site on the Arabian Peninsula
37 Scheduled
39 Letters on some college buildings
42 A.L. Central scoreboard abbr.
43 Little tricksters
44 Having good balance
45 Target of milk of magnesia
47 Informal demurral
48 Has a problem on the road
49 College in Claremont, Calif.
51 Tax burden?
53 It might go 7-5
54 Thing with a pressure point?
55 Grinder
56 Butterfly feature

DOWN

1 Totally unemotional type
2 Wheels
3 Things with rings
4 Further out of the woods?
5 Trick
6 One making waves
7 Kids' hideaway
8 Where many prints may be found
9 10-Down div.
10 Org. since 1910
11 Raked over the coals
12 Horse of a certain color
13 Occasions for baskets
15 Clairvoyant
21 Substitute: Abbr.
24 Abscissa
25 Barraged
28 "A Prairie Home Companion" co-star, 2006
29 "Odyssey" high point
30 "Star Wars" order
32 Fruit found among needles
33 Routinely
34 Battle of Put-in-Bay setting
35 16-Across, e.g.
36 General who prevailed over Carthage
38 Big name in ergonomic utensils
39 Settled
40 Shade deeper than heliotrope
41 Sonnet section
44 Flying predators of cold seas
46 "O mighty Caesar! ___ thou lie so low?": Shak.
48 Learned
50 "Tutte ___ cor vi sento" (Mozart aria)
52 ___ dog

by Mike Nothnagel

ACROSS

1 Classic sports lineup
11 All in favor
15 Antipathy
16 Not be fair?
17 "I hear ya!"
18 Regard impolitely
19 Low square
20 Work period
21 Intelligence problem
22 Winter fall, in Falkirk
23 Fortune 500 company founded in 1995
24 It's often administered orally
25 Needle holders
27 Power system
28 Birthplace of Evel Knievel and Martha Raye
29 Dill herb
30 "Follow the Fleet" co-star, 1936
32 Precursor to a historical "party"
34 Winner of four Oscars for musical scores
38 "Seems that way"
42 One-named singer with the 1960s Velvet Underground
43 Decision maker
46 Calls in a field
47 Proof word
48 Home of Gannon University
49 "I'll Be Doggone" singer, 1965
50 Lovelace who was called "The Enchantress of Numbers"
51 Cossacks' leader

52 Take the top off
54 Wild
55 Break
56 Enterprise
58 Natural healer
59 Decision maker
60 Revolutionary War general Thomas
61 Big name in foot care

DOWN

1 Dietary danger
2 Like some charms
3 Range, e.g.
4 Old character
5 Company keepers: Abbr.
6 Calendario units
7 Ribbons
8 Check

9 Preceder of many hockey games
10 Like a snood, commonly
11 Some dance honorees
12 Cousin of goulash
13 Like some old-fashioned lamps
14 Cold response?
26 1959 #1 hit for Lloyd Price
27 Track take
28 Cold response?
31 Corp. capital raisers
33 Breaking need
35 It's found in eggs
36 Like some streams in winter

37 "Isn't anyone interested?"
39 Like many supermarket lines?
40 Greet
41 Producer of some beads
43 It can give people flight reservations
44 Legendary Christian martyr
45 It's open for discussion
49 "Life Is Beautiful" hero
53 Spare change?
54 Buckling down
57 Org. with its own insurance agency

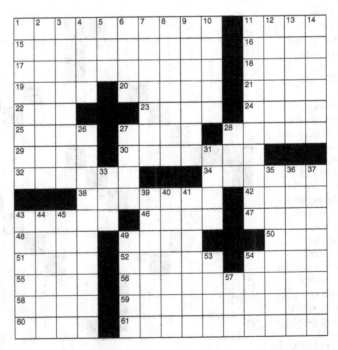

by Barry C. Silk

ACROSS

1 Windshield wipers
10 "Unbelievable!"
15 Darwin's home
16 Superrealist sculptor Hanson
17 Zip
18 They stand for something: Abbr.
19 Station info, briefly
20 Checks out
21 1984 hit parody of a 1983 hit song
22 Get moving, with "up"
23 Four-time Vardon Trophy winner
25 Area below the hairline
26 Lock changer?
29 Turn out
31 Narrows: Abbr.
32 Directory data: Abbr.
34 Clam
36 Bluster
40 Hardly humble homes
41 A bit much
43 Call in a calamity
44 No longer doing the job?: Abbr.
45 Bombards with junk
47 Become active
50 Pull out of ___ (produce suddenly)
52 Makes out
54 Fat cat, in England
56 Packs in stacks
58 Short distance
59 "Eight Is Enough" wife
60 Creator of lofty lines
61 Freshening naturally
63 Something to get a kick out of
64 Park gathering place
65 Starters
66 Garb symbolizing youth

DOWN

1 Not as touched
2 Like successful orators
3 James Forrestal was its last cabinet secy.
4 Portions of les années
5 Stat for a reliever
6 Slalom targets
7 Comic Boosler
8 Astronaut Collins and others
9 Toasted triangle topper
10 One of Jon Arbuckle's pets
11 Changsha is its capital
12 "Hang on!"
13 Eager
14 Things that may be shot in stages?
24 "La Reine Margot" novelist
27 ___'acte
28 Ways to go
30 Some shirts
33 Dishes out undaintily
35 Trailer's place
36 South Pacific island
37 Cry before storming out
38 "Lighten up, will ya?!"
39 Hiking aid
42 Hate, say
46 "Tristram Shandy" author
48 Natural
49 In the pink
51 10 kilogauss
53 Relish
55 Disk units
57 Bring to a standstill
59 Mar makeup
62 Letter run

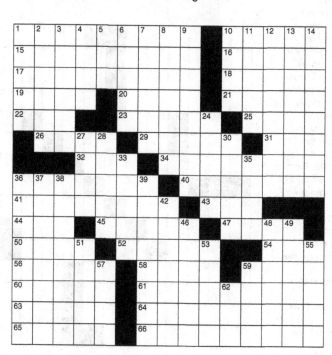

by Frederick J. Healy

ACROSS

1 Small suit
7 Cheese with a greenish tint
14 "The Outsiders" author
15 Band seen at parties
16 Available if needed
17 Aircraft for the Red Baron
18 Without reservation
19 "The Blessed Damozel" poet
20 "Mr. ___," 1983 comedy
21 Military classification
23 Result of a day at the beach?
24 "Infidel" author Ayaan Hirsi ___
25 ___ Island
26 Object of Oliver Twist's request for "more"
27 Semimonthly ocean occurrence
29 Somewhat
30 "___ and Janis" (comic strip)
31 Linguist Okrand who created the Klingon language
32 It's "heavier freight for the shipper than it is for the consignee": Augustus Thomas
35 Poem whose first, third and seventh lines are identical
39 Ready to explode
40 Garçon's counterpart
41 Application file extension
42 Big seller of smoothies
43 Economist who wrote "The Theory of the Leisure Class"
44 ___-Hulk (Marvel Comics character)
45 Goshen raceway's length
47 It's cleared for a debriefing
49 In a despicable way
50 Play a flute
51 Details
52 Book before Job
53 Future hunters
54 Does a landscaper's job

DOWN

1 Troupe leader
2 Camera obscura feature
3 Laudations
4 Bibliographical abbr.
5 National chain of everything-costs-the-same stores
6 Eloise of Kay Thompson books, e.g.
7 Made an effort
8 Become evident
9 Enlivens, with "up"
10 Figure seen in a store window
11 Pan American Games participant
12 Refined
13 Author of the 2006 best seller "Culture Warrior"
15 Big step
22 Disturbance
26 Typically green tube
28 Gaffe at a social gathering, in modern lingo
29 Often-unanswered missive
31 Tough's partner
32 Seemed particularly relevant
33 Pan's realm
34 Putting aside temporarily
35 Hearty entrée
36 Country of two million surrounded by a single other country
37 Let the air out, say
38 Betrays unsteadiness
40 Guys
43 See
46 Universal remote button
48 Breaks down

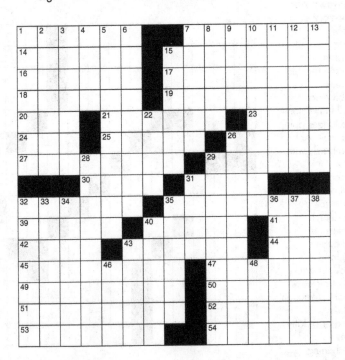

by Patrick Berry

ACROSS

1 News Corporation-owned Web site that's one of the 10 most visited sites in the world
8 Dirt on a person
14 Yellow fliers with large eyespots
15 "Cab," e.g.
16 Abscond
17 What the key of D minor has
18 Sponge
19 Driving distance is a concern in it
21 Dermal opening?
22 Miss Gulch biter
24 Height and such
25 Pet
26 Hostile
28 In advance of
29 Get a handle on?
30 They're played at the track
32 Buries
34 Brass
36 Walled city of the Mideast
37 "Let me live my own life!"
41 Gives a little, say
45 Wedding concern
46 Taper
48 Was sluggish?
49 Old Testament book: Abbr.
50 Reporting to
52 Vapid
53 1980s sitcom title role
54 Flips
56 Hiver's opposite
57 Not-so-good feeling
59 Former field food
61 Terminal timesaver
62 Its value is in creasing

63 Sprint acquisition of 2005
64 Crossword source since 1942: Abbr.

DOWN

1 Slip
2 Poem reader at the 2006 Olympics opening ceremony
3 Gaga
4 With 20-Down, waffle alternative
5 Capping
6 Finishes quickly, in a way
7 Groundskeeper's charge
8 Family group
9 ___-Neisse Line
10 Abbr. in personal ads
11 Center of Connecticut
12 All thrown together, say
13 Little women
15 Cheering section
20 See 4-Down
23 "Heavens!"
25 1963 Academy Awards host
27 He wrote "It's certain that fine women eat / A crazy salad with their meat"
29 Alb coverer
31 Sharp
33 Meal source
35 Lopsided court result
37 Ones paid to conceive?

38 Cartoon boss working at a quarry
39 Modern rental option
40 Sch. whose colors are "true blue" and gold
42 Cry upon arriving
43 Beau ideal
44 Burial place of many French kings
47 "Way to go, dude!"
50 Bernoulli family birthplace
51 Trouble
54 Raise
55 Not yet 58-Down
58 See 55-Down
60 ___ Friday's

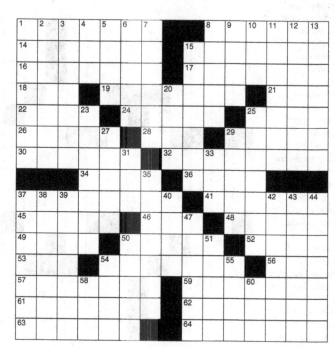

by David Quarfoot

114

ACROSS

1 Billionaire sports entrepreneur who heads HDNet
10 Like some seasonal helpers
15 Within the next few minutes, potentially
16 Some piano players
17 Case made for a shooter
18 Agitated
19 Real-estate ad statistic
20 Its motto is "All for our country": Abbr.
22 Go over
23 Orchestra section
25 Dr. Seuss's "Too Many ___"
27 Consumer protection grp.
28 Yokohama "yes"
30 Marathon runner Gebrselassie
32 It served the Mid-Atlantic until 1976
39 Classic laugh-inducing parlor game with writing or illustrations
40 Move on after a humiliating defeat
41 Claimed
42 Vintner's prefix
43 Kind of engr.
44 Member of a popular college frat
47 Parliament rival
52 Shot one on
54 Name for Quantum Computer Services since '89
55 Heavyweights compete in it
56 An overabundance
58 "You said it!"
62 Sent regrets, say
63 Help get settled
64 Priceless instrument
65 What green might ripen into

DOWN

1 Bird remarkable for its longevity
2 Breakout maker
3 Far Eastern bowlful
4 Manipulate, in a way
5 France's Saint-___-l'École
6 She played Martha in Broadway's "Who's Afraid of Virginia Woolf?"
7 One hanging around at Red Lobster?
8 Range option
9 Ben-Gurion setting
10 Stumble
11 "Happy Birthday" playwright
12 About-faces
13 Nervous
14 Band with the highest first-week album sales in music history
21 It'll get you somewhere
24 Some religious fundamentalists
25 Cook's words
26 Old settings for many out-of-tune pianos
29 Connecticut city on the Naugatuck
31 Factory seconds: Abbr.
32 Sport, for short
33 Foreignness
34 Old Spice alternative
35 Court stuff
36 Bus spec.
37 "The Mischievous Dog" author
38 ___ Peres (St. Louis suburb)
43 "Lady for a Day" director, 1933
45 One who's waited upon
46 Ecuador's southernmost coastal province
48 Provide an invitation for
49 Kind of cycle
50 Mug, e.g.
51 Cut
53 Firm part: Abbr.
57 Arms race plan: Abbr.
59 Takeaway game
60 Hot spot?
61 Gridiron datum

by Brendan Emmett Quigley

ACROSS

1 He had a hit with "The Joint Is Jumpin' "
11 Signs of neglect
15 First #1 hit by the Beach Boys
16 Like the sea
17 City on the Transcontinental Railroad
18 Some people have it for life
19 Not do the rite thing?
20 Requests for developers: Abbr.
21 Taylor of "Mystic Pizza"
22 Some cabbage
23 Dwell
24 Much
25 With 52- and 39-Across, gradually
26 Potentate
28 One of a primer pair
29 They're not originals
31 Materials used as inert paint fillers
33 Best people
34 El relative
35 Whole slew of
39 See 25-Across
43 Premium chargers, briefly
44 Like a well-maintained lawn
46 Discriminatory leader?
47 What "y" might become
48 Driver on a ranch
49 It's found in a chest
50 Fermentation locations
52 See 25-Across
53 19th-century territorial capital

54 Organs are located in it: Abbr.
55 Block head?
57 Delivery possibility
58 Committed a sports no-no
59 Due and sei
60 Succulent African shrub popular as a bonsai

DOWN

1 Internet Explorer alternative
2 Facial feature, later in life
3 Carpenter, at times
4 They're located on organs
5 Draw to a close
6 It may come after you
7 Hippie happenings
8 African city of 2.5+ million founded by the Portuguese
9 Infinite
10 Food figs.
11 Hanging setting
12 Big name in credit reports
13 Greyhounds may run in it
14 Wilde things?
23 "See ya!"
26 Year of St. Genevieve's death
27 Pitching
28 Fun
30 They're known for head-turning
32 Basketful
35 Fictional doctor
36 "This is no joke!"
37 Letter writing, some say

38 It was first observed in 1846
39 One taken in
40 Like some surgery
41 Group that starred in the 1968 film "Head," with "the"
42 Match-starting cry
45 Establishes
49 Challenge for a shortstop
51 Target of heavy W.W. II bombing, 1944
52 "That ___ . . ."
53 Comfortable
56 Discount designation: Abbr.

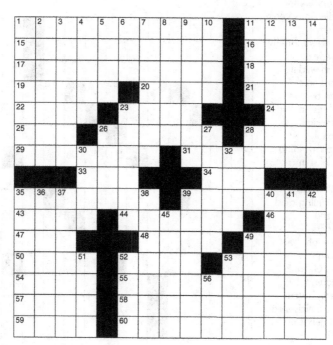

by Barry C. Silk

116

ACROSS

1 Sleuthing aid
11 Early education
15 Hammer wielder
16 Bangkok currency
17 YouTube phenomenon
18 ___ witness
19 Suffix with polymer
20 Walk-on parts?
21 Safari hazard
23 "Rhapsodie norvégienne" composer
24 Co-creator of Hulk and Thor
25 Napoleon, e.g.
28 Allergist's procedure
29 Lexicon listing
30 Relative of homespun
31 Century-ending Middle Ages year
32 Modern organizers, briefly
33 Judge, e.g.
34 Skittish wildlife
35 Record finish?
36 Fail to be
37 Food also called mostaccioli
38 Fictional Pulitzer-winning journalist in a 2006 film
40 Didn't fizzle
41 Aquatinting acid
42 Succeed
43 Grinders
44 One might be kidding
45 U.S.C.G. rank
48 "Madama Butterfly" wear
49 Much-anticipated Paris debut of 1992
52 Colleague of 38-Across
53 Place for trophies at an awards luncheon
54 Concert venues
55 1971 Elton John song

DOWN

1 Kind of bean
2 See 51-Down
3 Plot segment
4 Where folks go off and on: Abbr.
5 "View From the Summit" memoirist
6 Swell
7 ___ López de Loyola, founder of the Society of Jesus
8 People may get them before going to coll.
9 Part of a giggle
10 Hockey Hall-of-Famer Bryan
11 Not in the picture
12 Archer's post
13 Action thriller staple
14 Homey's acceptance
22 Innards of some clocks
23 Posts: Abbr.
24 Earth-shattering activity?
25 Casbah fugitive of French film
26 Noted diary words
27 Alternative to a rip cord
28 Coarse type
30 ___ Canal (connector of lakes Ontario and Huron)
33 It intersects the nave
34 Secretary, e.g.
36 Garden no-no, now
37 One of six pieces by Bach
39 Daisy variety
40 Like some questions
42 Vertiginous
44 Wink accompanier
45 "Power Lunch" channel
46 Legendary kicker
47 Legal hearing
50 Sch. in Kingston
51 With 2-Down, seat of Costilla County, Colo.

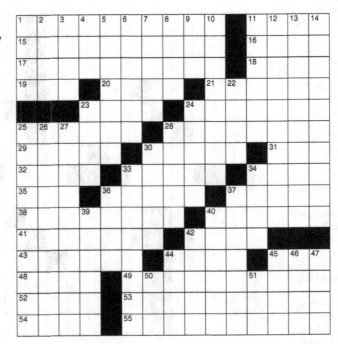

by Brad Wilber

ACROSS
1 Concerned query
6 Without a leg to stand on?
14 Vermont senator Sanders
15 It's a cinch
16 Pretentious
17 Without a match
18 "Pardon me"
19 Closing bid?
20 Peak
21 McCartney, to fans
24 Horror film that starts in a filthy lavatory
26 Weaken, in a way
29 Monotheistic Syrian
33 Most in need of toning
35 Top-rated, in a way
36 Slant
37 Get all histrionic
38 About 40°, for N.Y.C.
39 Hostel environments
40 Wore out
42 Some lap dogs
44 Result of a new TV series' renewal
46 A.A. discussion topic
48 Appoints as an agent
49 Roast pig side dish
52 Stands
55 Brew choice
56 Afro-Caribbean religion
58 Toeless creature in an Edward Lear verse
60 Engine manufacturer Briggs & ___
61 One with a second helping
62 Super Bowl XX champs
63 Personnel director, at times

DOWN
1 Hoped-for reply to 1-Across
2 Payment is often sent with one
3 Apt to say "So?"
4 Relative of -ish
5 Mauna ___
6 Missile with a mobile launcher
7 Product whose ads featured twins
8 Iroquois' foes
9 Lee Marvin TV oldie
10 Moldovan money
11 He or I, but not you: Abbr.
12 Ward of "Once and Again"
13 Deep river?
14 Sighing a lot, maybe
19 Some Nissans
22 "___ for Alibi"
23 ___ Pendragon, King Arthur's father
25 Call slip?
27 West African currency
28 Ponch player in 1970s–'80s TV
30 Too awful even to fix up, as an apartment
31 Octopus, e.g.
32 Take the cake?
34 Twit
36 Marcel Marceau character
41 Bush league?
43 City connected to the 4.1-mile long Sunshine Skyway Br.
45 Kitchen appliance brand
47 In a sense
49 "Over here"
50 Four-letter word, aptly
51 On
53 Pricey gown
54 McShane and McKellen
57 Bill
58 Sharable computer file, for short
59 Overseas agreement

by Henry Hook

118

ACROSS
1 Vegetable oil, e.g.
6 College major, briefly
10 Fog
14 Up
15 "Got it"
16 It's often marked with a number
17 Knee problem
19 Very small serving
20 ". . . ___ faith turn to despair": Romeo
21 Capital, usually
23 Leon who won both a Pulitzer and a National Book Award in 1963
24 Smith, e.g.
25 Symbols of freshness
27 Rogers Hornsby's nickname, with "the"
31 Senior ctr.?
33 Garage alternative
34 Before analysis, after "a"
35 Hangers-on
37 Select groups
38 Other drivers (never you, of course)
39 Following group
40 Character lineup
41 It's been put on before
42 Ammunition carrier on wheels
44 Windfall
46 Target of a rabbit punch
49 Like Y, e.g.
52 ___ francese
53 Crown
54 Soft, high-fiber dish
56 Red-bellied trout

57 Topic lead-in
58 Beehive division
59 Firm fear
60 "Saint Joan" playwright
61 Fisherman's basket

DOWN
1 Maker of a historic touchdown
2 Iota
3 Feature of many a big do
4 Neighbor of Monterey Park, briefly
5 Atlas info: Abbr.
6 Filling stations?
7 Had a causerie
8 The sacred bull Apis was his embodiment
9 They're proscribed
10 Jaunty
11 Botanist's angle
12 Fusilli alternative
13 Form of the French "to be"
18 #1 best sellers
22 Apes
26 "Right?"
28 Some clichéd writing
29 Some matériel
30 H.S. subject
31 Do something emotionally to
32 Word preceding various colors
34 Beat
36 They have nagging questions
37 It has valuable questions

39 Game derived from 500 rummy
42 Light carriage with a folding top
43 Even
45 Mexican uncle?
47 Part of the earth's outer layer
48 Oil holder
49 Halite, chemically
50 Be reminiscent of
51 Present occasion, informally
55 Multiple of LXX

by Dana Motley

ACROSS

1 Back-and-forth
6 One at the helm
15 "___ directed"
16 Product identifier
17 Apple storage devices
18 It maintains a proper attitude
19 "Western Star" poet
20 Mount ___, sacred Chinese site
21 Sunder
22 Source of support
23 Fragrant
27 Bbl. fraction
28 ___ rock (radio format)
30 Bills are in it: Abbr.
31 Deal-killing words
33 Bibliographical abbr.
34 Venue of many Richard Petty wins
36 First-class handouts?
38 Herd-thinning menace
42 Semirural, say
44 Time magazine Person of the Year, 2005
45 One working on a board
48 Party in Pretoria: Abbr.
49 Poses in a studio?
50 Photographer Goldin
51 Town on the Long Island Rail Road
54 Sprout
55 Channel blocker
57 Letters before a street name
58 "I'll give you ___ . . ."
60 Colloquial
63 Newswoman Poussaint
64 Logic's counterpart
65 Rich spreads
66 Trunk accumulation
67 Common dog name

DOWN

1 Nitpicking
2 Harshness
3 Relating to babes
4 ___ City, seat of Pasco County, Fla.
5 Right hands: Abbr.
6 1945 film musical with the song "It Might As Well Be Spring"
7 Cutting out?
8 Suffer a loss, slangily
9 Shogunate capital
10 Mouthpiece
11 Scissor
12 Costa del Sol port
13 Unprincipled
14 Green stinger
24 Creme Egg maker
25 Proclaim
26 Underbosses' bosses
29 1990s sitcom
32 Didn't get involved
35 Does, as business
37 Choppers
39 Probe
40 Bring about with some effort
41 Cavalier evaluation?
43 On the sundeck
45 Not yield
46 Corporate shark
47 Seeing the sites
52 Like muesli
53 Diamond protectors
56 Lug
59 Jalopy
61 It was deorbited in 2001
62 "Bel-___" (Maupassant novel)

by Chuck Deodene

120

ACROSS

1 Liniment ingredient
11 Certain copier
15 Presidents Adams, Fillmore and Taft
16 ". . . on the head of ___?"
17 Rap
18 "The Man Who Fell to Earth" director
19 Make a scene?
20 Put down some chips?
21 Minute buzzer
22 Detail on some tickets
24 Its banks are lined with nearly 200 palaces
26 Cousin of -trix
27 "Giuliani: Nasty Man" author
28 Booster of a rock band
29 Tackle box item
31 Ici ___ (here and there, to Thérèse)
32 "In the," in Italy
33 Nostalgia elicitor
36 Imprecise
38 Alma mater of Albert Sabin and Jonas Salk: Abbr.
39 You may get into it while shopping
43 Rx specification
44 Sinusitis studier's specialty: Abbr.
45 100 centimes, in Haiti
47 Like the Chrysler Building
51 Nightspots where the attraction is simply a gas
53 Characteristic quality
54 Direct
55 Makes a raucous noise
57 Project wrap-up?
58 Rolls roller
59 National Historic Landmark in Manhattan
61 Quarter division
62 Apropos
63 Pablo Neruda's "___ to Common Things"
64 Big name in Dakota history

DOWN

1 Parish leader
2 Its ads once showed hammers inside the head
3 One of a protective pair
4 Org. addressing class conflict
5 Occupiers of top spots
6 Like a bad spray-on tan
7 Score direction: Abbr.
8 Scottish cereal staple
9 Snarled
10 "Saving Private Ryan" craft, for short
11 Musical character who sings "My Favorite Things"
12 Player in a shirt pocket
13 Anticlimactic court outcomes
14 Lemony meringue concoction
21 Celtic Kevin with a retired jersey #32
23 Bank offering, briefly
25 Seventh-century year
30 It can help you keep your balance
33 Not many
34 Keen of vision
35 Like some airport shopping
37 Novus ___ seclorum (Great Seal phrase)
40 It goes on and on
41 Drinking fountain
42 Syllables to skip by
43 Willful state?
46 Character on trial in "A Passage to India"
48 People person?
49 Mint-family plant with bright-colored leaves and blue flowers
50 Goon's last words
52 Unlikely prom kings
56 "___ Ching" (classic book of Chinese poetry)
59 U.S.M.C. E-2
60 Ear: Prefix

by Brad Wilber

ACROSS

1 Bit of income for the Department of Motor Vehicles
11 Waist products
15 What someone might win after stumping a cultural group?
16 Russian car
17 Greek salad ingredient
18 Seventh-century year
19 Exhausted
20 Body repair sites, briefly
21 Indicated "Just teasing!"
23 Two-timing types
25 Target
26 Where Yankees were found at Shea
31 Dry out
32 They're taken to the cleaners
33 Dude
34 Y.M.C.A. member?: Abbr.
35 Ark contents
36 16 and Seventeen, for short
37 ___ tree
38 Hatch in politics
39 Doesn't quite mash
40 Fan fare?
43 Stinko
44 One-eighties
45 "Jeez!"
47 Amer. capital
48 Flawlessly
52 Corner piece
53 Axiom
56 Snatch, slangily
57 Witness to Anakin Skywalker and Padmé Amidala's secret wedding
58 When tripled, "et cetera"
59 Rod Laver won two

DOWN

1 ___ Mason (asset management firm)
2 "___, dislike it" (start of Marianne Moore's "Poetry")
3 Fictional character who first appeared in "The House Without a Key"
4 Begins
5 Robertson of CNN
6 Controversial 1980s–'90s baseball team owner
7 "A thousand pardons"
8 They're not for you
9 Big-headed sorts, for short
10 Big shoe spec
11 Candidate for the proverbial glue factory
12 Consecutive
13 Frivolous
14 Related
22 Don in the National Radio Hall of Fame
24 City where Cézanne was born
25 Cuisine that may be served with a chork
26 Hornet genus
27 "Everything's cool"
28 Ninth-century founder of the Russian monarchy
29 Id output
30 Put into a 35-Down
31 Smear
35 Waste product
36 Oldtime entertainer
38 Work
39 Skate
41 Start of a little daredevil's declaration
42 Food fish of Australia and New Zealand
45 Binge
46 Ciao, in Chile
47 Court org.
49 Make ___ check
50 Little bit
51 Wilson's vice pres. ___ Marshall
54 Sheet music abbr.
55 Cowboys' concerns, briefly

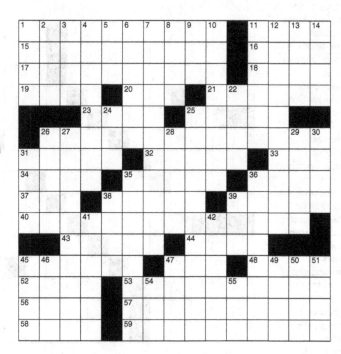

by Paula Gamache

122

ACROSS
1 Called for
10 Not get along
15 Common bank deposit?
16 Slow in scoring
17 1976–85 sitcom setting
18 Zealous
19 Philologists' work, for short
20 Rd. designer, e.g.
21 Begin energetically
22 Feed
24 Where things may be neatly ordered?
25 Doesn't belt it out
27 Unsettled sort
28 Lash with a whip
29 Source of political support
33 "Happy Days Are Here Again" composer
34 Three-time 1990s French Open winner
35 Israeli opera conductor Daniel
36 Encore setting
38 ___ Diamond, author of the 1998 Pulitzer-winning book "Guns, Germs, and Steel"
39 They may be done in a salon
40 Results of some glances
41 Onsets
44 Fast-food chain known for its floats
45 Distress call
46 Some shooters, briefly
47 Where to find "Rome," once

50 Lead-in to phobia
51 Drop off
53 Filibustered, say
54 Clumsy
55 "Why, what ___ am I!" (Hamlet soliloquy line)
56 Some Mozart works

DOWN
1 Pitcher who was the 1995 N.L. Rookie of the Year
2 Guarded weapon
3 They may accompany fevers
4 Part of a long and winding road?
5 It's usually spun first
6 Performs awfully

7 1980–'90s N.B.A. star Danny
8 Many a camper, informally
9 "___ out!"
10 Butcher's need
11 Display at a golf tournament
12 Provocation result
13 Draft holder
14 They frequently become locked
21 Shock aftermath
23 Open competitors, often
24 Kind of rack
25 Good secret-keeper
26 Unilever brand
27 7 and 11, in a casino
29 Storm sounds
30 Game sticker?

31 Look
32 Far left and far right
34 Perform superbly
37 Tropical reptiles
38 Star of TV's "The Fugitive"
40 King of pop
41 "Ten North Frederick" novelist
42 Duke of Cornwall's wife
43 Massey of film
44 Take in, e.g.
46 Loudness unit
48 Well around Trevi Fountain?
49 Goes (for)
51 They're found in a mess
52 Big Apple-bound luggage tag code

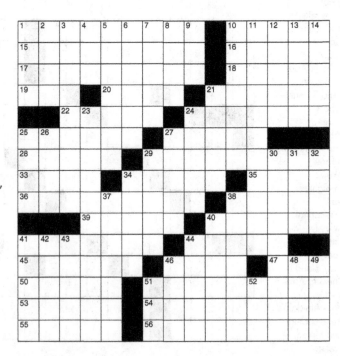

by Victor Fleming

ACROSS

1 Show signs of improvement
11 Second in a series
15 Indication of stress
16 1,575-mile river known to some locals as the Zhayyq
17 "Well, duh!"
18 Hitch
19 Supra
20 Syrup of ___
22 Caustic
23 Sci-fi author McIntyre
25 Bad ___, German resort
26 With eyes open
30 Mr. Levy of 1920s Broadway fame
32 Holders of big pads
33 Marker
34 W.S.J. subjects
35 "It's ___!" ("You're on!")
36 Alt. spelling
37 Slam
38 Dictionary data
39 Minimal change
40 Cloth workers?
42 Big-league
43 Sculptor Oldenburg
44 Dive
46 Game craze of the late 1980s and '90s
49 Direct
51 Island nicknamed the Gathering Place
52 Jump the gun
55 Senior moment?
56 One who's happy when things look black
57 Blunt
58 Undergo a change of habit?

DOWN

1 Olympics item . . . or the winning word in the 1984 National Spelling Bee
2 Civilians eligible to be drafted
3 ___ Line (German/Polish border)
4 Bitter fruit
5 Queues
6 Name on a bottle of Beyond Paradise
7 Sch. staffer
8 French pronoun
9 Suffix with south
10 Sparks a second time
11 Department
12 Greenland colonizer
13 "I did it!"
14 Pianist Templeton
21 Visual PC-to-PC files
23 Appearances
24 Classic Packard model with a numerical name
26 Pompadour, for one
27 Prerecorded
28 Advance
29 Tentlike dwelling with a conical roof
30 Like some electric circuits
31 Be angry as heck
32 "Nothing to it"
38 Hybrid fruit
39 Where cooler heads prevail?
41 Fritz the Cat illustrator
42 Paid (up)
44 Locker room habitués
45 Rain gear brand
46 Maximally
47 Pull down
48 Grand total?
49 Plural suffix with beat or neat
50 Kind of pronoun: Abbr.
53 Clause connector
54 Unduly

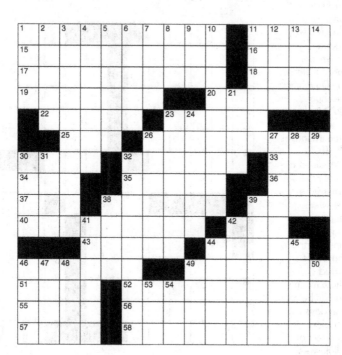

by Henry Hook

124

ACROSS

1 Choirs' neighbors
6 Lung covering
12 Publicized
14 Phrase of interest
16 Producer of fine threads
17 Source of more pay or more play
18 Baseball Hall-of-Famer Orlando ___
19 Grapevine exhortation
20 Liveliness
21 Veterinarian, at times
22 Stagnant conditions
23 Banes
24 Liliaceous plants
25 Solo, in a way
26 Bananas
28 Webers per square meter
33 "The Daughters of Joshua ___" (1972 Buddy Ebsen film)
35 Southern loaves
37 Pull off
41 He declined a Nobel Prize in Literature
42 One who's getting on
43 Pull in
44 Winner's pride
45 John Deere product
46 Where much info can be found these days
47 Melodious
48 Producers of wall flowers?
49 Most Indians

50 Limestone regions with deep fissures and sinkholes
51 Call-waiting alerts

DOWN

1 Sore spot
2 Something for Santa Claus to bite
3 Gear teeth trouble
4 Prince William, e.g.
5 Maximally mangy
6 Cachet
7 Wolf ___, captain in Jack London's "The Sea-Wolf"
8 Livelong
9 Merger
10 Products of some "mills"

11 Comment of concurrence
13 Comments of annoyance
14 Works with everyday objects
15 Gauge
25 Fawning type
27 Cigarette smoke byproducts
29 Cookout item usually eaten with two hands
30 Nancy's home
31 Direct opposite
32 Dishes out
34 Military wear
36 "The Prophecy of the ___" (Eddic poem)
37 Dualistic deity
38 Skyhook dropper, briefly

39 Stills
40 Receive
41 ___ Gamp, nurse in "Martin Chuzzlewit"
44 Clock sound

by Robert H. Wolfe

ACROSS

1 Confectioner's offering
8 Affecting the heart
15 Item in a 1-Across
16 Two-character Mamet play
17 Cause of overreactions?
18 Matching accessory for a slicker
19 Traditional Monday meal in Creole cuisine
21 "Oh! Susanna" closer
22 World Cup highlight
23 Podiatric problem, for some
24 Urges
25 Grand Lodge Convention attendees
26 Big tier?
27 Fair diversion
28 Time off
29 First major-league team to sign Satchel Paige
33 1992 New Hampshire primary winner
35 Intimidate
36 Frequent Styne collaborator
37 Speaks with a pleasing rhythm
38 Bundle up
39 Jimi Hendrix's style
43 Reese's "Legally Blonde" role
44 Synagogue cabinets
45 Timer sound
46 He said "How can anyone govern a nation that has 246 kinds of cheese?"
50 Underground nesters

51 Required reading for 007
52 Offering just the right amount of resistance
53 Wire, at times
54 Give a whirl
55 They hold at least two cups each

DOWN

1 Radar's radio contact on "M*A*S*H"
2 Longtime "What's My Line?" name
3 Brando's "On the Waterfront" co-star
4 First-year men
5 Money replaced by euros
6 Practice
7 Noted English portraitist

8 Beach shop souvenirs
9 Playwright Ayckbourn
10 Frist's successor as majority leader
11 TV host who told viewers "Look that up in your Funk & Wagnalls!"
12 Lying low
13 Montana county seat named for a nonnative creature
14 Hosts' hirees
20 Purpose
26 1982 film and arcade game
27 "I hate it when that happens!"
29 Cocktail party exchanges
30 Board opening?

31 Intellectuals' opposites
32 Site site
33 Had a one-sided conversation with
34 1976 Hall & Oates hit
36 Funny fellow
38 Dog breed whose name literally means "rather low"
39 Wrongs
40 Ocelot, for one
41 Come around
42 Palais Garnier offerings
47 Celebrity who testified at the 2005 Michael Jackson trial
48 Some famous last words
49 Four-legged Hammett character

by Patrick Berry

ACROSS

1 Second African-American in the Baseball Hall of Fame
11 They feature creatures
15 Some planets may be seen with it
16 "You can stop trying to wake me now!"
17 Simon Legree
18 League heading: Abbr.
19 Linemen next to centers: Abbr.
20 Taj Mahal attractions
21 "My Life on Trial" autobiographer
22 Stat that's better when lower
23 Undivided
24 Pillowcase material
25 Loose overcoat
28 Some home theater systems
30 Fangorn Forest dweller
31 Makeup problem
32 1961 top 10 hit for the Everly Brothers
34 1966 album that's #2 on Rolling Stone's all-time greatest albums list
36 2001 Microsoft debut
39 Web developer?
43 The same beginning?
44 Willingly
45 Melodramatic cry
46 Engine using a stream of compressed air
48 Pay stub?
50 Sequel title starter
51 Gets to work on Time?
52 Spread news of

54 Block buster?
55 Cager Kukoc
56 It appears first in China
58 ___ Sea (shrinking body of water)
59 Lexicographic enlighteners
60 Achiever of many goals
61 It's no longer working

DOWN

1 Sharp workers?
2 Cheaters, to teachers
3 Remove knots from, maybe
4 Water follower, commercially
5 Wearers of four stars: Abbr.
6 Comic Kevin

7 60-Across's real first name
8 Option for DVD viewing
9 Products of wood ashes
10 Flying start?
11 Fan club reading, briefly
12 Either of two father-and-son Dodgers owners
13 Silhouette
14 First-aid equipment
21 When there are lots of errands to run, say
24 "Doctor Faustus" novelist
26 Pacific force, for short
27 Spaces between leaf veins

29 Great move
32 Caesarean being
33 Book before Job: Abbr.
35 Dweeb
36 Conversation piece?
37 Early screenwriter Bernstein
38 Insignificant
40 How some people die
41 Durable athletes
42 Match
45 Many a circular
47 It's worth 8 points in Scrabble
49 Composer Boccherini
52 Mean
53 Northumberland river
56 Creature feature
57 Annuaire listing

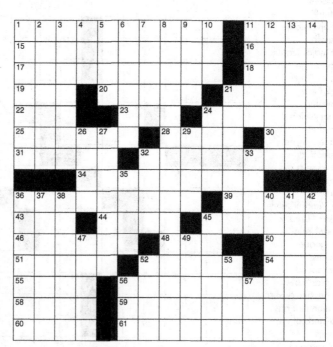

by Barry C. Silk

ACROSS

1 Deadlock
8 Watches in astonishment
15 Went for unhesitatingly
16 Luxembourg grand duke in whose name an annual art prize is awarded
17 Tropical spots
18 Plant material used for fuel
19 Brawl-ending cry
20 Beta tester, e.g.
21 Commandment word
22 French city where William the Conqueror is buried
24 Work an aisle, slangily
26 Monk's title
29 Ba preceder
31 "Salome" role
35 Snap out of it
38 Much work to get done
39 Place for good deals
40 Some bridge players
41 Titan's place
42 Blade
43 "Baudolino" novelist
45 It may be kept in a boot
47 Hand tool
50 Unclear
52 Spill the beans
57 Cook first, as pie crust
59 Cardiff Giant or Piltdown man
60 Went through
61 Away
62 University with campuses in New York and Rome
63 Zealots have them

DOWN

1 Sorry situations
2 Gist
3 Guam's ___ Bay
4 Each
5 Bite-the-bullet type
6 Leader of the Alamo siege
7 "The X-Files" subj.
8 Schmoozes
9 Something to bid
10 Dilapidation
11 Gypsy moth target
12 Period of time
13 "Now I see!"
14 See 36-Down
20 Neighbor of Hoboken, N.J.
23 Singer John and others
25 "Fuhgeddaboudit!"
26 Renaissance artist Piero ___ Francesca

27 Relatives of the Missouria
28 Change
30 Without hindrance
32 Steer stopper
33 Sea ___, denizen of the North Pacific
34 Wayne W. ___, author of "Your Erroneous Zones"
35 Tear
36 With 14-Down, something that can have you seeing things
37 Keeping company with
44 Of a durable wood
46 It's seen on the back of a U.S. quarter
47 Some programs, briefly

48 Judge's order
49 Actor ___ Cobb
51 British ends
53 "And so?"
54 Loathsome sort
55 Flow in a coulee
56 Two from sixty-six?
58 Bart, to Maggie
59 Feather ___

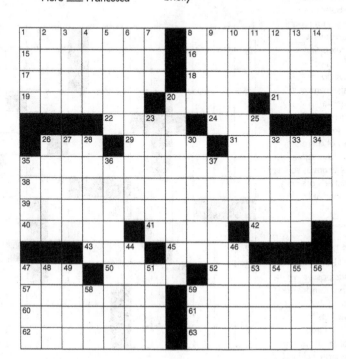

by Manny Nosowsky

ACROSS

1 They get sore easily
9 6'5" All-Star relief ace with identical first two initials
15 Pretty poor chances
16 Pro's remark
17 Shake
18 1970s–'80s Australian P.M.
19 They're lit
20 Places to make notes
22 ___-Aztecan language
23 Itinerary abbr.
24 Up to snuff
25 Take off
26 Rivals for the folks' attention, maybe
28 Wasn't straight
29 Part of some disguises
30 Org. that fought warrantless wiretapping
31 Words of expectation
33 Raise canines?
35 Meanie
39 Ingredients in a protein shake
43 Part of a French 101 conjugation
44 Get bronze, say
47 Butcher's offering
48 Mother of Hades
49 Dumps
50 "A Chapter on Ears" essayist
51 Where Mt. Tabor is: Abbr.
52 Paris possessive
53 What reindeer do
55 Pro fighter
56 "Enough!"
58 Fail to keep
60 Not at all close to
61 Dessert of chilled fruit and coconut
62 Liszt's "Paganini ___"
63 They're fried

DOWN

1 Filled in for a vacationer, in a way
2 Warned
3 Subject to an assessment?
4 Rushes
5 Fangorn Forest dweller
6 Caseworkers?: Abbr.
7 Muscle named for its shape
8 Didn't proceed forthrightly
9 Flash
10 Jostles
11 Org. with aces and chips
12 Sci-fi author Le Guin
13 Be about to fall
14 Took dead aim, with "in"
21 They come and go
25 Tributary
27 Buddhist teachings
28 Eponymous theater mogul
29 Top piece
32 Grp. with a common purpose
34 "I'm sorry, Dave" speaker of sci-fi
36 "Probably"
37 Gets the job done
38 Catherine I and others
40 ___ Peterson, lead role in "Bells Are Ringing"
41 Beginning with vigor
42 Composer Puccini
44 Certain ball
45 Order to leave
46 1957 RKO purchaser
50 "Symphony in Black" and others
53 Main route
54 Low points
55 "Rent-___"
57 Rx instruction
59 "___ sine scientia nihil est" (old Latin motto)

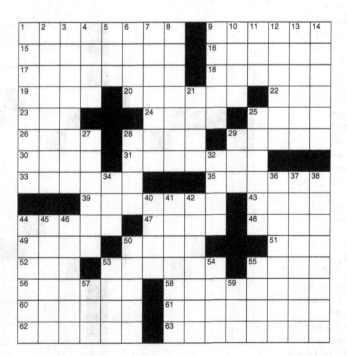

by Rich Norris

ACROSS

1 Musical genre that uses a flatted fifth
6 Violin attachments
15 It vibrates during snoring
16 Novel that nobody reads
17 Four-time U.S. presidential candidate
18 Net sales?
19 Multigallon container
21 Grave mound
22 Hostage holder
23 Endearing, as a smile
24 King's successor as S.C.L.C. president
27 Shrink
28 Member of the 500 Home Run Club
29 Cannibal of Anglo-Saxon legend
31 "Science made clear": Cocteau
32 Stole, slangily
33 Sweetums
36 Perseveres
37 You may need it going in
38 Union station?
41 Seven-foot star of 1960s TV
43 They may raise some people's spirits
45 Films that require a lot of shooting?
46 Sentence ender
47 Their work stinks
49 What a lack of evidence of forced entry might indicate
51 Send to the front?
53 Unchangeable situation

54 Van ___ ("Jump" band)
55 Orthodox Church council
56 Inception

DOWN

1 Roll
2 Actress who was the voice of Duchess in "The Aristocats"
3 The Pearl of the Danube
4 Sucrose polyester, more familiarly
5 "Travelin' Thru" singer
6 City largely destroyed by the Normandy campaign
7 Literary pal of Tom
8 Witness statement
9 Rain clouds
10 Worked one's wiles on
11 Longtime NBC sports exec
12 "Man of Constant ___" (old folk standard)
13 On the way
14 Stick on the grill
20 One of Ferdinand II's kingdoms
22 House on a hacienda
23 One of the Marsalis brothers
25 "Wild Thing" band, with "the"
26 1946 Literature Nobelist
30 University of North Texas home
32 Product lines?
33 Who's left?
34 Assessment paid only by those who benefit
35 Moving vehicles
36 Without apparent effort
37 Bonus Army member
38 Venomous
39 Cabin addition
40 Heel bone, e.g.
42 Bridge declaration
44 "Politics is the ___ of the imagination": Ian McEwan
47 Oz visitor
48 Supine, possibly
50 Dutch painter Steen
52 "We Know Drama" sloganeer

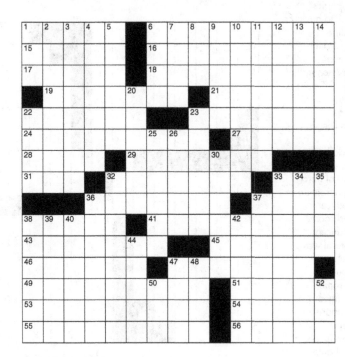

by Patrick Berry

130

ACROSS

1 Lobby, say
9 Where one can retire young?
13 Made further advances?
14 Singles player
15 Lofty pursuit
16 Really moving, musically
17 "The Treachery of Images" painter
18 Whipps candy bar maker
19 Some Tuscans
20 Caret indication
21 Sporting news
22 French teacher
23 Gizmo that measures gas properties
25 Back to back: Fr.
31 Online registration creations
32 Tony-nominated "Pippin" actress
34 Watergate judge
35 San Diego suburb
40 Deck figure
41 Puts down
43 Kind of hero
44 Big herbicide producer
46 Mushroom producers
47 Natural wave catcher
48 Impetuses for some outrageous acts
49 Comparison basis
50 They, in São Paulo
51 Eyeballs

DOWN

1 Perhaps a little too neat
2 "His eyes are ___ fire with weeping": Shak.
3 Creditor's writ
4 One on the way up?
5 Kansas city
6 One
7 Is relaxed
8 Dick Thornburgh's predecessor in the cabinet
9 Worse in quality, slangily
10 Artist who was a founder of the Pre-Raphaelites
11 Encrypted?
12 Stages of space exploration
14 Tom, Dick or Harry
16 Upper parts of piano duets
24 Roadsters
25 Opposite of encourage
26 ___ shorthair (cat breed)
27 Que follower
28 Hostilities
29 Transfers to another vessel, maybe
30 Long-armed redheads
33 Colorado city on the Rio Grande
36 Targets of those catching some rays?
37 Early Palestinian
38 Museum of archaeology display
39 Son of Aphrodite
42 Indication of wonderment
45 Traffic regs., e.g.

by Harvey Estes

ACROSS

1 Algonquian Indian tribe
6 Went sniggling
11 Singer with the #1 hit "All I Have"
14 Sci-fi character whose name is an anagram of CAROLINA ISLANDS
16 Otoscope user, for short
17 Have quite enough for
18 MedWatch agcy.
19 "I'm ready for the weekend!"
21 Chalon-sur-___, France
22 "The Da Vinci Code" priory
23 "Half ___ . . ."
25 Bygone Ford
26 Place to find a C-note?
27 Climber's support
29 Indian pastries
31 ___ Herbert, TV's Mr. Wizard
32 100 qintars
33 Hands out
37 Constellation between Cygnus and Pisces
41 They're plucked
42 Bird: Prefix
44 Star ___
45 "___ of Six" (Joseph Conrad story collection)
46 "A parlor utensil for subduing the impenitent visitor": Ambrose Bierce
48 1950s British P.M.
49 Mooring site
50 Stuffed with cheese, in Mexican cooking
52 D-Day arena: Abbr.
53 Some licensed practitioners
56 Exercise animal?
57 Hopscotch
58 Tough to dig into, as soil

DOWN

1 Notice
2 Home of many of the 1-Across: Abbr.
3 A long time in Lisbon
4 Fuchsite and alurgite
5 Assuming even that
6 They'll give you the run-around
7 Illuminati
8 Place, e.g.
9 7-in. platters
10 More than exalts
11 Sound of change
12 Mr. Rosewater in Kurt Vonnegut's "God Bless You, Mr. Rosewater"
13 "Butterfly" actress, 1981
14 Clear the way to
15 Some babysitters
20 South Beach, e.g.
22 Northwest tribe
24 2004 Sondheim musical, with "The"
26 Corinthian conclusion
28 Country ___
30 It can fill a yard
33 Elevator button
34 1968 hit whose title is repeated three times with "Oh" and then again after "Baby I love you"
35 Make hot
36 Passes effortlessly
37 Miss badly
38 Seaman in a ceremonial honor guard
39 Excise on some out-of-state purchases
40 Mr. abroad
43 Pluck
46 Extra benefits
47 When a football may be hiked
50 Geom. figure
51 "This is disastrous!"
54 Pulitzer category, briefly
55 Red ___ (young amphibian)

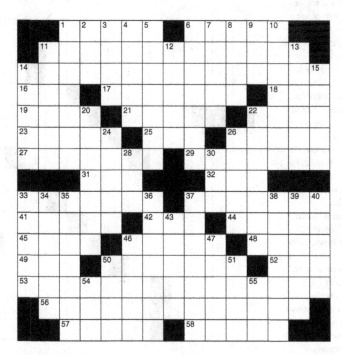

by John Farmer

132

ACROSS

1 Modesty preserver, in some films
11 "___ wondrous pitiful": "Othello"
15 Old form of Italian musical drama
16 "___ Nobody" (1983 Chaka Khan hit)
17 Public appearance preparers
18 Introduction to Chinese?
19 Pixar's first feature-length film
20 Finger or toe
22 Mass appeals: Abbr.
23 You may be lost in the middle of it
24 McKinley's first vice president
27 It has a smaller degree of loft than a mashie
28 Cupule's contents
29 Sparkling
30 List in a book's front: Abbr.
31 Like racehorses
32 Spanish city that gave sherry its name
33 ___ Harker, heroine of "Bram Stoker's Dracula"
34 Rocket datum: Abbr.
35 Where to pick up dates?
36 Fall production
37 Rich mine or other source of great wealth
39 Shuffles
40 Margay cousins
41 Siege site
42 Mountain sheep
43 Initiations
47 Graffitists' scrawls

48 Unexpected turn of events, as in a literary work
50 Puts away
51 See-through sheets
52 Banks of note
53 Grant's position in presidential history

DOWN

1 Shell, e.g.
2 Hair-raiser?
3 Bunch
4 Uniform armband
5 You can make light of it
6 Squire
7 Draft picks
8 Private group
9 Even numbers
10 Fliers, e.g.
11 Meditative exercise
12 End-of-year festival
13 "Common Nonsense" author, 2002
14 Insurance Institute for Highway Safety concern
21 Catawampus
23 Scoring units
24 Tries something
25 Mob rule
26 One running for work?
27 Latin land descriptor
29 Joins
32 Scolding wife: Var.
33 Handle incorrectly?
35 Price-manipulating group
36 Retinue
38 Top-of-the-line
39 Rug rat
41 It may be blind
43 Gasconade
44 Name equivalent to Hans or Ivan
45 Tear up
46 Military band
49 Father of Hophni and Phinehas, in the Bible

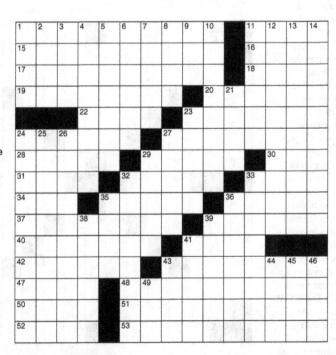

by Bob Klahn

ACROSS

1 Doesn't this beat all?
7 Eastern royal
11 U.S. ambassador to the Soviet Union during W.W. II
13 Take back
15 Home of a literary ghost
16 Currency replaced by the euro
17 Enthrones
18 Region of southern England on the English Channel
19 A telephone technician might perform one
20 Smooth
21 Bland quality
22 Work in a cabin, say
23 Cultural institution
25 Old-fashioned warning
30 Bet both ways
31 Halloween game of biting fruit dangling on a string
33 Not over the line
34 Protective plastic sheet
40 Not forget
41 Civic club member
43 Muzzle packer
44 Make a member of little by little
45 Title heroine with a turtle named Skipperdee
46 Volunteered
47 Like some big banks

48 Properly deals with after an exhumation
49 Holiday
50 Severity

DOWN

1 "Larry King Live," for one
2 Poisonous element: Prefix
3 Shrub often used to mark a boundary
4 The hit of a party?
5 Engages in melodrama
6 One cannot take it at face value
7 Motion starter
8 Growing
9 Revolt

10 Not far out
11 Contemptible one
12 Home maker
13 Sign of anger
14 Go this way and that
24 "Love is just around" it in a Bing Crosby song
25 Glassworker, at times
26 Checkmate
27 Places for combs
28 Ham's equipment
29 No longer in first place
31 Light reddish-brown
32 Storage spot
35 And more

36 Shooting marbles
37 Upper cruster
38 Photographic worker
39 Restaurant clientele
42 Go-aheads

by Raymond C. Young

134

ACROSS

1 Opposite of 58-Across
10 Evidence of trauma
15 Took off without a sound
16 Mel Tormé's "___ Home Baby"
17 "Doesn't that beat all?!"
18 Betel palm
19 Camp sight
21 Matching tops, maybe
25 Creeks, e.g.
26 Lapsed
27 Sitcom about a Texas soccer mom
28 Condition
29 Call up
34 Take ___ view of
35 Cartier rival
36 Crimson rivals
37 Information holders
39 Home of the Knights Hospitalers
40 Wasn't straight
41 More lean and muscular
42 It bites
46 Mean dude's quality
47 Procrastinator's aid
49 Philadelphia's first black mayor, 1984–92
50 What a mail order merchant wants
55 Guitarist's gizmo
56 Like wire transfers
57 Station postings, briefly
58 Opposite of 1-Across

DOWN

1 Where Sydney is: Abbr.
2 Opposite of hiver
3 Console abbr.
4 Old cloth measure
5 It's newly available, but not new
6 Knocker
7 Big-eyed baby
8 "Streamers" playwright
9 Seeing things
10 What a gate may be attached to?
11 Literally, "dwarf dog"
12 Simple life?
13 San Juan native, slangily
14 Annoying things to hit
20 Work site
21 It includes a third and a fifth
22 Rockabilly queen Jackson
23 Certain Greenlander
24 Bellini's title priestess
27 Commanded anew
29 "The Dick Van Dyke Show" actress
30 Soak up
31 Matriarch of an '80s prime-time soap
32 Subpoenas, say
33 Reds' old foes
35 Collect, as funds
38 Some Chevys
39 A few hours after dawn, in verse
41 Water, vis-à-vis wood
42 Some N.C.O.'s
43 Actress Aimée
44 ABC's Arledge
45 Requiring cracking, perhaps
46 Wallop
48 Time to give up?
51 Warriors' grp.
52 "An all 'round good fellow," in song
53 In the U.S.M.C., e.g.
54 Shade of blue

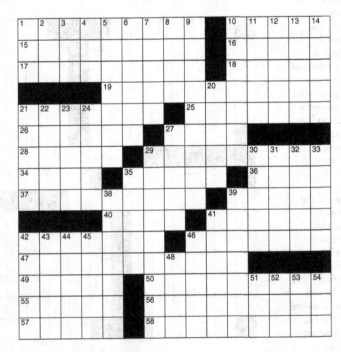

by Stella Daily and Bruce Venzke

ACROSS

1 Senator who wrote "Dreams From My Father"
6 The spy in "The Spy Who Came In From the Cold"
10 Oral verse
14 Hang
15 Ambassador or Statesman, once
16 It had "well-kept acres," in a classic novel
17 "Wait your turn!"
19 Religious philosopher Watts
20 Game ender, perhaps
21 Nonstop connection
23 Sharp things
24 Flattening
25 Ours, in Umbria
29 Tipped trips
32 On occasion
34 N.Y. engineering sch.
35 Beauties
36 Bony part
37 TV tavern that sells Duff Beer
38 Epsilon ___ (the planet Vulcan's star)
39 N.B.A. star who was on the cover of Sports Illustrated while still in high school
41 Some shots
43 Potherb plant
44 1940s Italian Fascist leader
45 Targeting need
46 One may have an arrow
49 One sacred to ancient Egyptians
53 Tippling evidence
54 "Seems likely"

56 Where I-5 crosses I-10
57 Buck
58 Sticks in a bathroom
59 Stress, say
60 Suffix with couch
61 "Crime and Punishment" heroine

DOWN

1 Eager student's cry
2 One-named rocker
3 Maintain
4 Suggest
5 The "her" in Beethoven's question "Who comprehends her?"
6 The opposition

7 Refuge
8 Title girl of a "Nine Stories" story
9 It may be avoided by keeping one's balance
10 Latin list-ender
11 Bob, e.g.
12 Bar garnish
13 Dropped
18 Fair warning
22 Divided
23 La lead-in
25 Beersheba locale
26 Problem addressed by a drama coach
27 Zero halved
28 ___-80 (old computer)
29 "It Must Be Him" singer and others

30 Monumental year?
31 Bruiser's antithesis
33 "___ careful"
37 Buddy
39 Ancestry
40 "Herman" cartoonist Unger
42 Self-proclaimed conqueror
45 "Only ___" (NPR program)
46 Some Muslims
47 Channel buildup
48 "While ___ it . . ."
49 Digging
50 Peaceful gathering, '60s-style
51 Kids play it
52 Dominican slugger
55 Head counts?

by David Levinson Wilk

136

ACROSS
1 Address
8 Rapper's beat
15 From China, e.g.
16 Stuck
17 "Not so!"
18 Stand that a politician might take
19 Sleeping unit?
20 Makes up, in a way
22 Heelless shoe, for short
23 Dohnányi who composed "Ruralia Hungarica"
25 Delhi chestful
26 Detroit's ___ Arena
27 Millennium starter
29 Dark side of China
30 Upset
31 "Doesn't bother me"
34 Kind of agreement
35 2003 Sandler/ Nicholson movie
41 Robert Frost farm site
42 Big Japanese computer firm
43 Defense device
44 "Finlandia" composer Sibelius
45 Must, slangily
47 Sister ___, title character of a 1970 film
48 Funny
49 Flimsy, as chances go
51 Mr. abroad
52 With no time to lose
54 Fifth, e.g.

56 Beer drinker's terse critique
57 Not knowing
58 In myth, loser of a shouting match with Hermes
59 Oath-taker

DOWN
1 Take suddenly
2 Longtime Penn State football coach
3 Ascetics of yore
4 ___ tilt
5 Sea palm or badderlocks
6 Singing groups
7 Somehow
8 Causes for penalties
9 Some parodists

10 Tic-___ (candies)
11 Court figure: Abbr.
12 Singing effect
13 Microbiology topic
14 CBers' numerical system
21 Commercial fishing aids
24 Forest plant with triangular fronds
26 Some duplexes
28 Blog predecessor
30 U-Haul competitor
32 Game played with counters
33 Zine
35 Lies next to
36 Is unobliged to

37 Make a subtle transformation, as in color
38 "The Bronx Zoo" star
39 Tell tales
40 Movie extra
45 Relish
46 Play to ___ (tie)
49 Dethrone
50 Emmy winner Falco
53 Avoided bloodshed
55 ___ Toguri (Tokyo Rose)

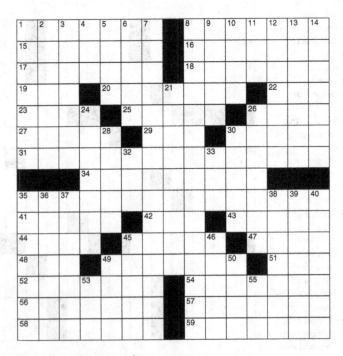

by Manny Nosowsky

ACROSS

1 Flu symptom
5 Spirited
9 Things let out
14 1990 N.C.A.A. hoops champs
15 Steamed
16 Rock and Roll Hall of Fame designer
17 Family term of endearment
18 ___ fruit
19 One noted for long drives
20 Make understandable
22 Burton's 1977 miniseries role
23 Catch 50 winks?
24 Join
25 Western national forest
28 Promise
30 Out of whack
33 Cole Porter's "___ Men"
34 They're behind some actions
36 "Shampoo" screenwriter Robert
37 Advocates
38 Bats
39 Pastoral
40 No one in particular
41 Folded like a fan
45 Edna St. Vincent Millay's "Love ___ All"
48 Team leaders
50 "Why Can't the English?" composer
51 All the things you are: Abbr.
52 What's taken in
53 First name in architecture
54 Something sunk
55 Primo
56 "The Bait" poet
57 Fictional pirate
58 Unfashioned

DOWN

1 Some kin
2 Twist
3 Skeleton parts
4 Fleeting
5 Time's 2001 Person of the Year
6 They're often pulled out in church
7 Do-re-mi
8 Comic strip canine
9 Uncertainty
10 Book in the Book of Mormon
11 Scrim feature
12 Human, by nature
13 Place plant nutrients near the roots of a growing crop
21 Purviews
26 Land, in another land
27 Protection from enemy fire
28 "Go fly a kite!"
29 Choice for durable wooden fencing
30 Beat at sea
31 Performed helplessly?
32 Home of the Univ. of St. Francis
35 Brasserie dish
42 Facetious group?
43 Economists' concern
44 Forename in fragrances
46 Glendower who revolted against Henry IV
47 Marketing leader?
48 They have scales
49 Ancient one

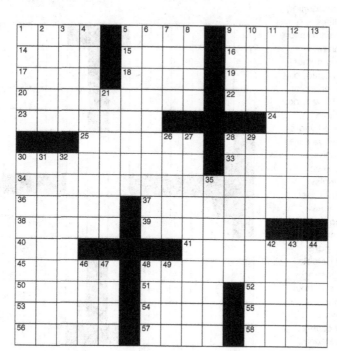

by Ed Early

138

ACROSS
1 Heavy overcoat
7 Pet that's likely to purr
13 Wandering rogues, as in Cervantes stories
15 Tax max
16 It hangs over the ocean
17 Prince ___ Land (historical Canadian region that drains into Hudson Bay)
18 Movie preview, e.g.
19 Having a knack for
20 One way of seasoning
21 Some card players
22 Earth-scanning satellites, e.g.
24 Certain furniture ensembles
25 Indian author ___ Mehta, a staff writer for The New Yorker for more than 30 years
26 Occult sciences, collectively
34 Little-seen examples
36 Cubist Léger
37 Ate quickly, slangily
39 Big name in auto parts
40 Not suitable for passing
41 Revel without restraint
42 Rouyn-___, city and county of Quebec
43 ___ Last Stand
44 Small laugh

45 Ancient Spartan magistrates
46 Has the wheel

DOWN
1 Surprise at the polls
2 Certain claimant
3 Beat it
4 ___ Trail (Everglades highway)
5 Explorer from ca. A.D. 1000
6 Floral ornament
7 Crescendos
8 Play the peacemaker
9 Plan in advance
10 Former first family
11 Perfume ingredients

12 Lab work
14 They're often found near busy intersections
15 Bookstore books
23 Keeps in print, in a way
26 Not very cushiony
27 Automaker Maserati
28 Make further modifications to
29 Kitchen gizmos
30 Producers of major reports
31 Be willed
32 Amount deducted from the price of goods to compensate for loss
33 Gallimaufry

34 Get back
35 One going to the post office
36 Ridiculous sham
38 Kind souls

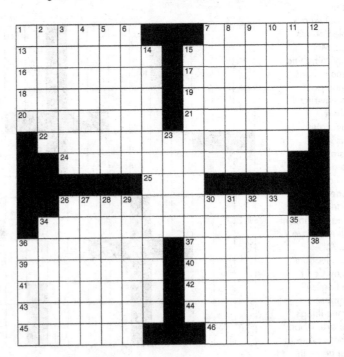

by Frank Longo

ACROSS

1 Hit hard
10 Strength
15 Native of a European capital
16 Not keep one's feelings pent up
17 No small favor
18 "Enough!"
19 Antarctica's ___ Ice Shelf
20 Sign of hostility
22 Doc ___, Spider-Man foe
23 Large amount of fudge?
24 "The Last Days of Pompeii" heroine
25 Kind of torch
26 W.W. II org.
27 Pigeonlike birds
30 Travels freely around the world
32 Sole options
33 Governmental suffix
34 "Breaking ___ Hard to Do"
35 Unveiling phrase
38 People who call themselves the Diné
42 It provides a light finish
44 Employer of Walter Cronkite and David Brinkley, once
45 Book part
46 Record keeper's concern
47 Range part: Abbr.
48 Like Schubert's Mass No. 2
49 Org. for the Denver Gold and Chicago Blitz
50 Set pieces?
53 Advocate of "justicialismo"
55 Z stands for it in electronics
57 Mystic
58 Primitive capacitor
59 Terraplane's predecessor, in old autodom
60 Weapon that Reagan called the "Peacekeeper"

DOWN

1 Starting breakfast drink
2 Funk
3 Love, as "thou" might do in a hymn
4 Some touch screens, briefly
5 End of many a string
6 The Phoenix of the Southern Conference
7 Grp. that has agony over ecstasy?
8 Like mustangs, for example
9 Ribbing
10 Small ticks?
11 "Hallelujah, ___ Bum" (Al Jolson film)
12 Ideal for engines and audio equipment
13 Contemporary travel convenience
14 Sign of warm affection
21 Three-time L.P.G.A. champ born in Korea
24 Land development?
25 Home of the Jaycees' national headquarters
27 See 52-Down
28 Flummoxed
29 Tartar sauce ingredient
31 Knock, with "at"
35 Cover-up at the highest levels?
36 Prime time follower
37 Pep pills?
39 1995 Robin Williams film
40 Kind of glass
41 Not forced
43 Baja cuisine
49 System for servers
50 Start to care?
51 Some tributes
52 With 27-Down, like some letters
54 Lament of Lady Capulet
56 English novelist Barbara

by Byron Walden

140

ACROSS

1 "Doonesbury" reporter Hedley
7 Chesterfield, e.g.
15 Where many jokes are set
16 Small amount
17 Take up
18 Light
19 Scraps
20 ___-Shan, ship in Conrad's "Typhoon"
21 ___ City, Fla.
22 Grocery section
23 Beside
25 Title lady of a 1932 Ethel Merman song
27 Simplifies
31 Berlin, for one
35 Nun's wear
36 Ferdinand III's daughter
37 First one out on the track
38 Enter drop by drop
39 Spring cleaning follow-up, perhaps
40 He sat in front of Nimoy and Shatner
41 "The Lower Depths" playwright
42 Inflexible
44 Señor's speech
48 Sky over the Seine
51 It's picked
52 Mark who won the 1998 Masters and British Open
54 Generally
56 No-good
57 Tartish treat
58 Meandered
59 Pulitzer-winning William Kennedy novel
60 Corsair, Ranger and Pacer

DOWN

1 Ebro y otros
2 "___-Year Day" ("The Pajama Game" tune)
3 Milk: Prefix
4 Neighbors
5 He was defeated and captured at Sedan
6 April to September, in southern Africa
7 Like some markets
8 Sports analyst who wrote "Living a Dream"
9 Prefix with -centric
10 Way: Abbr.
11 They often involve drawing
12 Most eligible, in a way
13 Ens. producer
14 Phony start?
24 Grammy winner for "Jonathan Livingston Seagull"
26 German article
28 Shelter provider: Abbr.
29 Big international carrier
30 Like a desert
31 "___ la guerre"
32 Olive genus
33 Unlikely to raise a ruckus
34 George Plimpton book
35 Productive one
37 Hole stat
39 Sang on high?
41 Opposite of macho
43 Snap
45 They're not final releases
46 Applesauce-topped treat
47 Dizzy
48 Valle del Cauca's capital
49 Robert of "The Sopranos"
50 Zoe's friend, on "Sesame Street"
53 Added stipulations
55 Weather report abbr.

by Eric Berlin

ACROSS

1 Sea monster of Greek myth able to make whirlpools
10 Show of compassion?
15 Golden Grain product
16 "I'm impressed!"
17 Utah's Grand Staircase-___ National Monument
18 Ill-kempt
19 Short cracks
20 Full set of bicuspids, e.g.
21 Proceed furtively
22 Around the bend
24 River whose name means "river"
25 Comply with
26 Hear something about
28 Subject of some of 32-Down's writings
29 Applesauce
30 Computer company with the slogan "Imagine it. Done."
31 Sticks up
32 Hose problem
33 Urban problem
36 Cataract site
37 Some chest-pumping, for short
40 Autumn Harvest Uprising leader
42 Cheshire cat's hangout
43 Help
44 Cosmetic procedure
45 Primitive percussion instrument
46 Not going bankrupt

48 Connect to
50 Honeycombed
51 Australia/New Zealand separator
52 Decree
53 Least comfortable
54 Old-fashioned symbol of authority
55 Playroom fixtures

DOWN

1 Wood tar derivative
2 Mocking title for an autocrat
3 Gave consent
4 Remark of exasperation
5 Bush or Kerry
6 Fiber
7 Steak orderer's specification

8 "To be honest . . ."
9 Rest of the afternoon
10 Cognizant of
11 Fighting opponent?
12 Discombobulates
13 Word of encouragement
14 Girly girls' opposites
23 Swinging about
26 Renaissance Fair vessel
27 Post houses
29 Archaic greetings
31 Cluttered room
32 Author who, with his friends, famously formed the Merry Pranksters
33 Multivehicle collision

34 Stupid oaf
35 Green-blooded "Star Trek" entity
36 Old crime syndicate head called "Lucky"
37 Fancy getaways
38 Showing the most vivacity
39 Cardinals' wear
41 Lofty reproof
42 College party crasher, maybe
45 Grind
47 Salon applications
49 All-in-one computer

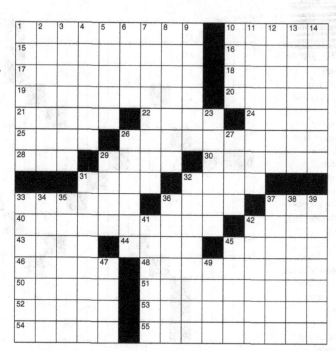

by Patrick Berry

142

ACROSS

1. Tom Wolfe catchphrase popularized in the 1970s
12. Loan periods: Abbr.
15. Like some corporate stock
16. Letters for soldiers
17. Many people read at these
18. Very cool
19. Pronounced
20. Deals in
21. Abbr. on a certain elevator button
22. Coasters
24. Trade grp. formed in the late 1950s
25. Two times, to Tomás
26. Relig. affiliation of 2½ million Americans
27. Ready to go free
30. ___ Monroe, "Green Acres" role
31. No ___ (street sign)
32. Pronoun not in the king's English
36. Big name in desserts
37. Going out in waves?
39. French pronoun
40. Major disasters
42. Little dog, for short
45. St. ___ Beach (Sunshine State vacation locale)
46. Water tester: Abbr.
47. Stand out
49. Impressionist
50. Center of a ball, maybe
52. Red letters?
53. Alphabet trio
54. Enthused out loud
56. Literary monogram
57. "None of the above," essentially
58. D.C. bigwig
59. Office meeting place

DOWN

1. Old "Best by taste test" sloganeer
2. "When the angry trumpet sounds ___": Shak.
3. Faltering condition
4. Basket fiber
5. Frame that's sometimes framed
6. Stout ones
7. Where les leçons are taught
8. Places with fireplaces
9. Shrews
10. Troubles
11. Some Amazon.com sales, for short
12. Went free, at least for now
13. It's not busy
14. Gentleness
21. Fathers, familiarly
23. Angers
25. Bring down
28. Follower of rule or court
29. "___ Alice" (classic 1971 antidrug teen "diary")
30. More pallid
32. 1970s fashion item
33. At peace
34. San Quentin or Attica
35. Where to beat the heat?
38. Brimming
41. Guggenheim sculptor
42. Epitome of hotness
43. Like some inspections
44. "Moon River" lyricist
48. Baja breakfast order
50. "A Fool There Was" star, 1915
51. Grander than grand
54. Net letters
55. Musician Yoko

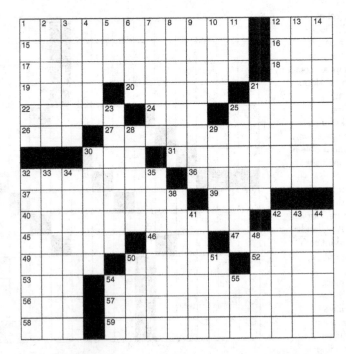

by Robert Bridges

ACROSS

1 Automatic, e.g.
8 Band-aid
15 Part of Italian East Africa
16 Millennium Falcon pilot
17 Military policy
19 Winged being, in Germany
20 Sequence sung by kids
21 Find out
22 Some Bourbons, par exemple
23 Grain sorghum variety
24 W.W. II service acronym
25 Foster son of the comics
26 Times when Mexico and Brazil celebrate their independence: Abbr.
27 "Meet John Doe" director
28 Concern of 55-Across
30 Least colorful
31 Press conference response
33 Many a monk, once
36 Like some radiation
40 Cries for attention
41 Some bolt holders
42 "Flower Drum Song" actor
43 Lock giant
44 Nucleus
45 Mideast capital
46 It may be polit.
47 Turn red, maybe
48 Training ship trainee
49 Song from "A Chorus Line"

52 Former English royal house
53 Powerless to progress
54 Workers with horse sense?
55 People getting into briefs?

DOWN

1 Like post-Revolutionary architecture
2 Refined find
3 Like certain endorsements
4 Ending with Rock
5 ___ Sea, known in ancient times as Oxianus Lacus
6 Monitor stat.
7 Brown-nose
8 Smiths

9 "Goldfinger" actress Mallet
10 Able to see through
11 Ore. is on it
12 Comes unglued
13 Very attentive
14 Relative of a sable
18 Lecherous
23 Clear for takeoff
24 Move breezily
26 Ones who may be wearing spotted ties?
27 ___ Major
29 Modern film genre
30 Board game played with stones
32 Wearing black, perhaps

33 Response to a dubious assertion
34 Dances with a shuffle-step
35 Self-___
37 ___ Freleng, creator of Bugs Bunny and Daffy Duck
38 Emphatic rejection
39 Facial features
41 Tropical animals
44 Kind of press
45 Off-color
47 Bank of Paris
48 Avian food holder
50 "___'able David" (classic silent film)
51 W.W. II agcy.

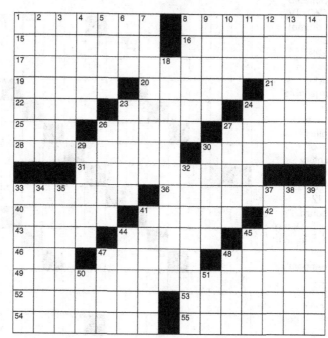

by Sherry O. Blackard

144

ACROSS

1 Gorged
8 Game with Spectacular Seven scoring
15 Cause of anomie
17 Pester
18 "I've had enough!"
19 Redbook rival
20 ___ grano salis
21 Unthinking
22 Caffe additive
23 "I can only ___ much"
24 South of Spain
25 Horse fathers
26 "Let's Fall in Love" song composer
27 Modern travel aids
29 Lightheaded?
30 "___ Hundred" (early '60s TV police drama)
31 Flourish
32 Mind set?
34 University in Massachusetts
37 "Unforgettable" singers
38 Batman, to his mother?
39 Middle of this century
40 ". . . the cruel venom of ___": Deut. 32
41 Ship board
42 A–B or C–D, e.g.
43 ___ Club (military hangout)
44 Finish smoothly
45 Dog-___
46 Line of agreement
49 Line of business
50 Rants
51 Emulated Amazon

DOWN

1 Damn
2 Vote count
3 Current delivery
4 Dickens title starter
5 Vermeer's "Woman With a ___"
6 Seamy matter
7 Servers' trolleys
8 "Ivanhoe" events
9 Cartoon art genre
10 "In that case . . ."
11 It goes before the carte, not the horse
12 Landmark made with blocks of white Georgia marble
13 Charged
14 Top of the agenda
16 Big gambler's pile
22 Some claims
23 Dickens title character
25 Heavens above
26 Unrivaled
28 Locks up
29 Forbidding, as 25-Down
31 Clairol option
32 "No way!"
33 Pool great Willie
34 Bald-faced
35 Brobdingnagian
36 Hammered hard
38 Blasts
41 Hat decoration
42 Sulu portrayer, in "Star Trek"
44 Fine
45 First name in singing
47 First name in singing
48 Quick

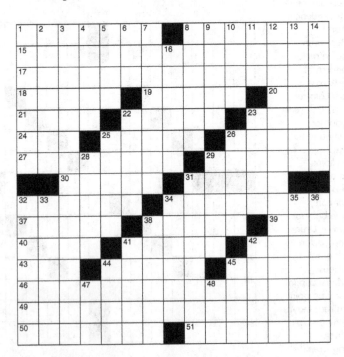

by Manny Nosowsky

ACROSS

1 Finish, with "up"
4 Benefiting from benzoyl peroxide
9 Run
14 Common course penalty
16 No family fare
17 1871 sequel to a classic 1868 novel
18 Conclude by
19 Got going
20 Unpleasantly involve
21 Checks
22 Phoenician love goddess
23 Campaign mgr.?
24 Monks, at times
25 It may be congested
28 Saxony seaport
29 Year the Liang dynasty began in China
30 Major oil refinery port
31 Jerusalem artichoke, e.g.
32 Attention
33 Appliance setting
34 Eppie's guardian, in an Eliot classic
35 Simile's end?
36 Caught
38 Wagner's "___ fliegende Holländer"
39 One proceeding confidently
40 Captures again, in a way
44 Trailer units
45 Long-distance service with fixed rates for fixed zones

46 One of a crime-fighting TV pair
47 Wasn't silly
48 Steaming
49 Gathers quotes on
50 1666 London fire chronicler
51 Struck down
52 Romantic lead-in

DOWN

1 One may be crowned
2 Standing by
3 ___ di pollo (chicken breasts)
4 World records?
5 No Einstein
6 The "Julius" of Gaius Julius Caesar, e.g.
7 Squeezed

8 Place to kick back
9 Used to buy
10 Cheat
11 Called for delivery
12 Under one's control
13 Not in front or back
15 Zapper
20 Dimethyl sulfate, e.g.
22 Home of the Cordillera Real
24 Comment from a tough guy
25 Return requirement
26 "Whatever"
27 Just the headlines
28 Formulator of the quadratic reciprocity law

31 Targets of inflation
32 Portrayer of Lt. Rodriguez on "NYPD Blue"
34 Part of a forlorn face
35 Deliberator's words
37 You can get cited for doing it
38 Notice
40 Call
41 Attach, in a way
42 Result
43 Handle
45 Friendly
47 "M*A*S*H" extras, for short

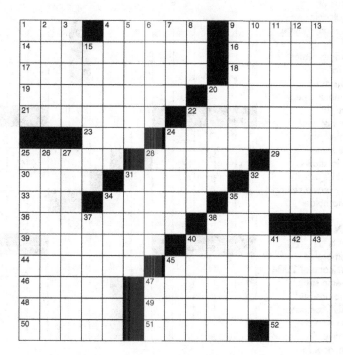

by Joe DiPietro

146

ACROSS

1 Rural strip
9 Recharging one's batteries, so to speak
15 Veto
16 Filler of many shoes
17 Shut up
18 Paying guest
19 They're far from any port
21 Mount with spirit
22 Some techies
32 Away
33 Prevaricate
34 Just for fun
37 Like many a resort
38 How some things are available
40 French site of Roman ruins
41 Result of a volcanic eruption, maybe
44 U.S. Army training center in Va.
45 It winds up
55 Commune near Perugia
56 Got hot, then cooled off
57 Like some radio shows
58 Monk's activity
59 War movie setting
60 Song holder

DOWN

1 Points
2 Memorable hurricane of 2004
3 Solemn stretch
4 "Thomas and Sally" composer
5 Backwoods relative
6 Penchant for taking off?
7 "Old Deuteronomy" writer and family
8 Conference site
9 Wartime dispatch carrier
10 Big city problem
11 First of a string of 13
12 Sailor's saint
13 Fairyland
14 Course guides?
20 Québec's Lévesque and others
22 Paparazzo sort
23 Department of central France
24 German town
25 Home subcontractor
26 As a friend, to François
27 Plain of the Southwest
28 First name in Mideast politics
29 Snail trail
30 They roll in
31 Biblical view
35 Disposing of at a church fair, maybe
36 Leg warmers, e.g.
39 Triangular
42 "I Love a Mystery" actress Lund
43 Bluffs
45 Some egg containers
46 E.T.S. offering
47 Cuba, por ejemplo
48 Lunar trench
49 Indian's home
50 Vintage vehicles
51 Knobstick
52 Settled down
53 Cast
54 Beat slightly

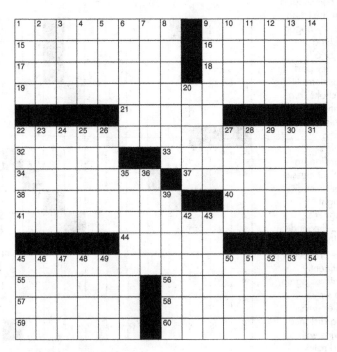

by Harvey Estes

ACROSS

1 Long, narrow cloud
10 Symbol of life
14 Tough thing to master at the Masters
16 Island do
17 Scuola di San Rocco muralist
18 Legal speeders, for short
19 Global positioning meas.
20 They look for a good body
22 End notes?
24 Digital file holder: Abbr.
25 Pet
26 Microwave button
28 Accessory for Wonder Woman
30 Groove-billed ___
31 Green emcee
33 College student's option
35 Spanish pronoun
37 Identifying mark
38 Effervesces
42 It's hard to understand
46 Corner piece
47 "No kidding"
49 Serfs of old
50 Remedial agents
52 Symbol of deficit
54 Something to scale, in Somme
55 1979 Broadway musical that celebrated old-style vaudeville
58 One that's tired?
59 Big star, say
60 Teatro dal Verme premiere of 1892
62 Impatient person's dread
63 Make it legal
64 Verb with vous
65 Tables or shelves

DOWN

1 Fictional defense attorney
2 Not at all sour
3 One living on investment income
4 Med. focus
5 Bulk transporter
6 Like most washers
7 "The Origins of Totalitarianism" author
8 Gap
9 Leon with three Super Bowl rings
10 Comic strip queen
11 Figure
12 "The Legend of Sleepy Hollow" maiden
13 Noted capture of 2003
15 Drag, e.g.
21 Navigational route
23 One good at breaking
27 Not as certain
29 Robert Louis Stevenson's "___ Triplex"
32 Blusters
34 Periscope part
36 One of 100: Abbr.
38 Permanently attached, as a barnacle
39 Enthusiastic approval
40 Spent
41 Potassium ___ (food preservative)
43 Trattoria dumplings
44 Rattled one's saber at
45 In the saddle
48 Import
51 Low points
53 Links locales
56 Pithecologists' study
57 ___ spell
61 Some are in windows: Abbr.

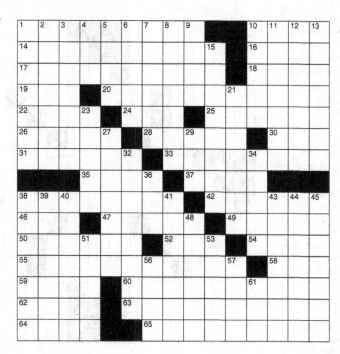

by Brad Wilber

148

ACROSS

1 Tom, to Samuel F. B. Morse
7 Not let the lees settle
13 Throughway
14 Exploitative employer
15 Some urban legends
16 Front
17 Kind of moth
18 Late-night host since 1993
20 Numbers preceder: Abbr.
21 Creep
22 Folk singer John
23 French chef's mushroom
24 Take ___ breath
26 11-time 1930s–'40s All-Star
27 There are 745.7 of them in one horsepower
28 Levelheaded
31 Film technique
32 Hotel amenity
33 Case for a podiatrist
34 Part of le printemps
35 Line of cliffs
39 Spanish pronoun
40 English philosopher George Henry ___
42 Scoundrel
43 ___ al-Khaimah (one of the United Arab Emirates)
44 Early in the morning
45 48-Across feature
46 Carrier of devastating cargo

48 Verdi work whose title character is a bandit
50 Lee of literature
51 In final form, as a film
52 Reporter who uses shoe leather
53 Meet people

DOWN

1 Pale violet
2 Here and there
3 Golf lesson topic
4 Most dice
5 Up until
6 Techie administrator
7 Peep show
8 Isn't that just perfect?

9 High class?: Abbr.
10 Act of dressing and grooming oneself
11 Rigorous
12 "Superman and the Mole Men" star, 1951
14 Angle
16 Waste
19 Award for showing
23 One who may adjust a belt
25 Lays
27 Some noncombatants, for short
29 First name in horror
30 Joseph C. Lincoln's "Cap'n ___"

31 Dirt-cheap
32 Singer Cash
33 Total, e.g.
36 Make sparkling
37 "Fatal Instinct" director
38 They're checked
40 Wearer of three stars: Abbr.
41 Unkind look
44 Rubáiyát stanza scheme
47 Skedaddle
49 Package info: Abbr.

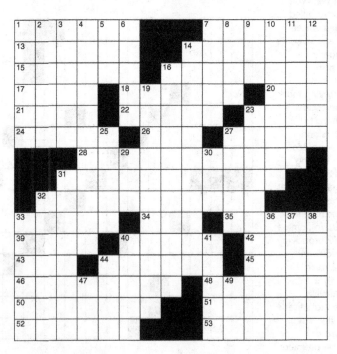

by Eric Berlin

ACROSS

1 It can be ear-piercing
5 Command to go
9 Trainee
14 N.B.A. star Kukoc
15 One foot
16 It may be stuck in a bar
17 Company whose cars don't use gasoline
18 PX users
19 Organism bodies
20 Snack item
22 Tearful
23 "___ Es el Amor" (Spanish song hit)
24 Relative of -let
25 One easily moved
26 Sheets
28 Nursery output
30 Beluga delicacy
31 Food items introduced to the United States by Samuel Thomas circa 1880
35 Pellet shooter
36 It has 646 members
41 Auto features, briefly
42 Book end?
43 "No, you're not" retort
45 Better waterproof
48 Former White House inits.
49 Gulager of "McQ," 1974
50 One going out
51 Iron
54 Page of un calendario
55 Outdoor feast
56 Is Spanish?
57 Follower of a duck, pig or cow

58 "Who ___?"
59 Tout's antithesis
60 "Days of Our Lives" setting
61 Coordinate
62 "Oliver!" composer Lionel ___

DOWN

1 Cameos, e.g.
2 Way of seasoning
3 Lion's combatant for the crown, in "Through the Looking-Glass"
4 Good-looker
5 Company with a brontosaur logo
6 Stockpile
7 Parisian possessive

8 One sip, maybe: Abbr.
9 George Jetson's boss
10 Cool
11 Film composer Tiomkin
12 Dodge
13 Final participants
21 Extend
25 "Well, whaddya know!"
27 Bygone dignitaries
28 Any-way link
29 "I know not why I ___ sad": Shak.
32 Concerns of some bathers: Abbr.
33 Fire up
34 Showman Ziegfeld and others

36 Fast-food chain
37 Orwellian setting
38 Corp. headquartered in Pittsburgh
39 Mediterranean capital
40 9-Across, at times
44 Like some genes
46 Chilling
47 "Get ___!"
48 Some horses
51 Poor
52 Guiding genius
53 Cicely, e.g.

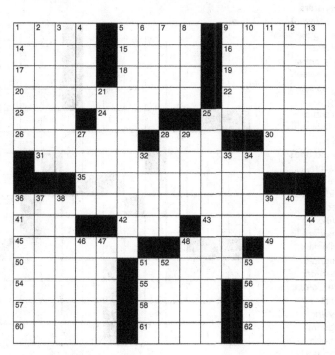

by Jim Page

150

ACROSS

1 Candy that, in urban legend, can be lethal when mixed with soda
9 Put under
15 It's exactly a foot long
16 Many an "S.N.L." cast member
17 Short musical composition
18 À la King?
19 Comforting words
20 Drinks akin to americanos
21 Plant that's a traditional symbol of remembrance
23 One to grow on
27 Remark to whisperers
31 In ___ (even)
32 Brits' "governors"
33 Remove
34 Ratify anew
36 What some singers sing in
37 Long series of troubles
38 Medical suffix
41 Pen fill
42 Beyond one's persona
44 Deal a low blow
45 Quickly recites
47 Special intuition, in modern lingo
50 Excitements
55 Designate
56 Field work
57 "The Conscious Lovers" playwright, 1722
58 Pregnant
59 Part of a safari party
60 Like some fruit

DOWN

1 Furtive summons
2 Cry of excitement
3 Southern bread
4 Stern
5 Musk maker
6 Marine animals like the sea lily and feather star
7 Orson Welles's Wisconsin birthplace
8 Irish moss, e.g.
9 Of some monuments
10 Principal McGee's portrayer in "Grease"
11 Fast one
12 Mine access
13 Lacquered metalware
14 Bridge expert Culbertson and others
22 Some degs.
23 Tehrani tongue
24 Saved on supper, perhaps
25 Not as green
26 Just bread and water, e.g.
28 Sports
29 Concertedly
30 English 101 subject
35 Coastal flier
36 Resort to violence
38 Wicked
39 Medicinal teas
40 Start of a strong opinion
43 "How to Handle a Woman" lyricist
46 Was ready to blow, say
47 Have a sudden inspiration?
48 Communiqué segue
49 Scene of heavy W.W. I fighting
51 Windmill arm
52 "Artaxerxes" composer
53 Focus of some workouts
54 Goes with

by Myles Callum

The New York Times

SMART PUZZLES

PRESENTED WITH STYLE

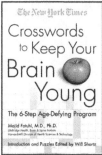

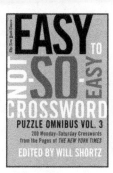

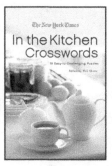

Available at your local bookstore or online at www.nytimes.com/nytstore

 St. Martin's Griffin

Solutions

Solutions

1

```
G O N Z O J O U R N A L I S M
T H A I R E S T A U R A N T S
B E T T E R G E T M O V I N G
R D S ■ S R O ■ A B M ■ S S R
■ ■ ■ A T Y O U ■ S A W ■ ■ ■
F O S T E R D A D ■ S H E D S
A C T I I I I ■ R O I ■ O B E Y
T H E S A C K ■ O B O I S T S
W E E K ■ E O S ■ U N S E A T
A R L E S ■ P A W P R I N T S
■ ■ ■ T E A ■ C A R E T ■ ■ ■
T D S ■ E L L ■ S O C ■ N R A
H O T E N O U G H F O R Y O U
I T A L I A N A M E R I C A N
S E C O N D A M E N D M E N T
```

2

```
O C T A N T S ■ S T E R E O S
P L A T O O N S E R G E A N T
P O R T R A I T P A I N T E R
O O Z E D ■ V A T ■ S T Y L I
S T A N ■ B E G I N ■ S O A P
E I N ■ T E L E C O M ■ U N E
R E T O O L E D ■ M I T R E D
■ ■ H H O U R ■ S I N G H ■ ■
B O E I N G ■ A U N T I E E M
O R A ■ S A L I N E S ■ A R I
T I P I ■ S A R R E ■ S R A S
A N E R A ■ R I O ■ M A T S U
N O M O R E I L O V E Y O U S
I C A N T S A Y F O R S U R E
C O N S I S T ■ S W E A T E D
```

3

```
D A T E ■ A M B I ■ A H E M S
E V O C A T I O N ■ M O V I E
F E L L F O R I T ■ A R E S T
I N D I A N E L E P H A N T S
E G Y P T ■ ■ R A S T E R ■
S E A S ■ B L A S S ■ I D A S
■ ■ E L L I O T T G O U L D
A S A ■ B A G L A D Y ■ P S I
E L O I ■ A T R E E ■ N A S H
■ T E N O N S ■ ■ A T T H E
F I V E S T A R G E N E R A L
A N E A R ■ B U L L S N A K E
T E R R I ■ E M U L A T I O N
A S A B C ■ R P M S ■ E N S E
```

4

```
M M M M G O O D ■ ■ O F F E D
A A A M E M B E R ■ P R O N E
T E L L S A L I E ■ T E R R A
T W A ■ T H A T S T O O B A D
H E R R ■ A D I O S ■ N A G S
A S I A N ■ I E R E ■ D E E
U T A H A N ■ S T T E R E S A
■ ■ A T O R ■ S S N S ■ ■
E X P L O D E S ■ E N V I E D
X E R ■ I C E T ■ A P P L E
P R O B ■ C H E R I ■ S A A B
L O T U S E A T E R S ■ N I E
O X E Y E ■ L O V E S C E N E
R E G I S ■ L I O N T A M E R
E D E N S ■ T R E S P A S S
```

5

```
S H O P P E ■ A S T R I N G S
C U R L U P ■ S P O O N O U T
A R C A N A ■ T E A T A B L E
B L A N C ■ D R A T ■ M I L L
■ ■ O H L O O K ■ F O S S E
T E D ■ E A R ■ V O N ■ ■
A L A N D T I P P E R G O R E
C A M E T O T H E R E S C U E
O N E W A Y O R A N O T H E R
■ S P A ■ H O R ■ S D S
E L I S E ■ B R E N D A
L E N T ■ P E O N ■ A P L U S
L I M A P E R U ■ R I S E T O
I C A N T S E E ■ I N E V E R
S A N D L O T S ■ A S S I S T
```

6

ETTU · SEAMOSS
DIRTS · CASTANET
INUIT · MONTAIGNE
TESLA · AFTERNOON
HASITINFOR · MIRO
RESURGES · HANES
RETILE · ZINGS
ONESHOT
TERRA · LARSEN
DALEY · TERRINES
EREV · JOEMONTANA
TAKELEAVE · GATOS
ENTRUSTED · LINOS
STRESSES · ELIZA
TOASTEE · SKED

7

PAUSED · ITSATRAP
ERNANI · BOWLGAME
DELTAS · ONELITER
ANARCH · SKAT · ANS
LOCATOR · ARISTAE
STEPONIT · MIAMI
RECONNECTED
ICES · SERIO · SSNS
MAGICTRICKS
PROMO · SHIELDED
OPTIMAL · EDMEESE
SHR · EDIT · DIGITS
TOILSOME · INASEC
ONPATROL · NATTER
RESPONSE · GLOSSY

8

LAMB · OWLET · ILLS
ASEA · RHODE · NOOK
DIAL · GEOMETRYII
LANDMARKS · ROAST
ENTWINES · PEAL
ISSUE · RADISH
SPANS · NEMOS · SHE
WETSUIT · EDUCTOR
ANA · GROSZ · ROSES
GAGMAN · AZTEC
LANA · TARRAGON
AWARD · KINESCOPE
SANTAMARIA · OTIS
AGCY · TRENT · LUNT
PEER · MOSEY · APES

9

ASFARASTHATGOES
TURNUPTHEVOLUME
THATSTHEWAYITIS
RACES · EWES · BONA
ARTS · ALERTS · FEM
CTA · TRESS · EZINE
TOLERANT · KNOTTS
LABS · IMTO
ETHICS · CRABMEAT
MOIST · GLORY · DIR
ERN · SPLINT · MIRY
TEDS · RICH · PACTS
ILLTHINKABOUTIT
CLEAREDONESNAME
SIGNEDANDSEALED

10

STRATA · OBSTACLE
TEASEL · PETUNIAS
ATRIAL · EVENINGS
GREASE · NEPALESE
EARNER · ALS
GUNS · MADAM
PLAYDEAD · CANINE
LINEONESPOCKETS
ADDLES · HUSHHUSH
TOILS · RUNT
CAT · AMPULE
ISOTONIC · RAINED
MARIPOSA · ILLINI
PREDATES · CELTIC
SAMEHERE · ASSENT

11

```
S I T U A T I O N C O M E D Y
T R A N S I S T O R R A D I O
O K L A H O M A S O O N E R S
. S I N E . . Y E N . . I N K .
. . I S E E . . S E L F . . .
S P A M . N A M . S I E S T A
E U R O . O R E O . P S H A W
T R O U B L E S H O O T I N G
T E N S E . D A Y O . D E K E
E R I C A S . S E Z . E R S E
. . H U T T . . S E T S . . .
. C P O . R A M . . A T T O .
M A R I T I M E N A T I O N S
C R O C O D I L E D U N D E E
L O V E M E L O V E M Y D O G
```

12

```
A I R G U I T A R . . C O C A
S N O O P D O G G . L A P A Z
T E S T A T O R S . A M E M O
A R I . T A T E . . Z O N E .
I R E S . G E E . A Y M A R A
R O T C S . D R O P S I N O N
E R H A R D . S H O U L D N T
. E R I E S . M O S E S . .
F I R E L A N E . R A T H E R
A N I T A L O O S . N E U R O
S A V A N T . L E A . A T M S
. H E C K . . I N D S . C I I
C O T T A . I T S A P L A N E
O L E I N . T H E M A S S E S
M E R C . E S S A Y T E S T
```

13

```
C A S T L E G A T E S . W I T
A N T I O X I D A N T . E N O
L E O N P A N E T T A . B S A
. M O D E M S . E R A S E S
F I L E R S . D E R E L I C T
L A I R S . K I X . D I T T Y
U S E . S I N E W A V E S
. E N U M E R A T E
M I L E P O S T S . . S T N
R I G I D . N O S . C A M R Y
E D N O R T O N . S O B E I T
E D I T O R . D A M A T O
V A T . R U M M A G E S A L E
E Y E . E L A I N E B E N E S
S S S . M Y S T E R Y D A T E
```

14

```
. S T U D I O R E M A K E S
. J U N I O R P A R T N E R S
W A S T E N O T W A N T N O T
U N H . S T N S . . S E N D A
R U I N . S O F A S . D E E R
S A B E R . N O S E S . L D S
T R A V I S . R E A P S .
S Y R I A N S . A L L E G R O
. S T O O P . S A T E E N
A G S . A W R A P . T A N T E
S O A P . S T R O M . E D I E
S O C A L . O L E G . A R Y
A G R E E T O D I S A G R E E
Y O U S A I D I T N O T M E
S O M E P L A C E E L S E
```

15

```
S E I J I O Z A W A . M I S T
W A T E R C O L O R . O N C E
E S C R I T O I R E . N Y A H
E T H O S . M E N S S T O R E
. B E H I N D . H A U T E
A S N O . E N T O . A G R I
W H O A M I . O W N S . F S U
L E M M I N G . N O T P A S S
S E D . M E L O . C A U C U S
. R E P O . I N C H . B E E R
T A P A S . S E A E E L .
U G L Y A S S I N . R I A T A
R O U E . K A R A T E C H O P
O N M E . I D O D E C L A R E
W Y E S . P E N A L T Y B O X
```

16

```
  S T A T I O N S     A M P S
I H A D A D R E A M   B O I L
N E V E R A G A I N   B O Z O
T R E   A H A   L O R E N Z
O P R Y   O N D O P E   W A S
W A N E   A Z U R   S T A P H
      M O N A D S   P O L I O
B E T E L S     B U N K E D
E L A N D   S T A I N S
R A D I I   H O S S   I S N T
T S P   S C A T H E   L A I R
  T O W H O M   A C T   M E A
M I L E   U P I N T H E S K Y
A C E S   P O S T E R I O R S
P S S T     O H I D U N N O
```

17

```
C A S T A S I D E   B A G E L
A D H O M I N E M   E B O L I
T E A K E T T L E   G E T A T
E L L E N   E A R   S T O L I
S E E N   M A Y A S   S W A G
      P A R S L E Y   A M A
F E S T E R S   D E E P S E T
A V A I L S     P A T T I E
N A M E T A G   W I T S E N D
C P A   S L O S H E S
Y O R E   A F T E R   N A R C
T R I N A   O R E   H O M E R
H A T E D   R I D E A L O N E
A T A R I   I D L E H A N D S
T E N O N   T E E N A N G S T
```

18

```
I N C A H O O T S   R A M P S
A I R W O R T H Y   I M A R I
S T A N D F I R M   P E R I L
I R T   S E T I   R O S C O E
M A I D   O I L C A N   E R N
O T O E S   S L O T   B A T T
V E N I C E   A R E Y O U O K
    C A R D I N D E X
B L U E M O O N   R A C I S M
B A K R   D I M S   N A R C O
Q T R   D E T A I L   R E I N
P E A P O D   N E E T   L E I
I F I L L   P I G G Y B A N K
T E N E T   C L E A R A N C E
S E E D S   T A L L O R D E R
```

19

```
J O B L E S S   H O L Y W A R
A C R O B A T   O N L E A V E
S T U M B L E   W E A R I E D
M A B   S E V E N A M   T R E
I V E S   S I L O   A S S A Y
N E C K   W E A V E   L O G E
E S K I M O   L E G B O N E S
    J A M B   L O E W
N O N U S E R S   C L I M E S
I M A M   N O L T E   S A X E
T I P P I   K A H N   H D T V
P C T   T H E P I T S   I R E
I R I S H E R   G R E A S E R
C O M P A R E   H I T H O M E
K N E A D E D   S C A N N E D
```

20

```
Q U I D P R O Q U O   G E T A
U L T R A S O U N D   O X E N
I T S I N T H E R E   O P E N
V I A     L S A T   D O T O
E M T S   M A T T S   A S H Y
R A R A   A L E E   K N E E S
E T A T   S A D D L E D
D E P I C T     I N E V E R
    N O S C O R E   V E N I
J E S S E   O N A N   I N S T
A M A H   G N A W S   L E N Z
C O T E   A C T H     R A I
O T O E   S E E I F I C A R E
B E R T   E R A D I C A T E S
I S I S   S T R E S S T E S T
```

21

E	T	R	A	D	E			L	A	S	A	G	N	A
S	H	O	R	E	S		P	A	R	A	K	E	E	T
T	R	U	M	P	E	D	U	P	C	H	A	R	G	E
H	I	T	A	T		E	D	S	E	L		B	A	S
E	V	E	N	H	A	N	D	E	D		W	I	T	T
T	E	R	I		M	I	L	D		P	O	L	E	S
E	D	S		P	O	S	E		G	U	E	S	S	
		B	L	U	E	J	E	A	N	S				
	P	R	I	E	R		U	M	P	S		B	E	L
P	R	A	D	A		E	M	M	E		R	E	N	E
R	O	P	E		P	I	P	E	D	R	E	A	M	S
A	S	H		B	I	D	E	T		E	S	T	A	S
W	H	A	T	E	V	E	R	T	H	E	C	O	S	T
N	O	E	R	R	O	R	S		U	S	A	U	S	A
S	P	L	I	N	T	S		R	E	N	T	E	R	

22

C	U	D	D	L	E		T	A	R	P	A	P	E	R
A	N	O	R	A	K		A	G	U	I	L	E	R	A
M	I	M	I	N	G		R	U	S	T	L	E	R	S
S	T	I	N	K		R	E	S	T	S	T	O	P	
H	A	N	K		L	A	Y	S	I	S	T	E	R	S
A	R	A	M	E	A	N			A	B	A			
F	I	N	E	R	I	E	S			U	R	G	E	D
T	A	C		A	T	W	A	T	E	R		E	L	I
S	N	E	A	D		P	R	O	G	R	A	M	S	
		N	I	N			I	N	H	E	R	E	D	
P	O	L	I	C	E	D	O	G	S		M	I	R	A
A	V	E	M	A	R	I	A			H	E	N	R	I
M	A	M	A	B	E	A	R		R	U	N	G	I	N
P	L	O	T	L	I	N	E		I	L	D	U	C	E
A	S	N	E	E	D	E	D		G	A	S	P	E	D

23

	B	E	A	S	T			S	K	I	P		
	M	A	C	H	I	N	E	G	U	N	N	E	R
O	U	R	L	I	T	T	L	E	S	E	C	R	E	T
S	N	E	A	K	S		E	R	I	E		S	C	H
R	I	N	S	E		A	C	R	E		B	O	E	R
I	C	E	S		A	R	T	Y		G	E	N	I	E
C	I	C		W	H	I	R		C	L	E	A	V	E
	P	E	R	I	O	D	I	C	T	A	B	L	E	
R	A	S	H	L	Y		C	A	R	D		H	O	Y
E	L	S	O	L		G	R	A	S		E	Y	R	E
I	B	I	S		A	L	A	N		M	A	G	D	A
N	O	T		A	M	E	N		B	U	R	I	E	R
K	N	I	T	T	I	N	G	P	A	T	T	E	R	N
	D	E	S	I	G	N	E	R	J	E	A	N	S	
	S	E	T	A			S	A	R	G	E			

24

C	H	A	T	S	U	P		T	R	A	U	M	A	S
R	A	D	I	O	F	R	E	E	E	U	R	O	P	E
I	T	S	A	C	O	I	N	C	I	D	E	N	C	E
S	T	O	R	K		O	M	A	N	I		G	A	S
T	E	R	A		C	R	E	T	E		M	O	R	T
O	R	B		G	E	E	S	E		Q	U	O	T	A
		H	A	R	S	H			C	U	R	S	E	R
R	E	S	I	Z	E	S		C	H	O	K	E	R	S
E	X	U	D	E	S		L	A	I	T	Y			
D	I	N	E	R		T	I	S	C	H		P	S	I
S	T	D	S		C	H	E	S	S		C	O	A	T
O	F	O		A	L	A	N	A		C	H	I	L	I
N	E	W	A	G	E	M	O	V	E	M	E	N	T	S
J	E	N	N	I	F	E	R	A	N	I	S	T	O	N
A	S	S	E	N	T	S		S	E	X	T	A	N	T

25

C	A	P		S	W	A	I	N	S		A	S	S	T
A	B	E		T	A	L	B	O	T		M	A	H	I
M	I	D		O	N	L	I	N	E		A	N	O	N
P	L	A	C	I	D	O	D	O	M	I	N	G	O	
H	E	L	L	C	A	T			N	A	F	T	A	
O	N	E	A			S	T	A	N	D	S	O	U	T
R	E	D	I	G	S		A	L	O	U		R	P	M
			M	A	K	E	P	E	A	C	E			
D	E	C		M	I	K	E		M	E	N	S	C	H
E	X	A	M	I	N	E	R	S			N	O	R	A
S	I	T	O	N				P	O	P	U	L	U	S
	S	E	R	E	N	A	W	I	L	L	I	A	M	S
O	T	R	A		A	M	A	N	D	A		C	P	L
V	E	E	S		P	I	L	E	I	N		E	E	E
A	D	D	S		S	E	T	T	E	E		S	T	D

26

THINK

T	THOSE	TAD	IRONON
H	HIKES	ORR	SEEMTO
I	ITALS	SENATESEAT	
N	OPLACETOGO		
K	KNIT	AAH	LOGICAL

SOAR · ANI · ASAMI
CEL · ENAMORED
OUTSIDETHEBOX
ENLISTED · ABA
WEAVE · NYC · ARNO
ERNESTO · OIL · OMIT
OVERFLOWETH
DREAMWORKS · FARSI
EILEEN · MEA · FITIN
ECHOES · ARY · STANK

THINK

27

DALAILAMA · SNOBS
ERINMORAN · MOVIE
TETEATETE · ADAPT
ATRAS · UMBRELLA
CHER · LARIAT · TAP
HAS · DEJECT · PINA
LEVAR · ASNER
SYNONYM · SEXIEST
POORS · ANAIS
ISBN · VIGORS · CST
NEL · DISOWN · NOLA
SMEARSON · ROGER
TIMMY · MIAMIHEAT
ETAIL · EZIOPINZA
RENNY · REDLETTER

28

PASSBY · LASCASAS
ENTIRE · EDNABEST
STENOS · TOOLCASE
THEIDIOTBOX · PUG
LIPSYNCHED · MOAN
ELLE · DEES · VERGE
SLY · WEAR · JESTER
IRENECARA
TRACED · BAMA · MEG
SEVEN · PERE · MAYA
ORES · MILESTONES
NOR · DAVIDCARUSO
GUIDEDOG · ASIMOV
ATLENGTH · ATTIRE
SELFTEST · NEATEN

29

BEST · HITANDMISS
UVEA · IKIDYOUNOT
REAP · REDJASMINE
INSECT · YULE · TAP
ANIMA · LIRA · BINS
LODESTONE · DRACO
SWEATHOG · WOOLEN
SIAM · PORK
TUMULT · WARMEDUP
ENURE · HOLEINONE
ARNE · FUME · CHIDE
BAD · CODA · FEELER
AVAGARDNER · AIRE
GENERALLEE · REGS
SLEEPYEYED · TSOS

30

SLIPRINGS · TEAMS
LEMONTART · AXMAN
INALATHER · CAPRA
DOME · GEEKCHIC
BRANT · HONKYTONK
YENTA · URGE · ARAB
APPLYTO · SARA
RUT · EEL · HUG · EAR
ANIT · SAGETEA
TINA · EBAN · ADAMS
ROCKSTARS · RANAT
ANTEHALL · SONO
CRUSE · LASTSTRAW
EERIE · ONAVERAGE
SPENT · ODDSMAKER

31

E	Y	E	L	A	S	H	■	■	U	N	S	A	I	D
S	O	D	A	S	H	O	P	■	R	E	P	I	N	E
C	H	I	P	P	E	W	A	■	B	O	A	R	D	S
R	O	T	S	■	E	T	Y	M	A	■	S	P	I	T
O	H	O	■	P	R	I	S	O	N	S	■	L	A	I
W	O	R	S	E	■	M	A	N	■	A	G	A	I	N
■	■	A	P	R	E	T	T	Y	P	E	N	N	Y	■
■	D	A	Y	S	O	F	T	H	E	W	E	E	K	■
T	E	N	N	I	S	L	E	S	S	O	N	■	■	■
A	S	S	O	C	■	I	N	N	■	O	A	T	H	S
N	E	W	■	O	N	E	T	O	E	D	■	R	E	O
T	R	E	S	■	I	S	I	T	I	■	S	U	L	U
A	T	R	I	S	K	■	O	I	L	L	A	M	P	S
R	E	T	A	K	E	■	N	C	A	A	G	A	M	E
A	R	O	M	A	S	■	■	E	T	H	A	N	E	S

32

S	P	A	C	E	C	A	D	E	T	S	■	A	S	H
N	O	T	E	L	L	M	O	T	E	L	■	R	T	E
O	R	A	L	H	I	S	T	O	R	Y	■	M	A	S
B	O	X	■	I	O	T	A	■	M	E	T	E	R	S
S	U	I	T	■	S	E	G	A	■	R	O	N	D	O
■	S	A	U	D	■	L	E	M	S	■	M	I	A	S
■	■	R	A	J	■	S	A	L	T	B	A	T	H	■
G	A	G	A	R	I	N	■	T	O	U	R	N	E	Y
I	L	L	N	E	V	E	R	■	W	B	A	■	■	■
R	O	A	D	■	E	W	E	S	■	B	D	R	M	■
L	E	R	O	I	■	S	F	P	D	■	Y	E	O	H
Y	V	E	T	T	E	■	R	I	E	L	■	G	R	O
M	E	D	■	A	S	I	A	N	F	U	S	I	O	N
A	R	A	■	L	A	V	I	E	E	N	R	O	S	E
N	A	T	■	L	I	O	N	T	R	A	I	N	E	R

33

A	P	E	S	■	J	A	B	B	A	■	I	F	F	Y
D	R	A	T	■	O	T	R	O	S	■	D	O	L	E
D	O	R	A	T	H	E	E	X	P	L	O	R	E	R
O	P	T	I	O	N	■	S	C	I	E	N	C	E	S
N	E	H	R	U	■	P	L	A	C	A	T	E	■	■
S	L	Y	■	R	E	A	I	R	■	S	K	O	A	L
■	■	F	I	T	I	N	■	M	E	N	U	D	O	■
D	E	B	A	S	E	D	■	I	M	H	O	T	E	P
E	X	A	L	T	S	■	E	N	D	O	W	■	■	■
P	E	P	S	I	■	U	N	T	I	L	■	J	E	D
■	■	T	E	N	A	N	T	S	■	D	E	E	R	E
S	P	I	T	F	I	R	E	■	P	E	R	M	I	T
C	U	S	T	O	M	E	R	S	E	R	V	I	C	E
O	P	T	O	■	T	E	E	U	P	■	I	M	A	C
W	U	S	S	■	O	L	D	I	E	■	N	A	S	T

34

A	P	T	■	P	A	R	■	■	S	P	I	R	A	L
L	A	H	D	I	D	A	H	■	L	O	N	E	L	Y
I	N	E	U	R	O	P	E	■	A	R	C	S	I	N
C	A	S	C	A	R	A	S	■	S	T	A	T	E	N
E	M	I	T	T	E	R	S	■	H	E	M	A	N	■
■	A	S	S	E	R	T	■	R	E	N	E	G	E	S
■	■	■	S	I	D	E	S	T	R	E	E	T	■	■
L	A	N	E	S	■	S	E	A	■	S	A	S	S	Y
I	C	E	S	K	A	T	E	R	S	■	■	■	■	■
B	E	T	T	E	R	S	■	M	O	P	S	U	P	■
■	S	P	I	L	T	■	B	A	R	R	A	G	E	S
H	O	R	M	E	L	■	A	M	B	U	L	A	N	T
A	V	I	A	T	E	■	L	E	A	N	O	N	M	E
R	E	C	T	O	S	■	I	N	T	E	N	D	E	R
P	R	E	E	N	S	■	■	T	E	D	■	A	N	N

35

Q	U	I	N	T	U	P	L	E	T	■	A	T	A	D
T	H	R	E	E	S	C	O	R	E	■	F	I	F	I
R	O	M	A	N	E	S	Q	U	E	■	I	N	T	R
S	H	A	R	P	S	■	U	P	M	A	R	K	E	T
■	■	■	L	A	P	A	T	■	B	E	E	R	Y	■
I	T	A	L	Y	■	I	T	S	O	N	■	R	A	J
S	A	R	I	■	W	E	S	■	B	E	I	T	S	O
U	N	A	R	M	E	D	■	F	O	R	S	O	O	K
S	C	R	E	E	N	■	M	A	E	■	L	Y	R	E
P	O	E	■	O	T	O	E	S	■	C	A	S	T	S
E	L	B	O	W	■	P	A	T	C	H	■	■	■	■
C	O	R	P	S	M	E	N	■	L	I	G	A	T	E
T	R	E	E	■	O	N	T	H	E	R	O	P	E	S
S	E	E	D	■	O	U	T	O	F	P	R	I	N	T
O	D	D	S	■	S	P	O	R	T	S	P	A	G	E

36

P	A	S	T	A	S	A	L	A	D	■	T	S	P	S
A	R	M	O	R	P	L	A	T	E	■	W	E	R	T
D	E	E	P	S	E	A	T	E	D	■	O	N	E	A
S	A	W	T	E	E	T	H	■	U	N	E	A	S	Y
■	■	■	E	N	D	E	■	I	C	E	D	T	E	A
B	O	N	N	I	E	■	E	M	E	R	G	E	N	T
A	P	U	■	C	R	E	M	E	■	D	E	P	T	H
C	E	D	E	■	S	L	A	T	S	■	D	A	D	O
K	R	I	S	S	■	M	I	A	T	A	■	G	A	M
P	A	S	T	O	R	A	L	■	R	I	B	E	Y	E
E	S	T	E	F	A	N	■	C	A	M	O	■	■	■
D	E	C	L	A	W	■	R	O	T	E	N	O	N	E
A	R	A	L	■	B	O	O	K	E	D	I	T	O	R
L	I	M	E	■	A	B	N	E	G	A	T	O	R	S
S	A	P	S	■	R	E	A	D	Y	T	O	E	A	T

37

I	B	E	F	O	R	E	E	■	C	D	R	O	M	S
R	E	D	D	F	O	X	X	■	A	I	R	B	U	S
I	T	S	A	F	A	C	T	■	M	E	R	E	S	T
S	H	E	A	■	N	E	R	V	E	S	■	Y	E	S
H	E	L	P	S	■	P	A	I	R	E	D	■	■	■
■	■	■	P	L	A	T	■	P	A	L	O	M	A	R
L	U	B	R	I	C	A	N	T	■	■	M	O	N	A
A	T	O	O	T	H	F	O	R	A	T	O	O	T	H
M	A	R	V	■	■	T	H	E	S	T	A	T	E	S
S	H	E	A	T	H	E	■	A	T	O	R	■	■	■
■	■	■	L	E	A	R	N	T	■	P	I	P	P	A
A	D	D	■	E	N	C	A	M	P	■	G	A	L	L
B	E	R	E	T	S	■	N	E	E	D	A	N	A	P
C	L	I	C	H	E	■	A	N	N	O	T	A	T	E
S	E	Q	U	E	L	■	S	T	T	H	O	M	A	S

38

F	R	A	N	Z	K	A	F	K	A	■	N	A	T	S
L	I	M	E	S	T	R	E	E	T	■	E	T	U	I
I	C	E	C	A	S	T	L	E	S	■	E	T	N	A
T	E	N	K	■	■	P	I	P	E	D	R	E	A	M
E	D	D	■	S	P	A	N	I	A	R	D	S	■	■
■	■	S	H	A	P	E	N	■	C	O	T	T	A	■
D	I	S	P	O	S	E	S	■	P	A	W	S	A	T
A	L	T	E	R	E	R	■	B	A	R	E	T	T	A
H	E	R	E	T	O	■	C	A	R	T	L	O	A	D
S	T	A	D	T	■	P	A	R	C	E	L	■	■	■
■	■	P	R	O	T	E	S	T	E	R	■	C	A	M
D	O	P	E	N	A	N	C	E	■	■	C	I	T	I
A	V	I	A	■	S	T	A	N	L	A	U	R	E	L
V	E	N	D	■	S	A	R	D	I	N	E	C	A	N
E	R	G	S	■	E	X	A	S	P	E	R	A	T	E

39

H	I	T	P	A	R	A	D	E	■	A	W	A	R	E
E	C	H	I	N	A	C	E	A	■	S	I	N	E	W
R	E	A	L	I	T	I	E	S	■	S	C	O	N	E
D	R	I	L	L	I	N	S	T	R	U	C	T	O	R
■	■	■	B	I	N	G	■	S	A	R	A	H	■	■
R	E	H	U	N	G	■	L	I	K	E	N	E	S	S
I	M	A	G	E	■	T	I	D	E	S	■	R	A	T
S	I	N	S	■	Z	O	N	E	D	■	P	Y	L	E
E	L	K	■	T	A	P	E	R	■	W	O	O	E	R
R	E	Y	N	O	L	D	S	■	C	O	L	U	M	N
■	■	P	I	K	E	R	■	M	A	U	L	■	■	■
S	P	A	C	E	S	A	T	E	L	L	I	T	E	S
T	E	N	O	N	■	W	O	R	L	D	W	A	R	I
A	N	K	L	E	■	E	R	G	O	N	O	M	I	C
B	A	Y	E	D	■	R	O	E	N	T	G	E	N	S

40

J	A	C	K	K	N	I	F	E	■	I	D	E	A	L
A	L	A	N	L	O	M	A	X	■	S	O	C	K	O
V	A	R	I	E	G	A	T	E	■	B	A	S	I	E
A	B	A	T	E	■	B	I	G	O	N	■	E	H	S
M	A	V	S	■	L	U	G	E	D	■	G	I	S	■
A	M	A	■	B	E	M	U	S	E	S	■	A	T	E
N	A	N	T	E	S	■	E	I	T	H	E	R	O	R
■	■	O	N	T	V	■	S	O	O	T	■	■	■	■
M	A	D	E	I	R	A	S	■	J	O	C	O	S	E
A	X	E	■	N	A	V	A	J	O	S	■	L	E	V
R	O	T	■	D	A	V	E	Y	■	M	I	C	E	■
A	L	E	■	D	E	V	A	S	■	L	E	V	E	R
C	O	N	D	O	■	O	N	T	H	E	S	I	D	E
A	T	T	I	C	■	O	N	E	O	N	O	N	E	S
S	L	E	E	K	■	M	A	R	E	S	N	E	S	T

41

```
S T D E N I S ■ P O P T O P S
N I C E O N E ■ S U R E B E T
E M U L A T E ■ S T E L L A R
E E N ■ M E R C ■ O G L A L A
■ T I S ■ L E A D F O O T E D
T O T H E ■ D S O S ■ F E D S
A G E O L D ■ H T T P ■ ■ ■
G O D E L E S C H E R B A C H
■ ■ ■ O D O R ■ P O O R A T
A B M S ■ I D O L ■ B A R B S
T R E E S C A P E S ■ R E S ■
L I N G U A ■ S A L E ■ S T A
A D D U P T O ■ D I G I T A L
S L E E P E R ■ E M I N E N T
T E R S E S T ■ R E S E E D S
```

42

```
J O S H E D ■ J E R O B O A M
A P P E A R ■ I S A B E L L A
C E L E R Y ■ M O B I L I T Y
K R I L L ■ Z E T A S ■ V A N
F E N S ■ T E N E T ■ M I R O
I T T ■ R Y D E R ■ Y E A S T
S T E P U P ■ Z I P P Y ■ ■
H A R R I E D ■ C U R E A L L
■ ■ I N B O X ■ P E R D U E
P O E M S ■ V E E P S ■ R C A
U R S A ■ G E R R Y ■ P E R P
N I P ■ C O C O A ■ M O N E Y
J O R J A F O X ■ L A M A Z E
A L I E N A T E ■ A M E L I A
B E T T E R E D ■ V A S S A R
```

43

```
A C E R B ■ S P A R ■ A F A R
L A N A I ■ R O U E ■ R I D E
P R O D S ■ S T R I C T L A W
S P L I T S ■ E A C H ■ M M E
■ ■ O R K A N ■ H E P C A T
D I S C O U N T S ■ A R A ■
I O T A ■ A S I A ■ P O R E S
S W O R D S W A L L O W E R S
C A R B O ■ E L A L ■ R E A R
■ Y O N ■ R E D A L E R T S
H O B N O B ■ N A M E S ■ ■
O O O ■ R A C E ■ A T T L E E
W H A T S M O R E ■ S L U M P
S E R B ■ B E G S ■ G E N I E
O D D S ■ I D Y L ■ O R A T E
```

44

```
S E A L I N ■ S C R I P T S
A L B I N O S ■ P H A R A O H
P I C T U R E ■ E U T E R P E
I N T H R E E ■ R M S ■ I S A
D A V E E G G E R S ■ M E E T
■ ■ ■ R E L Y ■ F E T C H
■ B E R S E R K ■ C U R A R E
T O I L E T S ■ C A J O L E D
A N D E R S ■ Z A N I E S T ■
P A E S E ■ P A R A ■ ■ ■
A P R S ■ M A K E A S C E N E
S A D ■ G O B ■ E N A B L E R
B R O K E R S ■ R I N G S I N
A T W O R S T ■ S T A B I L E
R E N A M E S ■ E A S E L S
```

45

```
■ T H A T S O K ■ C L A P S ■
T H E M A I N E ■ H I R E O N
R E P A R T E E ■ A R M A D A
A B C ■ T E M P O R E ■ C O Y
D E A L ■ D O N U T ■ F E M S
E S T E S ■ R O N ■ M A N I A
■ ■ ■ S W E E T C H A R I T Y
R A I S E S T H E S T A K E S
O L D F A S H I O N E D ■ ■ ■
B L E A T ■ I N F ■ R A J A H
B E A T ■ A N G S T ■ Y U L E
E L L ■ B U G B E A R ■ T I A
R U I N E D ■ A N T E A T E R
S I S I S I ■ C S T U D E N T
■ A M T O O ■ K E Y P A D S
```

46

```
M A K E S A G R E A T G I F T
E D I T O R I A L W R I T E R
G E N E R A L D E L I V E R Y
A L G ■ A B A S E S ■ ■ E R R
B I T E R S ■ ■ ■ A N A I S
I N U S E ■ D E P O S I T E D
T E T E ■ L I V E L I N E S S
■ ■ ■ L O V E S E T ■ ■ ■
S P A R E P A R T S ■ E L E A
E A S E M E N T S ■ B R A Y S
M I S T S ■ ■ ■ S E N S E S
■ S O I ■ A C O R N S ■ T H U
G A R R I S O N K E I L L O R
E N T E N T E C O R D I A L E
L O S E S O N E S T E M P E R
```

47

```
J I F F Y ■ I D E A ■ N O B S
A M O C O ■ N U N N ■ B U O Y
C I R C U M N A V I G A T O R
O N T ■ R A I L ■ S P E R M
B E E B ■ R E C D ■ A R I E
■ ■ O H S ■ I U D ■ ■ G R E
C L O S E B U T N O C I G A R
P U R C H A S I N G A G E N T
O N T H E R A Z O R S E D G E
S C H ■ S I E ■ O A T
■ H O D S ■ R N A S ■ A Q U I
■ E D E N S ■ S U E Z ■ U S P
M O O N L I G H T S O N A T A
I N X S ■ N A I R ■ O A S E S
A S Y E ■ E S P Y ■ T W I N S
```

48

```
A L D A ■ S C A G ■ ■ L U F T
F O O T L O O S E ■ B E T A S
T I N H E L M E T ■ U N T I E
A N T E S U P ■ W A R I E R
■ ■ A L T O ■ A L T E R S
D I A R I E S ■ R M O N T H S
A C U T E S T ■ M A N T R A P
W A N ■ ■ ■ ■ ■ I K E
E N T I C E D ■ S C A L P E L
S T I M U L I ■ A R T I E S T
■ S E P S I S ■ N E O N ■
■ E M O T E S ■ R E N T A L S
L E A S E ■ E Y E P I E C E S
T I M E R ■ C A M E C L E A N
S T E S ■ T H O R ■ S S R S
```

49

```
O L D W H A T S H E R N A M E
Y O U H A V E N O C H O I C E
S A D O M A S O C H I S T I C
■ L E S S ■ ■ H O N E ■
■ S H E L ■ ■ ■ E R G S
E K E ■ A S F O R ■ R U N
R E A D S T H E R I O T A C T
N E V E R H A D A C H A N C E
S T E P S O N O N E S T O E S
T E T ■ L E N T S ■ L E T
■ R O A M ■ ■ ■ R O A D
■ C A R B ■ L O O N ■
O N E T H I N G A T A T I M E
A U R O R A A U S T R A L I S
S T A R E S I N T O S P A C E
```

50

```
C O C O A B E A N S ■ S H A H
O R A N G E T R E E ■ C A T E
O N T H E S T A G E ■ A N T A
P O T E N T A T E ■ O R D E R
■ ■ R T E ■ ■ V I O L I S T
C A S ■ R D A S ■ C H A N T S
A N T S Y ■ E C C E ■ T H E E
S N A P ■ T O I L S ■ T A D A
T A I L ■ I N F O ■ P I N T S
A B R A D E ■ I T E R ■ D O E
S E C T O R S ■ S E M ■
P L A T H ■ C E S T S I B O N
E L S E ■ R A D I A L T I R E
L E E R ■ G L I T T E R A T I
L E S S ■ S E T S E Y E S O N
```

51

```
B A D E G G S   C A R P E T S
E Q U E R R Y   O B E L I S K
G U L L I E S   M A Z U R K A
S A Y S M E   S E S A M E S T
      E N M E S H
A L T A   B E R I   P A T S Y
M A I N T E N A N C E F R E E
A L L T H A T G L I T T E R S
N A T I O N A L A V E R A G E
A W A C S   L I S I   A D E S
      B L O T C H
A S W E L L A S   D I L A T E
S H O R E U P   J U R Y B O X
T E R R I E S   U T E R I N E
O D D S A R E   G Y R A T E S
```

52

```
A T T H E O P E R A   E P H S
C R A Y O L A B O X   S L A P
H O L E S I N O N E   T E R R
O M E N   N I N   L A D I D A
O P R A H   C I S S Y   A L I
S E S   A L B E E   R O D I N
      A U G U S T   G E N E
H A N D S E T   I M P O S E D
A M O I   T E N T E D
D O N T S   O L M A N   C P L
A R F   D A N N O   N E A L E
S E A L I N   O T S   R E A S
E T T E   A E R I A L I S T S
A T A N   I N T O X I C A T E
T O L D   S C E N E T H R E E
```

53

```
A T A   U S A F   S H A N I A
G O D S P E L L   R E C O I L
A P A S S A G E T O I N D I A
N A P E   I D O   S E E
A Z T   M B A   E M T   P P S
    S A O   L A O   B O R O
E V I L U N D E R T H E S U N
R E T U R N O F T H E K I N G
E N E M Y A T T H E G A T E S
C A R P   R D S   R E A
T E A   F D A   E S L   S H E
    T I E   S P A   R O A M
R A I S E T H E T I T A N I C
A P O L L O   S U R E F I R E
H O N E S T   O P E N   A Y E
```

54

```
S E S T E T   T A J M A H A L
E X H A L E   S Q U I R E L Y
A P E M E N   Q U I C K I E S
B E L L E   B U I C K   F R I
O L L A   M E A N Y   L E O N
A L A   Z O R R O   V E R S E
R E C H A R G E   M I T
D E S E X E S   N U D I S T S
      L I S   P A R E N T A L
O A S I S   R O D E O   A M A
X B O X   R E M I X   A R A M
C U R   Q A T A R   M A T R I
A S T E R O I D   H E R O I N
R E I N S U R E   A M O U N T
T R E S T L E S   W O N T D O
```

55

```
H A V E N T W E M E T   G S T
O N E M O R E T I M E   E P I
W A R T S A N D A L L   S A N
A H A   Y I N   Y E A S T Y
R E N D   N E M O   X D O U T
D I D O S   R O M A   H E L I
  M A G E E   U N C L E S A M
      G A G W R I T E R
J P M O R G A N   S E E M S
A R A N   O W E S   S T U N S
M I N E S   A D E E   O N E A
P O N D E R   E X S   D E T
A R E   R O B E R T P E A R Y
C T R   B L A D E R U N N E R
K O S   S L A M D A N C E R S
```

56

```
G E L L E D . . A B L E S T
A Q U A V I T . C R I M E A
S U M M O N E R . R O S I N S
J A P A N E S E . E A T S A T
E T E R N I T Y . A D E S T E
T E R R E N C E . G E N I E S
. . . A S B E S T O S . . .
. C O S T S . A S T O N . .
. M A I T R E D S . . . . .
V A L L E E . R E D S T A R T
I R I S E S . A P O L O G I A
A L B E R T . W A T E R L O O
C E R E A L . L I T E R A T I
O N E D G E . R E V E R E S
M E S S E S . . D E S E R T
```

57

```
S T O M A C H A C H E . S T E
T E X A S H O L D E M . O R R
I N C I N E R A T E D . R A N
N S A . O A R S . A S C I I
G E R M . T I K I . S C E N E
S R T A S . D A R K H O R S E
. . . D U B . N E E . R E E L
G L E E F U L . D E S E R T S
O O N A . R A G . P U P .
D V D B U R N E R . M A D A M
S E G E R . D R I P . D R N O
G R A T A . M F R S . O K S
I B M . N A T A L I E C O L E
F O E . U P O N E S A L L E Y
T Y S . S T R E S S T E S T S
```

58

```
. F E L L S . T H E C O M I C
B O R E A L . H O N O L U L U
B R O N Z E M E D A L L I S T
L A S T Y E A R . M E A R A .
. . . . P I E C E S . . .
F L A T D E N I A L . R A J A
R E P A I R I N G . V E N A L
A I R M A S S . E C O C I D E
G L O P S . S O D A W A T E R
S A N A . P U S H E S P A S T
. . . A R E T E S . . .
. S E A T O . L A U R E L E D
T E R R I B L E T R A G E D Y
A L L C L E A R . A Y E A Y E
M A E S T R O S . S E R F S
```

59

```
C B E R S . . S C A P U L A
H E G E L . L A I D O P E N
E R O D E . G O L D E N R O D
S E T T E . L O V E S C E N E
S T R I P P O K E R . H A I R
. S I D E A R M S . H O R N S
. P E R S I A . F O S S E
. . S T A N C E S . .
. C A G E Y . O R A T E D
N O T I T . W H I T E N E D
I R O N . G R A S S S T A I N
C O N G A L I N E . S E D G E
K N E E B E N D S . I N S E T
E A R R I N G S . N T E S T
L E S S E N S . G E T T Y
```

60

```
S P O R T S B R A S . D I S H
H A V E A H E A R T . O N T O
I T A L I A N I C E . T S A R
M E L A L L E N . P U T O N S
. . . T O O T . C O L L U D E
A F F I R M . C O N N E C T S
P A R O S . J U L I A . I R E
P L A N . R O B O T . C A I N
A L T . C E D A R . N A N A S
R E E L E D I N . J O S T L E
I N R A N G E . R U T H .
T I N D E R . L A S T M I L E
I D I D . A N E S T H E S I A
O O Z E . P O E T L A R I A T
N L E R . E S S A Y T E S T S
```

61

```
S P E E D D A T I N G ■ O R T
L A T E A R R I V A L ■ N E H
E L E C T R I C E Y E ■ T B A
W E S ■ S U E S ■ S A C H E T
■ ■ C U T S ■ P A S T E L S
U N H U N H ■ S A Y O N A R A
S E A R S ■ L I N E N ■ L E M
A S I S ■ V O T E R ■ N E B O
I S R ■ M A R E S ■ R A R E R
R E P A I R E D ■ G E N T L E ■
F L I T S I N ■ G A M S ■ ■
O R E L S E ■ D A Y O ■ S A D
R O C ■ I T C O U L D N T B E
C D E ■ N A T A L I E C O L E
E E S ■ G L A S S B L O W E R
```

62

```
C A P E C O D ■ ■ S T A B S
O V E R U S E S ■ S T O R E S
H E R G R A C E ■ M A R T E N
E R S ■ E G O T R I P P E R S
R A P ■ R E C O I L L E S S ■
E G I S ■ S T U D I E D ■
D E R A T ■ S T E N T O N ■
■ D E L I S ■ G O N E R
■ D E M O T I C ■ N E W E L
■ S E N O R A S ■ T R U E
■ P I C C A L I L L I ■ E N S
T A L L A N D S L I M ■ G I S
A S S E R T ■ E S P O S I T O
C H A R D S ■ S T O N E M E N
T A S K S ■ ■ O N A G E R S
```

63

```
I S S U E A M A N I F E S T O
T R A N S L I T E R A T I O N
H O L D A L L T H E C A R D S
E S S O ■ A A H ■ D E L U D E
■ ■ D Y N E S ■ P S T
B A L L O ■ L E T H E
I N A U G U R A T I O N D A Y
A C H I L L E S T E N D O N S
S E R G E A N T O R O U R K E
■ I G N I S ■ R E F E R
T N N ■ N E R D S
R O U T E D ■ C O O ■ I K O N
A R T U R O T O S C A N I N I
C A S T I R O N S K I L L E T
T H O U S A N D I S L A N D S
```

64

```
T E A R G A S ■ F I E S T A S
A A M I L N E ■ A N D O R R A
P R E F A C E ■ R U D Y A R D
I F N E C E S S A R Y ■ D O S
N U R S E S A I D E ■ L E G O
S L A T ■ T W A S ■ R O D A N
■ P O E M ■ T I R I N G
C O W B I R D ■ M O M E N T S
O N I O N S ■ P A W S ■
R E L A Y ■ B U R N ■ A L G A
S O D S ■ M I N I M A L A R T
I N C ■ B A B Y M O N I T O R
C O A L O I L ■ B U G B I T E
A N T O I N E ■ A S S I S T S
N E S T L E S ■ S E T S H O T
```

65

```
T I M E W A R P ■ T A C T I C
E V A M A R I E ■ A M A R N A
J A L F R E D P R U F R O C K
A N O ■ T A E B O ■ M I L L E
N I N A S ■ S O L D ■ B L O W
O V E N ■ J O Y O U S ■ O V A
■ T H E U S ■ R A P P E L
C I N E A S T ■ D E K L E R K
R O O S T S ■ P O S S E ■
A L T ■ H E L L A S ■ N E I L
C A S E ■ L A O S ■ S A N T E
K N O C K ■ I S I A H ■ S S E
S T F R A N C I S X A V I E R
U H A U L S ■ V A L H A L L A
P E R S I A ■ E Y E S L E F T
```

66

```
. . C A N A L . B E S T S .
K E R O S E N E . I N L A W .
A L A N K I N G . A L I K E .
B I G T I M E R . S A M E A S
U S E R N A M E . T R I S T E
L A S A G N E S . I G E T I T
. . . A T P R E S E N T . . .
P I A S T E R . R E S T A G E
U N D E R R A T E . . . . . .
S T A L I N . O D O M E T E R
A R M A N I . P A L O M I N O
N E S S I E . S T I L E T T O
. P A S D E . P O N D E R E D
. I L I A L . O R D E R E R S
. D E E D S . T S A R S . . .
```

67

```
A B O R C . . M A Y B E N O T
S A N E R . B O N V O Y A G E
K R O N E . I T D E P E N D S
A G N E W . G I G S . . C E L
B R E W . S H O O . A R E N A
O A K . S O O N . A G E . . .
U P N . C U R T . S E N D S .
T H E R E S N O I I N T E A M
. S E I N E . D R A T . V I A
. . B E D . I A N S . I N T .
G L A S S . S S T S . B O T H
I O N . A H M E . V A U L T .
N O N P A R E I L . I S S U E
S P E A K E A S Y . S I L K S
U S E D C A R S . A S Y E T .
```

68

```
A M A Z E M E N T . J A R O D
L A T E L U N C H . E L E N I
F R O N T D O O R . R E S E T
R I M . O H S . O M I G O S H
E L A Y N E . I G O . A R T E
D Y N E . N O N S T A R T E R
O N T A P . L I N E S . S P Y
. . R O A D T E S T S . . . .
E D D . T U N I C . R U F U S
B E E F S T E A K S . V E N I
B A N A . O W L . P L A S M A
T R I C K S Y . V U E . T O M
I S S E I . O P E R A T I V E
D I O R S . R I N G D O V E S
E R N S T . K A T E S P A D E
```

69

```
DOG M A . V A M P S . DOG E A T DOG
CAT O N . A B E E T . S P R E E
C R I CAT O N I N E T A I L S
H A M P E R S . . C A L . . .
E L A L . T A R . R R A T E D
R E S O L E . A A U . B I T E
. . . T O R R I D . CAT S P A W
H U N CAT S A N D DOG S . S L Y
O H A R E . R I N G U P . . .
T O T O . H E N . I P E C A C
DOG H O U S E . G R E . S O L O
. . L A P . A B S O R B S
CAT C H A S CAT C H C A N . N E E
E V A D E . S I E G E DOG I T
R I D E S . T E R S E . S T S
```

70

```
S T O P C O C K . T S H I R T
E A S Y P O U R . H E E D E R
S M A L L F R Y . E T A L I I
T A K E . S T P . T A L O N S
E R A . A T B A T . V E T .
T A N S . D I O R S . V E D A
. . C R E N N A . G E T I T
A P H O T I C . I F O R O N E
S E E R S . A M N I O N . .
T R A N . F L I T E . A L T A
E S T . W I L D E . E R N .
R O W E R S . R A E . P N I N
I N A B I T . I S T H A T S O
S A V A T E . F E R O C I T Y
K E E N E D . F R E C K L E S
```

71

P	A	P	A	S	M	U	R	F		U	S	O	F	A
I	C	E	S	K	A	T	E	R		F	I	N	I	S
R	U	P	P	A	R	E	N	A		O	V	E	R	T
A	M	P	S		C	N	O	T	E		A	C	E	R
T	E	E		V	H	S		B	L	T		A	L	I
E	N	D		E	M	I		O	V	E	R	R	A	N
			H	E	A	L		Y	I	N	Y	A	N	G
A	B	O	A	R	D			S	P	A	T	E	S	
C	Y	C	L	O	N	E		S	P	A	N			
I	G	O	O	F	E	D		I	R	S		B	B	B
D	E	T		F	S	U		G	E	T		R	E	L
R	O	I	L		S	C	A	N	S		B	A	M	A
A	R	L	E	S		A	P	O	L	L	O	V	I	I
I	G	L	O	O		T	I	R	E	I	R	O	N	S
N	E	O	N	S		E	A	S	Y	T	O	S	E	E

72

S	C	R	A	P	E		P	O	S	T	C	A	R	D
T	I	E	D	I	N		L	I	M	A	O	H	I	O
E	V	A	D	E	D		A	L	A	N	L	A	D	D
P	I	N		R	E	I	N		R	O	T	T	E	D
C	L	I		C	A	N	T	A	T	A	S			
H	U	M	P	E	R	D	I	N	C	K		D	E	S
A	N	A	I	S		I	N	G	A		G	R	I	T
N	I	T	E		W	A	G	E	R		R	A	G	A
G	O	E	S		I	N	T	L		T	I	G	H	T
E	N	D		O	N	A	H	I	G	H	N	O	T	E
			E	M	I	N	E	N	C	E		N	O	T
O	M	E	L	E	T		S	A	L	T		F	U	R
B	I	G	A	R	A	D	E		E	R	M	I	N	E
I	C	A	N	T	L	I	E		F	I	E	R	C	E
S	A	N	D	A	L	E	D		S	P	R	E	E	S

73

M	R	B	O	J	A	N	G	L	E	S		B	B	S
A	I	R	F	O	R	C	E	O	N	E		A	R	T
P	L	A	Y	S	A	R	O	U	N	D		N	O	R
S	E	G	O			L	I	E	A	W	A	K	E	
		R	A	M	B	O	S		N	O	N	E	T	
S	P	E	E	D	B	A	G			M	A	R	C	
T	A	V		M	A	R	Y	J		H	A	R	S	H
A	R	I	D	E	S	T		E	M	A	N	A	T	E
T	A	L	O	N		H	A	D	I	T		M	I	R
E	M	I	L			W	I	N	E	S	A	P	S	
H	O	N	E	S		D	E	S	E	R	T			
O	U	T	D	A	T	E	S			U	F	O	S	
U	N	E		N	I	C	O	L	A	S	C	A	G	E
S	T	N		D	N	A	M	O	L	E	C	U	L	E
E	S	T		S	A	F	E	T	Y	Z	O	N	E	S

74

G	L	E	E	C	L	U	B		A	L	B	E	D	O
F	O	X	G	L	O	V	E		B	E	A	R	U	P
O	R	I	G	I	N	A	L		D	A	T	I	V	E
R	E	S	H	O	E			I	S	U	R	E	C	A	N
C	A	T	E	S		J	E	L	L		A	I	L	S
E	L	S	A		L	E	V	I		A	U	D	I	E
			D	I	A	Z	E	P	A	M		L	E	A
G	E	T	S	O	R	E		S	U	F	F	E	R	S
U	G	O		L	A	B	O	H	E	M	E			
N	O	L	T	E		E	C	O	L		A	H	A	B
S	M	E	W		F	L	E	D		P	R	I	M	E
M	A	R	I	P	O	S	A		M	E	S	S	R	S
I	N	A	N	E	R		N	E	U	R	O	S	I	S
T	I	N	G	E	D		U	L	T	I	M	A	T	E
H	A	T	E	R	S		S	K	E	L	E	T	A	L

75

G	R	A	N	O	L	A	B	A	R		M	V	P	S
R	E	N	O	N	E	V	A	D	A		C	A	L	I
E	V	I	T	A	P	E	R	O	N		S	N	A	G
N	O	M	E		E	N	R	A	G	E		U	S	N
A	K	A		R	U	I	N		N	E	A	T	O	
D	E	L	T	S		E	O	N		V	O	T	E	R
E	S	S	A	Y	S		S	I	N	E	C	U	R	E
			T	R	A	P		E	R	L	E			
O	L	D	T	I	M	E	R		C	O	N	T	R	A
P	A	U	L	A		T	E	D		P	E	R	E	S
E	B	S	E	N		S	T	U	D			A	D	S
N	E	T		S	A	T	I	R	E		B	I	D	E
B	L	U	E		H	O	R	O	S	C	O	P	E	R
A	L	P	S		E	R	E	C	T	O	R	S	E	T
R	E	S	T		M	E	S	S	E	N	G	E	R	S

76

```
S H E A R S   ■ S A W H O R S E
N E X T U P   ■ I C E Q U E E N
O R T E G A   ■ T H E S T A N D
W O R M S ■ C U E S ■ ■ E M T S
S N A P ■ G O A F T E R ■ ■ ■
■ ■ L O S E S T O ■ L E A P T
D N A ■ C A T E R ■ P A T I O
E A R N E R ■ ■ ■ F A R I N A
L T G E N ■ A P L U S ■ M E T
L O E W E ■ I R O N O R E ■ ■
■ ■ D I A M O N D ■ A T O B
A R T E ■ L E V I ■ C R O N E
P O O L S I D E ■ L I E D E R
S U S H I B A R ■ E N S I L E
E X H I B I T B ■ I Q T E S T
```

77

```
E Z P A S S   ■ L A T R O B E
L E E R A T   ■ R O T H I R A S
M A R I N E B I O L O G I S T
I L I E D ■ I P S A ■ A G E
R O S S I ■ B L E S S ■ I P O
A T H ■ E U L E R ■ L A N A I
■ ■ G R E Y ■ N O B A I L
L A P D O G S ■ J E W E L R Y
S N E E Z E ■ S E A N ■ ■
A S K T O ■ T I T L E ■ S I S
T W O ■ O P E N S ■ W H I N E
■ E E N ■ O N E K ■ S O L A R
M R T O A D S W I L D R I D E
S T E A D I E S ■ G A S C A N
G O A H E A D ■ A Y E A Y E
```

78

```
A B C D E F G ■ M A C R A M E
B O L O T I E ■ A L D O R A Y
O X I D A N T ■ N O T A O N E
U S M ■ S C H A A P ■ D U C T
N E A R ■ H O T L ■ S I E
D A T E D ■ T W I G ■ C E N S
S T E E L S ■ I V E H A D I T
■ ■ L I G H T E N U P ■ ■
H E R E I T I S ■ E N T A I L
O P E D ■ S T E P ■ G O N Z O
L I Z ■ ■ S N O B ■ R A Z E
S C O T ■ M O D U L E ■ P A S
T U N E D I N ■ T A R G E T S
E R E L O N G ■ E N M A S S E
R E D L E G S ■ R E A L T O R
```

79

```
T H E F O N Z ■ S T E I G ■
H E L L W E E K ■ A R E N O T
E A T A L O N E ■ R E N D E R
I R O N S ■ I N F I X ■ I S O
S E R ■ A T T O ■ B A H T
T R O Y ■ C H U R N ■ R I O T
■ ■ A P T ■ C A L L O N M E
A N A K I N S K Y W A L K E R
D E S K C O P Y ■ E M I ■ ■
J O S E ■ W A D E S ■ N A S L
O N E D ■ T E X T ■ F L U
I L S ■ Q B E R T ■ H A R U M
N A S H U A ■ B R A I N A G E
S M O R E S ■ Y A R D S I G N
■ P R E S S ■ S P E E D O S
```

80

```
P A L M ■ G I F T E D K I D S
O M O O ■ I N S I D E I N F O
L A C E ■ G U T T E R B A L L
E R A S ■ G R A I N ■ O L A V
M I L ■ A L E R ■ S I T E
I L L B R E D ■ D U C H E S S
C L A R E T ■ H U G O ■ ■
S O W O N E S W I L D O A T S
■ ■ A S H Y ■ Y E O M A N
I L P O S T O ■ U S R O U T E
N E A T ■ ■ U P C S ■ D E A
P E S O ■ P A R L E ■ D A R K
A L C O H O L B A N ■ A R T S
R E A L E S T A T E ■ B Y O B
T E L E P H O N E S ■ O A T Y
```

81

```
A B E V I G O D A ■ I D T A G
N I N E L I V E S ■ N A I V E
G O D S A V E T H E Q U E E N
O N U P ■ E R R O L ■ B O R E
L I R A S ■ T O R M E ■ N S F
A C E ■ L O O I E ■ A N E E L
■ ■ C O U N T ■ M R M O T O
C A P T U R E ■ C O M E N O W
O R I N G S ■ B O R A X ■ ■
S M A S H ■ M A L A R ■ A S L
T I N ■ S P I R O ■ K N U T E
U N O S ■ I S E R E ■ O T R A
M A K E A N E X A M P L E O F
E R E C T ■ R A D I O T U B E
S M Y T H ■ S M O L D E R E D
```

82

```
S P A C E C R A F T ■ A M O S
H E L L O H E L L O ■ M O L T
I N S I N U A T E S ■ O N M E
A T O M I C ■ W I R E T A P
■ B A K E D ■ R U B E N S
A R S O N ■ X I S ■ B A S R A
D O W N ■ P A S T E L ■ S I S
I L E ■ J A C C U S E ■ O V I
O L E ■ U N T A C K ■ M R E D
S E T O N ■ A R C ■ Z A I R E
A D E P T S ■ D O T E R ■
M O N T A N A ■ R A S S L E
I V E S ■ I N O C U L A T O R
G E R T ■ P I N A C O L A D A
O R S O ■ S T A T E T A X E S
```

83

```
B U T T H E N ■ J I G I S U P
E N R O U T E ■ O N A R O L L
S W I N G A T ■ I N G E N U E
T E P E E ■ S I N ■ E N O L A
B A L D ■ M A N E T ■ E R A S
E V E ■ W A L K M A N ■ A T E
T E X T I L E S ■ P A I N E D
■ U S E S ■ D I F F ■
B E I G E S ■ Z O O T S U I T
I Q S ■ R E B E C C A ■ P L Y
G U A T ■ X E N I A ■ F L O P
T I B E T ■ A O L ■ S L A V E
I N E R R O R ■ E T H A N E S
M E L R O S E ■ L I E I D L E
E S S A Y E R ■ Y E L L S A T
```

84

```
B R A D S H A W ■ P R I S M S
D E V I L I S H ■ A D R I A N
A V E M A R I A ■ C A S T R O
L E N ■ B E A T L E S ■ U A R
T N U T ■ E N S O R ■ H A N K
O G E E S ■ S T Y ■ B I T T E
N E S T L E ■ H A D A M E A L
■ H O R S E L E S S ■
F I R E B O M B ■ L I E S T O
O M A R S ■ E I N ■ E L L E R
R P M S ■ M A G I C ■ F O R D
G A P ■ M A R I N E R ■ G R E
I N A B I T ■ D O R A M A A R
V E N I C E ■ E N T R A N C E
E L T O R O ■ A S S E S S E D
```

85

```
A B O V E Z E R O ■ S E A L S
T U B E N O S E D ■ P L A I T
B E L L Y A C H E ■ L A R V A
A N I M A ■ I S L A N D E R
T O G A ■ J E R S E Y ■ W A G
S S E ■ P O L E A X ■ Z O L A
■ T A L K S ■ F E L I Z
S W E A R T O ■ L A T E F E E
Q A N D A ■ M O L L S ■
U R S A ■ S C A R A B ■ B A S
A W N ■ B A R R E N ■ G A W K
D E A D S P O T ■ O R T H O
C A R A T ■ W I K I P E D I A
A R E N A ■ D A R N I T A L L
R Y D E R ■ S N A K E E Y E S
```

86

S	T	E	P	F	A	T	H	E	R		M	A	N	S
N	I	N	E	O	N	E	O	N	E		A	M	O	I
A	T	T	E	N	D	A	N	T	S		N	O	T	E
P	L	E	N	T	Y	M	O	R	E		I	R	A	S
P	I	N	S			E	R	O	T	I	C	I	S	T
E	N	T		S	T	R	E	P		C	O	S	T	A
A	G	E	L	E	S	S		Y	V	E	T	T	E	S
			A	A	A			L	A	T				
A	N	T	W	E	R	P		T	A	X	I	C	A	B
S	E	A	L	A		R	I	O	D	E		L	T	R
S	U	P	E	R	H	E	R	O			S	O	T	O
I	T	I	S		O	P	E	R	A	M	U	S	I	C
G	R	O	S		H	A	N	D	C	A	M	E	R	A
N	A	C	L		O	R	I	E	N	T	A	T	E	D
S	L	A	Y		S	E	C	R	E	T	C	O	D	E

87

C	B	S	DUST	O	F	F	S		S	A	W	DUST
H	I	E	S		U	R	I	A	H		O	T	I	C
E	T	C	H		P	E	N	T	A		D	A	D	O
E	T	R	E		O	S	A	K	A		B	E	V	
C	H	E	E	S	E	S		H	O	R	M	O	N	E
H	E	C	T	O	R			T	R	I	E	R		
DUST	Y	S	P	R	I	N	G	F	I	E	L	D		
			P	O	L	I	T	I	C					
	I	N	T	E	R	S	T	E	L	L	A	R	DUST
C	R	E	E	D			C	E	L	E	B	S		
H	I	T	T	U	N	E	W	H	I	P	S	U	P
A	D	Z		P	E	N	N	E		H	O	S	E
L	I	E	S		A	D	O	B	E		A	L	T	E
K	U	R	T		L	I	V	E	N		S	E	E	D
DUST	M	O	P		S	T	A	R	DUST		D	R	Y

88

H	A	D		D	I	B	S		S	T	A	P	L	E	R
O	N	E	O	C	A	T		P	A	L	E	A	L	E
T	A	T	T	E	R	Y		A	R	B	O	R	E	D
T	H	E	E	D	G	E		S	T	E	P	D	A	D
E	E	N	S	I	E			A	R	L	E	N	E
S	I	T	O	N	I	T		E	N	T	E	R	O	N
T	M	E	N		N	A	I	L	S		S	S	R	S
				B	O	G							
N	I	L	S		E	O	S	I	N		M	O	S	H
O	N	A	T	E	A	R		N	O	T	A	L	I	E
W	A	G	I	N	G			N	I	K	O	L	A
W	R	A	N	G	L	E		C	H	E	E	R	E	D
H	U	S	K	I	E	R		L	E	S	S	O	N	S
A	S	S	E	N	T	S		A	R	T	I	S	T	E
T	H	E	R	E	S	T		R	O	O	T	O	U	T

89

M	A	Z	E	L	T	O	V		A	S	T	H	M	A
E	M	I	L	I	A	N	O		L	U	R	E	I	N
S	A	N	M	A	T	E	O		I	D	U	N	N	O
S	T	N		R	E	A	D	I	E	S		R	I	D
R	O	I	S		S	C	O	R	N		M	Y	M	Y
S	L	A	P	S		T	O	A		G	A	V	I	N
			R	I	B		E	Q	U	A	L	I	Z	E
F	I	B	O	N	A	C	C	I	S	E	R	I	E	S
I	N	N	U	E	N	D	O		O	L	A			
L	S	A	T	S		R	N	S		S	U	B	I	C
L	E	T	S		K	O	O	K	Y		X	E	N	A
I	C	U		J	A	M	M	I	E	S		T	E	R
N	U	R	S	E	R		I	T	S	A	L	I	V	E
G	R	A	H	A	M		C	O	W	H	I	D	E	S
S	E	L	E	N	A		S	W	E	L	T	E	R	S

90

B	E	F	O	R	E	T	H	E	O	T	H	E	R	S
I	T	A	L	I	A	N	A	L	P	H	A	B	E	T
G	I	R	L	F	R	O	M	I	P	A	N	E	M	A
D	E	M	I	T		T	A	C		D	O	R	A	G
O	N	C	E		B	E	N	I	N		I	L	I	E
S	N	L		B	U	S		T	U	G		E	N	D
	E	U	L	E	R		D	E	C	R	Y			
	B	E	A	R	D	E	D	L	A	D	Y			
	O	D	I	U	M		E	P	S	O	M			
U	N	A		S	T	N		H	U	E		D	O	L
S	O	P	S		O	K	R	A	S		B	E	N	E
B	R	I	T	T		T	A	S		S	A	L	T	S
A	M	E	R	I	C	A	N	S	T	U	D	I	E	S
N	I	C	O	T	I	N	E	L	O	Z	E	N	G	E
K	E	E	P	O	N	K	E	E	P	I	N	G	O	N

91

```
. B A N A N A S P L I T .
. M U S I C A L P I E C E S
B A S K E T B A L L T E A M S
A T T I C S . S A L T F R E E
B R I N E . S K Y S . L O R E
K O N G . P E A S . M O U S Y
A N G . S O A P . A R E T H A
. . G A L L E R I E S . . .
C L E R K S . N E R D . J O B
H I R E S . M I S S . C A R R
I N R E . G E N T . H O W I E
M E A N D E R S . S O R B E T
P U T T I N G U P A F R O N T
. P I E R R E L E N F A N T .
. C A K E S A N D A L E .
```

92

```
S H E B A N G . S T J A M E S
R O T A T O R . Y A R D A G E
T R U S T M E . M T S I N A I
A D D I S A B A B A . D I N S
S E E N . D E L I . V A C .
. . G D S . J O E I S U Z U
C O W E R . E A S Y A . R A P
F L O R E N Z Z I E G F E L D
O I L . S T I E S . R O D E O
S O F T S H O E . T A L .
. S H Y . P R E S . D I E M
R E B A . G I A N T P A N D A
O V A T I O N . G R A B B A G
B E N I T E Z . R A N L A T E
O L E S T R A . S P E E D E E
```

93

```
. S H A G C A R P E T S .
. S T E P T O T H E R E A R
C H A R L O T T E A M A L I E
H I N D U S . R A N A R A C E
A N D E S . Z A S U . I D O L
I B I D . D O C . T S E .
T O N . U I N T A . A S M A D
E N G A R D E . M I X T A P E
A E O N S . D A M M E . L P S
. . T A E . T A P . W A L K
H O P E . X M E N . H A Y E S
U R I C A C I D . G Y R A T E
T E L E V I S I O N P I L O T
. M E D I T E R R A N E A N .
. D E S E R T S T O R M .
```

94

```
. A S P C A . . C A M P E D
I N T E R N S . R E C A R V E
C O R R U G A T E D S T E E L
E D I T S . M I C E . A C R E
R E V E T . I N T . H O Y T
. S E R A . S T O A . A L O E
. . C R E E . B O R O N S
. C O M E U N D E R F I R E .
H A B E A S . G R A F . .
E L S A . E L L O . C O D S
P L O T . E A T . A W A C S
T A L C . S I S I . M E N A T
A H E A D O F S C H E D U L E
D A T S U N S . A E R O B A T
S N E E Z Y . S A N E R .
```

95

```
C B S . C O L T . U T A H A N
O R A T O R I O . N O S A L E
A U T O M A T E . C O S S E T
S N A P P L E . C O L I N .
T O N G A . B O N . S O L E
. U N I V E R S I T I E S
R A I N Y S E A S O N . D A S
E D S . M A R S A L A . E R A
T I O . E A S T G E R M A N Y
R E C O N C I L E D T O .
Y U R I . H O Y . I D E S T
. A L B A N . C A S E L A W
A R T E R Y . D O C T R I N E
C H E R I E . N O M I N A T E
T O S S E S . A L E C . S A D
```

96

```
T H E T H I N G I S ■ E N O W
S O C I A L C A L L ■ L O R I
A N O T H E R D A Y ■ I W O N
R E L O A N ■ ■ ■ E L A Y N E
■ ■ ■ S E W E R ■ A H O O T
C A S E ■ S E R U M S ■ U M A
E L M S T ■ B A B U S H K A S
A L A M O D E ■ I M E A N I T
S A L E M S L O T ■ S T O N E
E N L ■ C L O R I S ■ E W E R
F A T H A ■ S E N O R ■ ■ ■
I D I O T S ■ ■ R E G A L E
R A M S ■ U T N E R E A D E R
E L E E ■ R A G G E D Y A N N
S E R A ■ G O O G L Y E Y E S
```

97

```
A C T F O R ■ P R I C E T A G
M A H A L O ■ R I G H T A R M
O P E N E R ■ E C L E C T I C
R I C ■ G Y M S H O E S ■ ■
A T R A ■ A U T O S ■ S H H
L A U G H A T M E ■ E A P O E
■ S O U T H E R N C R O S S
C H A R G E ■ ■ D A N T E S
M A D A M E S P E A K E R ■
D I E S E ■ P I C K E T E R S
R R S ■ T O U G H ■ ■ T M E N
■ ■ D I R T P O O R ■ O D A
A B R O G A T E ■ D O O V E R
H E I G H T E N ■ D O T E L L
S T P E T E R S ■ S T O R M Y
```

98

```
P L A N B ■ T O T S ■ C C U P
E O L I A N H A R P ■ O R N E
P O I N D E X T E R ■ T E D S
E N T E R S ■ H O U S E P E T
■ ■ ■ R A C E S ■ C A D E T ■
R A M ■ P A X ■ S E R A P E S
A V I S ■ F I J I ■ O Z A R K
J A C Q U E L I N E D U P R E
A S K U P ■ E M I R ■ R E E D
S T E A D E D ■ S A S ■ R D S
■ M Y R O N ■ H E S H E ■
S A F E S I D E ■ M A L O N E
A T I C ■ G A S G U Z Z L E R
R E N U ■ M I S S S A I G O N
G Y N T ■ A S E A ■ M E A N S
```

99

```
S T O P S I N ■ Q U I V I V E
H O P I N T O ■ U N M O R A L
I R E P E A T ■ A C U T E L Y
A N N E E ■ A F R ■ S E L E S
T O S S ■ B R U T E ■ D A R E
S U E ■ F R I Z Z L E ■ N I E
U T A H J A Z Z ■ E L U D E S
■ M O N E Y B A G S ■
R E C O R D ■ M E N I S C U S
E P A ■ D E C A G O N ■ R K O
N I L E ■ D O T E R ■ B A R N
E T O N S ■ A H N ■ C O N A N
G O R E T E X ■ T W I N K I E
E M I R A T E ■ L A R G E N T
D E C O Y E D ■ E N C O D E S
```

100

```
E N T E B B E ■ W H A T A M I
S I E R R A S ■ N O W I S E R
T E N N E S S E E W A L K E R
A C T I V E I N T E R E S T S
R E S E E D E D ■
■ Z A N I N E S S
S P A N I S H O M E L E T T E
E U R O P E A N T H E A T E R
C R E A S E R E S I S T A N T
O L D H A N D S ■
■ E A R H O L E S
R E A L E S T A T E A G E N T
I S E A G E R T O P L E A S E
S A O T O M E ■ M O V E S U P
K I N E S I S ■ S T A S H E S
```

101

```
GOFORADIP   SOPOR
ABORIGINE   CLARO
VERKLEMPT   ASSAY
ARTIE  MRT  LOTTA
GOWN  QEII  ENROL
ENO  TURNER   ARI
   AHA  TSUNAMIS
AMBIENT  TSELIOT
QUIXOTIC  HAL
USA  AMULET  RAJ
ASSAD  ERAS  METO
TETRA  LAO  GATOS
IDIOT  ACTSALONE
CURSE  GAZASTRIP
SPEED  SOULPATCH
```

102

```
CLEW  HEATDAMAGE
LASH  ERRORRATES
ESPY  FRONTAXLES
OER  ETON    BANA
PRETZEL  CARAWAY
ABSURD  CHLOE
TESTA  DEADWRONG
RAO   PODIA   ROI
AMSTERDAM  CHASM
     ONAIR  BOATEL
RECLAME  LAPROBE
IDOL    SEIS  RAT
CURBAPPEAL  MINE
OCEANBORNE  BODY
HEARTSEASE  ESSE
```

103

```
ASBADASBADCANBE
THEREYOUGOAGAIN
LITTLEORNOTHING
 MAST  TRIM  AVGS
    CYS   ISEE
FAJITA   PIC
OVERANDDONEWITH
AIRAMERICARADIO
MAKEARESOLUTION
   LSD   INTONE
 PLIE   EKE
BAIN  KANE  JOAD
LIBERALDEMOCRAT
ANYPORTINASTORM
SEATTLESEAHAWKS
```

104

```
SPYVSSPY   COCCI
THENATION  BARON
PAMELASUE  SHANT
ELECTS  OWNSUPTO
TANKS  ONTAP  PAN
ENIS  SAL  POLICE
RXS  CITYSTREETS
    SATELLITE
SANATORIUMS  ELF
ONEMAN  VEE  CLEO
YOW  TIRED  CANAL
BISCOTTO  DARING
ENDON  ENDURANCE
ATARI  SCENEFOUR
NSYNC  EYETESTS
```

105

```
LEAVESABADTASTE
ARTAPPRECIATION
BYTRIALANDERROR
  AMC  OMEN  ORTO
LEGIST    TUPELO
AGIN  EKES  SHEET
TORT  TINAFEY
ESL  FONDLED  ALA
   GONDOLA  IRIS
FRERE  AWES  MMES
RAREST    TOEOUT
IMIN  RICE  MAR
ESCAPEMECHANISM
DEADASADOORNAIL
ASSESSMENTROLLS
```

106

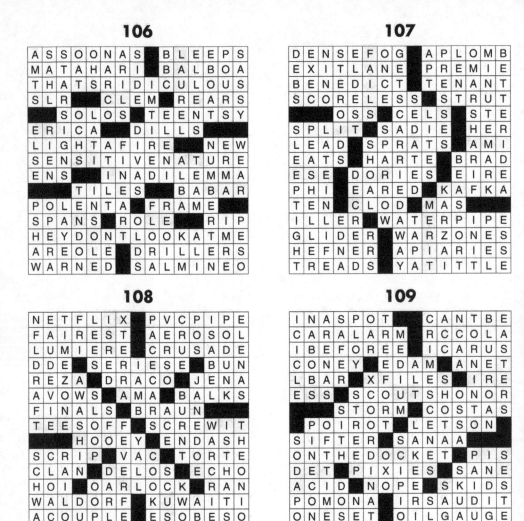

A	S	S	O	O	N	A	S		B	L	E	E	P	S
M	A	T	A	H	A	R	I		B	A	L	B	O	A
T	H	A	T	S	R	I	D	I	C	U	L	O	U	S
S	L	R			C	L	E	M		R	E	A	R	S
		S	O	L	O	S		T	E	E	N	T	S	Y
E	R	I	C	A			D	I	L	L	S			
L	I	G	H	T	A	F	I	R	E			N	E	W
S	E	N	S	I	T	I	V	E	N	A	T	U	R	E
E	N	S			I	N	A	D	I	L	E	M	M	A
			T	I	L	E	S			B	A	B	A	R
P	O	L	E	N	T	A		F	R	A	M	E		
S	P	A	N	S		R	O	L	E			R	I	P
H	E	Y	D	O	N	T	L	O	O	K	A	T	M	E
A	R	E	O	L	E		D	R	I	L	L	E	R	S
W	A	R	N	E	D		S	A	L	M	I	N	E	O

107

D	E	N	S	E	F	O	G		A	P	L	O	M	B
E	X	I	T	L	A	N	E		P	R	E	M	I	E
B	E	N	E	D	I	C	T		T	E	N	A	N	T
S	C	O	R	E	L	E	S	S		S	T	R	U	T
		O	S	S		C	E	L	S		S	T	E	
S	P	L	I	T		S	A	D	I	E		H	E	R
L	E	A	D		S	P	R	A	T	S		A	M	I
E	A	T	S		H	A	R	T	E		B	R	A	D
E	S	E		D	O	R	I	E	S		E	I	R	E
P	H	I		E	A	R	E	D		K	A	F	K	A
T	E	N		C	L	O	D		M	A	S			
I	L	L	E	R		W	A	T	E	R	P	I	P	E
G	L	I	D	E	R		W	A	R	Z	O	N	E	S
H	E	F	N	E	R		A	P	I	A	R	I	E	S
T	R	E	A	D	S		Y	A	T	I	T	T	L	E

108

N	E	T	F	L	I	X		P	V	C	P	I	P	E
F	A	I	R	E	S	T		A	E	R	O	S	O	L
L	U	M	I	E	R	E		C	R	U	S	A	D	E
D	D	E		S	E	R	I	E	S	E		B	U	N
R	E	Z	A		D	R	A	C	O		J	E	N	A
A	V	O	W	S		A	M	A		B	A	L	K	S
F	I	N	A	L	S		B	R	A	U	N			
T	E	E	S	O	F	F		S	C	R	E	W	I	T
			H	O	O	E	Y		E	N	D	A	S	H
S	C	R	I	P		V	A	C		T	O	R	T	E
C	L	A	N		D	E	L	O	S		E	C	H	O
H	O	I		O	A	R	L	O	C	K		R	A	N
W	A	L	D	O	R	F		K	U	W	A	I	T	I
A	C	O	U	P	L	E		E	S	O	B	E	S	O
B	A	N	D	S	A	W		D	I	N	E	S	O	N

109

I	N	A	S	P	O	T			C	A	N	T	B	E
C	A	R	A	L	A	R	M		R	C	C	O	L	A
I	B	E	F	O	R	E	E		I	C	A	R	U	S
C	O	N	E	Y		E	D	A	M		A	N	E	T
L	B	A	R		X	F	I	L	E	S		I	R	E
E	S	S		S	C	O	U	T	S	H	O	N	O	R
			S	T	O	R	M		C	O	S	T	A	S
		P	O	I	R	O	T		L	E	T	S	O	N
S	I	F	T	E	R		S	A	N	A	A			
O	N	T	H	E	D	O	C	K	E	T		P	I	S
D	E	T		P	I	X	I	E	S		S	A	N	E
A	C	I	D		N	O	P	E		S	K	I	D	S
P	O	M	O	N	A		I	R	S	A	U	D	I	T
O	N	E	S	E	T		O	I	L	G	A	U	G	E
P	E	S	T	L	E		E	Y	E	S	P	O	T	

110

T	F	O	R	M	A	T	I	O	N		P	R	O	S
R	E	P	U	G	N	A	N	C	E		R	A	I	N
A	M	E	N	T	O	T	H	A	T		O	G	L	E
N	I	N	E		S	T	I	N	T		M	O	L	E
S	N	A			E	B	A	Y		Q	U	I	Z	
F	I	R	S		G	R	I	D		B	U	T	T	E
A	N	E	T		A	S	T	A	I	R	E			
T	E	A	A	C	T			P	R	E	V	I	N	
		G	U	E	S	S	S	O		N	I	C	O	
J	U	D	G	E		C	A	W	S		S	T	E	T
E	R	I	E		G	A	Y	E			A	D	A	
T	S	A	R		U	N	H	A	T		A	M	O	K
L	U	L	L		I	N	I	T	I	A	T	I	V	E
A	L	O	E		D	E	T	E	R	M	I	N	E	R
G	A	G	E		O	D	O	R	E	A	T	E	R	S

111

S	Q	U	E	E	G	E	E	S		O	H	W	O	W
A	U	S	T	R	A	L	I	A		D	U	A	N	E
N	O	N	E	A	T	A	L	L		I	N	I	T	S
E	T	A	S		E	Y	E	S		E	A	T	I	T
R	E	V		S	N	E	A	D		N	A	P	E	
	D	Y	E	R		E	N	D	U	P		S	T	R
		N	O	S		S	I	M	O	L	E	O	N	
B	I	G	T	A	L	K		P	A	L	A	C	E	S
O	V	E	R	D	O	N	E		S	O	S			
R	E	T		S	P	A	M	S		S	T	I	R	
A	H	A	T		S	P	O	T	S		N	O	B	
B	A	L	E	S		S	T	E	P		A	B	B	Y
O	D	I	S	T		A	I	R	I	N	G	O	U	T
R	I	F	L	E		C	O	N	C	O	U	R	S	E
A	T	E	A	M		K	N	E	E	P	A	N	T	S

112

S	P	E	E	D	O		S	A	P	S	A	G	O
H	I	N	T	O	N		S	T	R	E	A	M	E	R
O	N	C	A	L	L		T	R	I	P	L	A	N	E
W	H	O	L	L	Y		R	O	S	S	E	T	T	I
M	O	M		A	C	T	I	V	E		P	E	E	L
A	L	I		R	H	O	D	E		G	R	U	E	L
N	E	A	P	T	I	D	E		F	A	I	R	L	Y
		A	R	L	O		M	A	R	C				
H	A	T	R	E	D		R	O	N	D	E	L	E	T
I	R	A	T	E		F	I	L	L	E		E	X	E
T	C	B	Y		V	E	B	L	E	N		S	H	E
H	A	L	F	M	I	L	E		T	H	R	O	A	T
O	D	I	O	U	S	L	Y		T	O	O	T	L	E
M	I	N	U	T	I	A	E		E	S	T	H	E	R
E	A	G	L	E	T	S		R	E	S	O	D	S	

113

M	Y	S	P	A	C	E		G	O	S	S	I	P
I	O	M	O	T	H	S		R	E	D	W	I	N	E
S	K	I	P	O	U	T		O	N	E	F	L	A	T
S	O	T		P	G	A	T	O	U	R		E	P	I
T	O	T	O		S	T	A	T	S		S	N	I	T
E	N	E	M	Y		E	R	E		T	I	T	L	E
P	O	N	I	E	S		T	R	O	U	N	C	E	S
		G	A	L	L		S	A	N	A				
I	M	N	O	T	Y	O	U		T	I	T	H	E	S
D	R	E	S	S		V	C	R		C	R	E	P	T
E	S	T	H		B	E	L	O	W		A	R	I	D
A	L	F		H	A	S	A	C	O	W		E	T	E
M	A	L	A	I	S	E		K	R	A	T	I	O	N
E	T	I	C	K	E	T		O	R	I	G	A	M	I
N	E	X	T	E	L		N	Y	T	I	M	E	S	

114

M	A	R	K	C	U	B	A	N		E	L	F	I	N
A	T	A	N	Y	T	I	M	E		R	O	L	L	S
C	A	M	E	R	A	B	A	G		R	O	I	L	Y
A	R	E	A			N	E	V		S	P	A	N	
W	I	N	D	S		D	A	V	E	S		F	T	C
			H	A	I		H	A	I	L	E			
R	E	A	D	I	N	G	R	A	I	L	R	O	A	D
E	X	Q	U	I	S	I	T	E	C	O	R	P	S	E
C	O	U	N	T	O	N	E	S	L	O	S	S	E	S
	T	A	K	E	N			O	E	N				
C	I	V		S	I	G	E	P		S	A	L	E	M
A	C	E	D		A	O	L		S	U	M	O		
P	I	L	E	S		D	O	N	T	I	K	N	O	W
R	S	V	P	D		O	R	I	E	N	T	A	T	E
A	M	A	T	I		T	O	M	A	T	O	R	E	D

115

F	A	T	S	W	A	L	L	E	R		W	E	B	S
I	G	E	T	A	R	O	U	N	D		A	Q	U	A
R	E	N	O	N	E	V	A	D	A		L	U	S	T
E	L	O	P	E		E	N	L	S		L	I	L	I
F	I	N	S		B	I	D	E		F	A	R		
O	N	E		D	Y	N	A	S	T		J	A	N	E
X	E	R	O	X	E	S		S	I	L	E	X	E	S
			W	I	N		L	O	S					
Z	I	L	L	I	O	N		A	T	A	T	I	M	E
H	M	O	S		W	E	E	D	E	D		N	O	N
I	E	S			P	R	O	D		L	U	N	G	
V	A	T	S		S	T	E	P		S	I	T	K	A
A	N	A	T		A	U	C	T	I	O	N	E	E	R
G	I	R	L		I	N	T	E	R	F	E	R	E	D
O	T	T	O		D	E	S	E	R	T	R	O	S	E

116

```
F L A S H L I G H T ▣ A B C S
A U C T I O N E E R ▣ B A H T
V I R A L V I D E O ▣ S T A R
A S E ▣ L E G S ▣ T S E T S E
▣ ▣ L A L O ▣ S T A N L E E
P A S T R Y ▣ S K I N T E S T
E N T R Y ▣ T W E E D ▣ M C C
P D A S ▣ T R I E R ▣ D E E R
E S T ▣ A R E N T ▣ P E N N E
L O I S L A N E ▣ L A S T E D
E T C H A N T ▣ W O R K ▣ ▣
M O L A R S ▣ G O A T ▣ C P O
O B I S ▣ E U R O D I S N E Y
K E N T ▣ P R I Z E T A B L E
O D E A ▣ T I N Y D A N C E R
```

117

```
▣ Y O U O K ▣ S T E M L E S S
B E R N I E ▣ C O R S E L E T
L A D I D A ▣ U N I Q U E L Y
A H E M ▣ A D I E U ▣ M A X
S I R P A U L ▣ S A W ▣ ▣
E M B R I T T L E ▣ D R U S E
▣ F L E S H I E S T ▣ O N E A
B I A S ▣ E M O T E ▣ N L A T
I N N S ▣ R A N R A G G E D ▣
P E K E S ▣ S E A S O N T W O
▣ ▣ D T S ▣ D E P U T E S
P O I ▣ P O D I A ▣ M A L T
S A N T E R I A ▣ P O B B L E
S T R A T T O N ▣ D U E L E R
T H E B E A R S ▣ F I R E R ▣
```

118

```
E S T E R ▣ E C O N ▣ D A Z E
A H E A D ▣ A H S O ▣ E X I T
G R A S S S T A I N ▣ B I T E
L E S T ▣ M E T R O P O L I S
E D E L ▣ A R T I S A N ▣ ▣
▣ D A I S I E S ▣ R A J A H
S C H ▣ S H E D ▣ P R I O R I
T O A D I E S ▣ Q U O R U M S
I D I O T S ▣ C U L T ▣ R S T
R E R U N ▣ C A I S S O N ▣
▣ B O N A N Z A ▣ N A P E
N E X T T O L A S T ▣ A L L A
A C M E ▣ M A S H E D P E A S
C H A R ▣ A S T O ▣ C A S T E
L O S S ▣ S H A W ▣ C R E E L
```

119

```
Q A N D A ▣ S T E E R S M A N
U S E A S ▣ T R A D E N A M E
I P O D S ▣ A U T O P I L O T
B E N E T ▣ T A I ▣ P A R T
B R A ▣ S C E N T E D ▣ G A L
L I T E ▣ A F C ▣ N O S A L E
E T A L ▣ D A Y T O N A ▣ ▣
S Y L L A B I ▣ R U S T L E R
▣ E X U R B A N ▣ B O N O
I R O N E R ▣ A N C ▣ Y O G A
N A N ▣ S Y O S S E T ▣ K I D
S I L T ▣ A K A ▣ A H I N T
I D I O M A T I C ▣ R E N E E
S E N T I M E N T ▣ P A T E S
T R E E R I N G S ▣ S P O R T
```

120

```
C A M P H O R O I L ▣ M I T A
U N I T A R I A N S ▣ A P I N
R A T A T A T T A T ▣ R O E G
A C T ▣ S N A C K ▣ M I D G E
T I E R ▣ G R A N D C A N A L
E N N E ▣ E D K O C H ▣ A M P
▣ F L Y ▣ E T L A ▣ N E I
O L D I E ▣ ▣ L O O S E ▣
N Y U ▣ D E B T ▣ T E R ▣
E N T ▣ G O U R D E ▣ D E C O
O X Y G E N B A R S ▣ O D O R
R E F E R ▣ B L A T S ▣ I L E
T Y R E ▣ P L A Z A H O T E L
W E E K ▣ F E L I C I T O U S
O D E S ▣ C R A Z Y H O R S E
```

121

```
L I C E N S E F E E   O B I S
E T H N I C V O T E   L A D A
G O A T C H E E S E   D C L I
G O N E   O R S   W I N K E D
      R A T S   A I M A T
  V I S I T O R S D U G O U T
D E T O X   S U I T S   B R O
A S S N   T O R A H   M A G S
U P A   O R R I N   R I C E S
B A L L P A R K F R A N K S
    L O U S Y   U E Y S
O H G O S H   U S D   T O A T
R O O K   B A S I C T R U T H
G L O M   A R T O O D E T O O
Y A D A   G R A N D S L A M S
```

122

```
N E C E S S A R Y   C L A S H
O P O S I T I V E   L E N T O
M E L S D I N E R   E A G E R
O E D   E N G R   W A D E I N
    S T O K E   T A V E R N S
C R O O N S   R O V E R
L A R U E   P O W E R B A S E
A G E R   S E L E S   O R E N
M U S I C H A L L   J A R E D
    N A I L S   C A R O M S
O R I G I N S   A A N D W
H E L P M E   S L R S   H B O
A G O R A   G O T O S L E E P
R A N O N   I N E L E G A N T
A N A S S   S E R E N A D E S
```

123

```
L O O K B E T T E R   B E T A
U N D E R S C O R E   U R A L
G E E Y A T H I N K   R I D E
E A R L I E R   I P E C A C
  S N I D E   V O N D A
    E M S   M I N D F U L L Y
A B I E   E A S E L S   I O U
C O S   A D A T E   V A R
D I S   U S A G E S   C E N T
C L E R G Y M E N   P R O
    C L A E S   J O I N T
T E T R I S   N O N S T O P
O A H U   A N T I C I P A T E
P R O M   B O O K K E E P E R
S N U B   C R O S S D R E S S
```

124

```
A P S E S       P L E U R A
B I L L E D   P E R A N N U M
S P I D E R   O V E R T I M E
C E P E D A   P A S S I T O N
E S P R I T   A L T E R E R
S T A S E S   R U I N E R S
S E G O S   S T A G
  M E N T A L   T E S L A S
      C A B E   P O N E S
  A C H I E V E   S A R T R E
  M O U N T E R   A R R I V E
T O P S C O R E   R E A P E R
O N T H E N E T   A R I O S E
C R E E P E R S   H I N D U S
K A R S T S       B E E P S
```

125

```
S A M P L E R   C A R D I A C
P R A L I N E   O L E A N N A
A L L E R G Y   R A I N H A T
R E D B E A N S A N D R I C E
K N E E   G O A L   O D O R
Y E N S   E L K S   T W I N E
      R I D E   R A N D R
I N D I A N S   T S O N G A S
D A U N T   C A H N
L I L T S   B A L E   A F R O
E L L E   A R K S   B E E P
C H A R L E S D E G A U L L E
H O R N E T S   D O S S I E R
A L D E N T E   A N T E N N A
T E S T O U T   T E A S E T S
```

126

C	A	M	P	A	N	E	L	L	A	■	Z	O	O	S
U	N	A	I	D	E	D	E	Y	E	■	I	M	U	P
T	A	S	K	M	A	S	T	E	R	■	N	A	T	L
L	G	S	■	S	L	O	T	S	■	B	E	L	L	I
E	R	A	■	O	N	E	■	M	U	S	L	I	N	
R	A	G	L	A	N	■	R	C	A	S	■	E	N	T
S	M	E	A	R	■	E	B	O	N	Y	E	Y	E	S
■	P	E	T	S	O	U	N	D	S	■				
W	I	N	D	O	W	S	X	P	■	A	T	T	I	C
I	S	O	■	L	I	E	F	■	M	Y	H	E	R	O
R	A	M	J	E	T	■	O	L	A	■	S	O	N	
E	D	I	T	S	■	B	R	U	I	T	■	T	N	T
T	O	N	I	■	F	A	M	I	L	Y	N	A	M	E
A	R	A	L	■	U	S	A	G	E	N	O	T	E	S
P	E	L	E	■	R	E	T	I	R	E	M	E	N	T

127

I	M	P	A	S	S	E	■	G	A	P	E	S	A	T
L	E	A	P	T	A	T	■	A	D	O	L	P	H	E
L	A	G	O	O	N	S	■	B	I	O	M	A	S	S
S	T	O	P	I	T	■	U	S	E	R	■	N	O	T
■	■	■	C	A	E	N	■	U	S	H	■			
■	D	O	M	■	A	L	I	F	■	H	E	R	O	D
R	E	T	U	R	N	T	O	R	E	A	L	I	T	Y
A	L	O	T	O	N	O	N	E	S	P	L	A	T	E
C	L	E	A	R	A	N	C	E	C	E	N	T	E	R
E	A	S	T	S	■	S	I	L	O	■	O	A	R	
■	E	C	O	■	T	Y	R	E	■					
A	W	L	■	H	A	Z	Y	■	T	A	T	T	L	E
P	R	E	B	A	K	E	■	B	I	G	H	O	A	X
P	I	E	R	C	E	D	■	O	N	L	E	A	V	E
S	T	J	O	H	N	S	■	A	G	E	N	D	A	S

128

H	O	T	H	E	A	D	S	■	J	J	P	U	T	Z
O	N	E	I	N	T	E	N	■	I	A	G	R	E	E
U	N	S	E	T	T	L	E	■	F	R	A	S	E	R
S	O	T	S	■	S	T	A	F	F	S	■	U	T	O
E	T	A	■	O	K	A	Y	■	F	L	E	E		
S	I	B	S	■	L	I	E	D	■	B	E	A	R	D
A	C	L	U	■	O	D	D	S	A	R	E	■		
T	E	E	T	H	E	■	S	A	D	I	S	T		
■	R	A	W	E	G	G	S	■	E	T	E	S		
M	E	D	A	L	■	L	O	I	N	■	R	H	E	A
A	X	E	S	■	E	L	I	A	■	I	S	R		
S	E	S	■	P	R	A	N	C	E	■	A	N	T	I
Q	U	I	T	I	T	■	G	O	B	A	C	K	O	N
U	N	L	I	K	E	■	A	M	B	R	O	S	I	A
E	T	U	D	E	S	■	T	O	S	S	P	O	T	S

129

B	E	B	O	P	■	C	H	I	N	R	E	S	T	S
U	V	U	L	A	■	A	U	D	I	O	B	O	O	K
N	A	D	E	R	■	E	C	O	M	M	E	R	C	E
■	G	A	S	T	A	N	K	■	B	A	R	R	O	W
C	A	P	T	O	R	■	W	I	N	S	O	M	E	
A	B	E	R	N	A	T	H	Y	■	C	O	W	E	R
S	O	S	A	■	G	R	E	N	D	E	L	■		
A	R	T	■	B	O	O	S	T	E	D	■	L	U	V
■	H	A	N	G	S	O	N	■	V	I	S	A		
A	L	T	A	R	■	G	E	N	T	L	E	B	E	N
S	E	A	N	C	E	S	■	O	A	T	E	R	S	
P	A	R	D	O	N	■	T	A	N	N	E	R	S	
I	N	S	I	D	E	J	O	B	■	D	R	A	F	T
S	T	A	L	E	M	A	T	E	■	H	A	L	E	N
H	O	L	Y	S	Y	N	O	D	■	O	N	S	E	T

130

P	R	E	S	S	U	R	E	■	C	R	I	B
R	E	L	O	A	N	E	D	■	P	H	O	N	O
I	D	E	A	L	I	S	M	■	P	R	E	S	T	O
M	A	G	R	I	T	T	E	■	R	E	E	S	E	S
■	S	I	E	N	E	S	E	■	I	N	S	E	R	T
■	T	R	A	D	E	S	■	M	A	I	T	R	E
■	A	E	R	O	M	E	T	E	R
D	O	S	A	D	O	S	■	U	S	E	R	I	D	S
I	R	E	N	E	R	Y	A	N	■
S	I	R	I	C	A	■	L	A	M	E	S	A	■
S	E	A	M	A	N	■	A	B	A	S	H	E	S
U	N	S	U	N	G	■	M	O	N	S	A	N	T	O
A	T	E	S	T	S	■	O	U	T	E	R	E	A	R
D	A	R	E	S	■	S	T	A	N	D	A	R	D
E	L	A	S	■	A	S	S	E	S	S	E	S

131

```
. M I A M I . E E L E D .
J E N N I F E R L O P E Z .
L A N D O C A L R I S S I A N
E N T . S A T I A T E . F D A
T G I F . S A O N E . S I O N
A L O A F . L T D . O P E R A
T E N D R I L . S A M O S A S
. . D O N . . . L E K . .
A S S I G N S . P E G A S U S
L U T E S . A V I . A N I S E
A S E T . P I A N O . E D E N
R I A . R E L L E N O . E T O
M E M B E R S O F T H E B A R
. Q U I C K B R O W N F O X .
. P O T S Y . R O O T Y .
```

132

```
B U B B L E B A T H . T W A S
O P E R A S E R I A . A I N T
A D V A N C E M E N . I N D O
T O Y S T O R Y . D A C T Y L
. . S E R S . N O W H E R E
H O B A R T . F O U R I R O N
A C O R N . W I T T Y . T O C
S H O D . X E R E S . M I N A
A L T . P A L M S . C I D E R
G O L C O N D A . M O S E Y S
O C E L O T S . F O R T .
A R G A L I . B A P T I S M S
T A G S . P E R I P E T E I A
I C E S . P L A T E G L A S S
T Y R A . E I G H T E E N T H
```

133

```
. C A P P E R . . R A N I .
H A R R I M A N . R E C A N T
E L S I N O R E . E S C U D O
E L E V A T E S . D O R S E T
L I N E T E S T . F L U E N T
. N O T A S T E . A V I A T E
. . A R T C E N T E R
. A L A R U M . H E D G E D
S N A P A P P L E .
O N S I D E . A C E T A T E
R E T A I N . R O T A R I A N
R A M R O D . D R A W I N T O
E L O I S E . E N L I S T E D
L E V E E D . R E I N T E R S
. R E S T . . R I G O R S
```

134

```
N E V E R M O R E . S C A R S
S T O L E A W A Y . C O M I N
W E L L I L L B E . A R E C A
. . . S L E E P I N G B A G
T W I N S E T . I N D I A N S
R A N O U T . R E B A .
I N U R E . R E C O L L E C T
A D I M . R O L E X . E L I S
D A T A B A S E S . M A L T A
. . L I E D . W I R I E R
S A R C A S M . B A D N E S S
S N O O Z E A L A R M .
G O O D E . R E S P O N S E S
T U N E R . I N T E R B A N K
S K E D S . E T E R N A L L Y
```

135

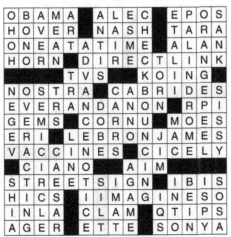

```
O B A M A . A L E C . E P O S
H O V E R . N A S H . T A R A
O N E A T A T I M E . A L A N
H O R N . D I R E C T L I N K
. . . T V S . K O I N G
N O S T R A . C A B R I D E S
E V E R A N D A N O N . R P I
G E M S . C O R N U . M O E S
E R I . L E B R O N J A M E S
V A C C I N E S . C I C E L Y
. C I A N O . A I M .
S T R E E T S I G N . I B I S
H I C S . I I M A G I N E S O
I N L A . C L A M . Q T I P S
A G E R . E T T E . S O N Y A
```

136

```
S P E A K T O ■ R A T A T A T
E A S T E R N ■ U P A T R E E
I T S A L I E ■ L E C T E R N
Z E E ■ P O W D E R S ■ M O C
E R N O ■ S A R I S ■ C O B O
O N E A D ■ Y I N ■ R I L E D
N O S K I N O F F M Y N O S E
■ F A I R T R A D E ■
A N G E R M A N A G E M E N T
D E R R Y ■ N E C ■ R A D A R
J E A N ■ G O T T A ■ S A R A
O D D ■ O U T S I D E ■ S R I
I N A R U S H ■ O R D I N A L
N O T A S T E ■ N A I V E T E
S T E N T O R ■ S W E A R E R
```

137

```
A G U E ■ G O G O ■ R O O M S
U N L V ■ I R E D ■ I M P E I
N A N A ■ U G L I ■ S N E A D
T R A N S L A T E ■ K I N T E
S L E E P I N ■ ■ W E D
■ S H A S T A ■ S W E A R
O F F C E N T E R ■ I H A T E
U L T E R I O R M O T I V E S
T O W N E ■ P R O M O T E R S
S W A T S ■ S E R E N E ■
A N Y ■ P L I C A T E
I S N O T ■ M U L E T E E R S
L O E W E ■ A N A T ■ D I E T
E L I E L ■ P U T T ■ A O N E
D O N N E ■ S M E E ■ R U D E
```

138

```
U L S T E R ■ L A P C A T
P I C A R O S ■ T O P R A T E
S E A M I S T ■ R U P E R T S
E N T I C E R ■ A D E P T A T
T O T A S T E ■ D E A L E R S
■ R E M O T E S E N S O R S
■ D I N E T T E S E T S
■ V E D ■
■ H E R M E T I C I S M
■ R A R E I N S T A N C E S
F E R N A N D ■ I N H A L E D
A C D E L C O ■ O N E L A N E
R O I S T E R ■ N O R A N D A
C U S T E R S ■ S N I G G E R
E P H O R S ■ S T E E R S
```

139

```
S M A C K E D U P ■ S I N E W
M A D R I L E N O ■ E M O T E
A L O T T O A S K ■ C A N I T
L A R S E N ■ H I S S ■ O C K
L I E ■ I O N E ■ T I K I
O S S ■ S A N D G R O U S E S
J E T S E T S ■ F I L L E T S
■ C R A T ■ U P I S ■
E T V O I L A ■ N A V A J O S
C H I F F O N C A K E ■ U P I
L E A F ■ S T A T ■ M T N
I N G ■ U S F L ■ M O S A I C
P E R O N ■ I M P E D A N C E
S W A M I ■ L E Y D E N J A R
E S S E X ■ M X M I S S I L E
```

140

```
R O L A N D ■ O V E R C O A T
I N A B A R ■ P I T T A N C E
O C C U P Y ■ E T H E R E A L
S E T T O S ■ N A N ■ D A D E
■ A I S L E ■ A L O N G
■ E A D I E ■ E A S E S
C O M P O S E R ■ W I M P L E
E L E A N O R ■ P O L E C A R
S E E P I N ■ Y A R D S A L E
T A K E I ■ G O R K I ■
■ R I G I D ■ H A B L A
C I E L ■ O R E ■ O M E A R A
A L L I N A L L ■ R O T T E N
L E M O N P I E ■ S N A K E D
I R O N W E E D ■ E D S E L S
```

141

```
C H A R Y B D I S   O P R A H
R I C E A R O N I   N E A T O
E S C A L A N T E   T A T T Y
O N E L I N E R S   O C T A D
S I D L E   N U T S   E L B E
O B E Y   G E T A L I N E O N
L S D   B O S H   U N I S Y S
      R O B S   K I N K
S P R A W L   L E N S   C P R
M A O T S E T U N G   T R E E
A L M S   T U C K   G O U R D
S O U N D   T I E I N W I T H
H O L E Y   T A S M A N S E A
U K A S E   U N E A S I E S T
P A N T S   T O Y C H E S T S
```

142

```
R A D I C A L C H I C   M O S
C L O S E L Y H E L D   A P O
C A T T L E C A L L S   D E F
O R A L   S E L L S   P E N T
L U G E S   E E C   D O B L E
A M E   P O S T A G E P A I D
      A L F   S T O P P I N G
H I S S E L F   S A R A L E E
O N T H E A I R   S E S
T R A I N W R E C K S   P O M
P E T E S   E P A   S H I N E
A P E R   B E L L E   U S S R
N O P   W A X E D P O E T I C
T S E   W R I T E I N V O T E
S E N   W A T E R C O O L E R
```

143

```
F I R E A R M   S T O P G A P
E R I T R E A   H A N S O L O
D O N T A S K D O N T T E L L
E N G E L   E I E I O   S E E
R O I S   D U R R A   W A A C
A R N   S E P T S   C A P R A
L E G A L I T Y   P A L E S T
      N O C O M M E N T
S C R I B E   I O N I Z I N G
A H E M S   T N U T S   S O O
Y A L E   C A D R E   S A N A
S C I   R I P E N   C A D E T
W H A T I D I D F O R L O V E
H A N O V E R   U P A T R E E
O S T L E R S   L A W Y E R S
```

144

```
A T E A L O T   J A I A L A I
C U L T U R E C O N F L I C T
C R E A T E A N U I S A N C E
U N C L E   C O S M O   C U M
R O T E   L A T T E   D O S O
S U R   S I R E S   A R L E N
E T I C K E T S   B L O N D E
      C A I N S   B L O O M
I M A G E S   B R A N D E I S
C O L E S   B R U C E   M M L
A S P S   P L A N K   T O M E
N C O   G L A Z E   E A R E D
N O W Y O U R E T A L K I N G
O N E M O M E N T P L E A S E
T I R A D E S   E T A I L E D
```

145

```
M O P   A C N E D   S C O O T
O N E S T R O K E   P O R N O
L I T T L E M E N   E N D A T
A C T U A T E D   E N M E S H
R E I N S I N   A S T A R T E
        G E N   I N T O N E R S
S I N U S   E M D E N   D I I
A D E N   T U B E R   M I N D
L O W   S I L A S   L O N G E
E N S N A R E D   D E R
S T R I D E R   R E T A P E S
S C E N E S   W A T S L I N E
L A C E Y   M A D E S E N S E
I R A T E   P R I C E S O U T
P E P Y S   S M O T E   N E O
```

146

L	I	L	A	B	N	E	R		A	S	L	E	E	P
O	V	E	R	R	U	L	E		I	M	E	L	D	A
C	A	N	N	E	D	I	T		R	O	O	M	E	R
I	N	T	E	R	I	O	R	R	E	G	I	O	N	S
					S	T	E	E	D					
S	Y	S	T	E	M	S	A	N	A	L	Y	S	T	S
N	O	T	I	N			T	E	L	L	A	L	I	E
O	N	A	L	A	R	K		S	E	A	S	I	D	E
O	N	D	E	M	A	N	D			N	I	M	E	S
P	E	T	R	I	F	I	E	D	F	O	R	E	S	T
				F	T	L	E	E						
S	P	I	R	A	L	S	T	A	I	R	C	A	S	E
A	S	S	I	S	I		A	N	N	E	A	L	E	D
C	A	L	L	I	N		I	N	T	O	N	I	N	G
S	T	A	L	A	G		C	A	S	S	E	T	T	E

147

M	A	R	E	S	T	A	I	L			A	N	K	H
A	M	E	N	C	O	R	N	E	R		L	U	A	U
T	I	N	T	O	R	E	T	T	O		E	M	T	S
L	A	T		W	I	N	E	T	A	S	T	E	R	S
O	B	I	T		C	D	R		D	E	A	R	I	E
C	L	E	A	R		T	I	A	R	A		A	N	I
K	E	R	M	I	T		M	E	A	L	P	L	A	N
			E	S	A	S		S	C	A	R			
S	P	A	R	K	L	E	S		E	N	I	G	M	A
E	L	L		I	K	N	O	W		E	S	N	E	S
S	A	L	V	E	S		R	E	D		M	O	N	T
S	U	G	A	R	B	A	B	I	E	S		C	A	R
I	D	O	L		I	P	A	G	L	I	A	C	C	I
L	I	N	E		G	E	T	H	I	T	C	H	E	D
E	T	E	S			S	E	T	S	A	S	I	D	E

148

D	A	S	H	E	S			R	E	S	T	I	R
A	R	T	E	R	Y		P	A	D	R	O	N	E
H	O	A	X	E	S		F	O	R	E	S	I	D	E
L	U	N	A		O	B	R	I	E	N		L	E	V
I	N	C	H		P	R	I	N	E		C	E	P	E
A	D	E	E	P		O	T	T		W	A	T	T	S
			D	O	W	N	T	O	E	A	R	T	H	
		F	R	E	E	Z	E	F	R	A	M	E		
	R	O	O	M	S	E	R	V	I	C	E			
C	O	R	N	S		M	A	I		S	C	A	R	P
E	S	A	S		L	E	W	E	S		H	E	E	L
R	A	S		A	T	D	A	W	N		A	R	I	A
E	N	O	L	A	G	A	Y		E	R	N	A	N	I
A	N	N	A	B	E	L		E	D	I	T	E	D	
L	E	G	M	A	N			R	A	C	E	R	S	

149

S	T	U	D		S	C	A	T		C	A	D	E	T
T	O	N	I		I	A	M	B		O	L	I	V	E
O	T	I	S		N	C	O	S		S	O	M	A	S
N	A	C	H	O	C	H	I	P		M	O	I	S	T
E	S	O		U	L	E		S	O	F	T	I	E	
S	T	R	A	T	A		W	A	H			R	O	E
	E	N	G	L	I	S	H	M	U	F	F	I	N	S
		A	I	R	P	I	S	T	O	L				
H	O	U	S	E	O	F	C	O	M	M	O	N	S	
A	C	S			I	S	H		Y	E	S	I	A	M
R	E	S	E	A	L		R	M	N		C	L	U	
D	A	T	E	R		S	M	O	O	T	H	O	U	T
E	N	E	R	O		L	U	A	U		E	S	T	A
E	I	E	I	O		I	S	N	T		R	I	E	N
S	A	L	E	M		M	E	S	H		B	A	R	T

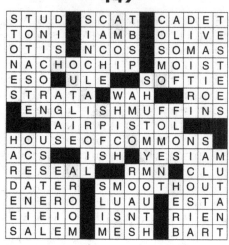

150

P	O	P	R	O	C	K	S		S	E	D	A	T	E
S	H	O	E	T	R	E	E		T	V	I	D	O	L
S	O	N	A	T	I	N	A		E	E	R	I	L	Y
T	H	E	R	E	N	O	W		L	A	T	T	E	S
				R	O	S	E	M	A	R	Y			
F	A	R	M		I	H	E	A	R	D	T	H	A	T
A	T	I	E		D	A	D	S		E	R	A	S	E
R	E	P	A	S	S			U	N	I	S	O	N	
S	I	E	G	E		I	T	I	S		C	O	N	S
I	N	R	E	A	L	L	I	F	E		K	N	E	E
			R	E	E	L	S	O	F	F				
G	A	Y	D	A	R		A	R	O	U	S	A	L	S
A	S	S	I	G	N		N	O	R	M	A	R	A	E
S	T	E	E	L	E		E	N	C	E	I	N	T	E
P	O	R	T	E	R		S	E	E	D	L	E	S	S